ARIZONA SHERIFFS

ARIZONA SHERIFFS

Badges and
Bad Men

 Jane Eppinga

Foreword by
Asa Bushnell

RIO NUEVO PUBLISHERS
TUCSON, ARIZONA

Rio Nuevo Publishers®
P.O. Box 5250, Tucson, Arizona 85703-0250
(520) 623-9558, www.rionuevo.com

Library of Congress Cataloging-in-Publication Data

Eppinga, Jane.
Arizona sheriffs : badges and bad men / Jane Eppinga ; foreword by Asa Bushnell.
    p. cm.
Includes index.
ISBN-13: 978-1-887896-21-4
ISBN-10: 1-887896-21-X
1. Sheriffs—Arizona. 2. Criminals—Arizona. I. Title.
HV8145.A7E67 2006
363.28'209791—dc22
                                    2006024485

Design: Karen Schober, Seattle, Washington

Printed in Canada.

10   9   8   7   6   5   4   3   2

CONTENTS

Foreword

It has been a long time coming, but *Arizona Sheriffs* indisputably is well worth the wait. Right off the bat, it smacks of an incredible amount of research, woven artfully into the story of fabled as well as foibled lawmen who have left their marks on the history of the Southwest over the past century and a half. By the end, its exciting, edifying chapters reveal the obvious: most of these sheriffs have served for the better, only a few for the worse.

The author of *Arizona Sheriffs,* to no one's surprise, is Jane Eppinga, for whom the compelling subject matter has become a career labor of love. Indeed, she is noted for a seemingly endless series of published sheriff profiles that is unmatched in its scope and its scholarship. Her new book is the happy realization of a recurrent dream.

In the pages that follow, readers will track the fascinating trail Arizona sheriffs have left behind while moving forward from Territorial days, to statehood and the many changes, bringing us to modern times. Each aspect of the top lawman's fascinating position is laid bare as we encounter courage, bravery, heroism, ineptitude, deceit, corruption, and every imaginable trait of the human condition along the way.

Indeed, the stage is set through two very different, yet difficult, confrontations between sheriffs and feuding factions, the first exposing vividly the violence, challenges, and hardships existing in the Arizona Territory, and the second underscoring the extremely dangerous and demanding nature of a sheriff's job at the turn of the twentieth century into the birth of a new state.

Subsequent chapters will reveal the early sheriffs as executioners—a duty their successors gladly forfeited to state government—and as "politicians," doing their darnedest to please oft-volatile constituencies, while wondering why a law-enforcement position is subject to partisanship in the first place. Also, readers may be surprised to learn that the jail, though it has progressed from primitive and unsafe to state-of-the-art and virtually escape-proof status, is still a major headache to sheriffs because it represents a huge percentage of their annual budgets and it always is just a costly mistake away from a public scandal.

Intriguing facts and colorful quotes abound as we discover the importance of rodeos as a breeding ground for well-prepared lawmen (and outlaws) and the significance of manhunts, whether by horseback then or auto and airplane now, in bringing culprits to justice. And how could the author possibly overlook the varied vices tolerated or exploited by a small minority of sheriffs that have succumbed to temptation and wound up with tarnished badges since 1863?

Toward the end of the trail, readers will come upon two final chapters devoted to a pair of emerging phenomena that has taxed the wits and resources of Arizona sheriffs for more than the past half-century: zealots who break state laws under the banner of "freedom of religion" and juveniles in alarming numbers who commit wanton, heinous acts of criminal behavior that warrant stringent prosecution and punishment as adults.

Arizona Sheriffs offers an entertaining, informative, full-speed-ahead trip from its starting point in once not-so-pleasant Pleasant Valley via surprising twists and turns throughout the state's storied landmarks to an unforgettable ending at an ill-fated Buddhist temple in Maricopa County. Enjoy the ride!

—ASA BUSHNELL
Former community relations manager,
Pima County Sheriff's Department

Introduction

The office of the High Sheriff originated during the Middle Ages in England, when the "shire of the reeve" represented the Crown in local government. Like his modern counterpart, the shire-reeve (sheriff) kept the peace. He also held court and commanded the local militia. Because the shire-reeve amassed and exercised vast power, subsequent kings sought to limit his authority by removing his power to preside over local courts.

When the English settled along the east coast of North America, the sheriff's office became a common feature of the local colonies. These Colonial sheriffs, generally chosen from among the landowners, served legal papers, kept the peace, maintained the jail, and collected taxes. After the American Revolution, the sheriff became a familiar lawman on the Western frontier. Each new territory officially legislated this office into existence. As municipalities increased in population, the office of town marshal, constable, and ultimately a police department were added, but the sheriff came to represent not only law enforcement, but a way of life unique to the West.

Before achieving a separate status as a territory in February 1863, what is now Arizona had been part of the New Mexico Territory. New Mexico's Doña Ana County Sheriff Samuel G. Bean had observed sometime in the late 1850s, "My jurisdiction was not as large as [that of] the Czar of Russia, but it extended from Texas to California." Tucson and Tubac were 250 miles from Mesilla, the county seat. Outlaws fleeing the Texas and California law flocked to this remote land. The creation of the Arizona Territory in 1863 provided for the first county and federal law enforcement.

Upon formation of the Arizona Territory in 1863, Arizona's first set of codified laws, drafted by Judge William T. Howell of Michigan, prescribed that one of the sheriff's duties was to call the parties, witnesses, and jurors to trial as required. The 400-page document, originally known as the Howell Code, eventually became the Arizona Statutes, which are still revised periodically. Sheriffs were paid on a piecework basis and frequently had to ride into dangerous country to summon jurors, who resented having to leave their farms and ranches for any length of time. If, on the other hand, the sheriff failed to serve a summons the judge might be forced to draw from a pool of loiterers around the court. The sheriff was also to make the opening and adjourning proclamations in court, and he played an important part in jury selection.

The most visible identification of the sheriff's office was his badge—apparently a holdover from the shields of the era of knighthood in medieval England. In America's early West, "drummers" (traveling salesmen) peddled badges in various sizes and shapes. If no badge was available, the sheriff himself stamped one out of tin, thus the term "tin star." Many badges became as famous as their owners. Pima County Sheriff Waldon Burr, who left the office in disgrace in 1971, sported a magnificent diamond-studded badge. Even today a sheriff may select a badge design of his personal choice.

Comparatively few men made much money from the office. While some viewed it as a burdensome duty, others eagerly sought it. Until the 1950s, Arizona sheriffs were elected for two-year terms, which meant that much of their time was involved in electioneering and political maneuvering. Qualifications, besides popularity, included familiarity with the weapons of the day, knowledge of the vast jurisdiction, a good horse, and a willingness to put one's life on the line if need be.

ARIZONA COUNTIES AND COUNTY SEATS

UTAH

▲ Hildale, UT
▲ Short Creek/ ▲ Fredonia
Colorado City

Colorado River

COCONINO

NEVADA

APACHE

MOHAVE

Colorado River

NAVAJO

NEW MEXICO

• Kingman

▲ Bullhead
City

▲ Williams • Flagstaff

▲ Needles,
CA

YAVAPAI

• Prescott

MOGOLLON RIM

• Holbrook

• St. Johns

PLEASANT VALLEY

CALIFORNIA

• Parker

LA PAZ

MARICOPA

▲ Waddell

GILA

★ Phoenix
▲ Scottsdale
▲ Mesa
▲ Tempe

• Globe

GREENLEE

• Clifton

YUMA

• Florence

PINAL

GALIURO MOUNTAINS

GRAHAM

• Safford

• Yuma

PIMA

• Tucson

▲ Willcox

COCHISE

▲ Tombstone

SANTA
CRUZ

Miracle
Valley

• Bisbee

SONORA, MEXICO

• Nogales

▲ Palominas ▲ Douglas

▲ Nogales, Sonora

▲ Agua Prieta,
Sonora

CHAPTER 1.
The Pleasant Valley War

The Blevins cottage in Holbrook.

Today, when one views the Mogollon Rim—that magnificent escarpment hurled sky-ward through the eons of time—and in its shadow, Pleasant Valley in the Tonto Basin, with its lush pine forests, verdant pastures, purple mountains, orange sunsets, and pristine flowing creeks, it is easy to see how Pleasant Valley got its name. It is hard to conceive that in the 1880s, anywhere from twenty-five to seventy-five men were mur-dered during the Pleasant Valley War, also known as the Graham-Tewksbury Feud.

The number of casualties will never be accurately determined, in part because of the many nameless strangers who were perhaps in the wrong place at the wrong time. Fortunately, nowadays a Pleasant Valley cowboy, upon seeing an approaching horse-man, is not likely to dismount, lay his rifle across the saddle, and scrutinize a stranger until he determines whether it is friend or foe.

In the 1880s, Pleasant Valley served as the backdrop for the bloodiest feud in Arizona's history. Yavapai County Sheriff William "Billy" Mulvenon and Apache County Sheriff Commodore Perry Owens were charged with stopping the killings and arresting the guilty. As in the Hatfield-McCoy and other famous feuds, lawmen could not stop the killing, because the participants obeyed a strict code of silence. Those who did not found lonely graves in the remote stretches of Pleasant Valley.

As late as 1920, old-timers were still reluctant to discuss the feud with author Zane Grey while he prepared his fictional account of the vendetta in *To the Last Man*. Although he had been just a child at the time of the conflict, Bob Voris still worried about breaking the code of silence in 1957. He talked to Globe (Arizona) historian Clara Woody about the Pleasant Valley War on the condition that his story remained sealed until twenty-five years after his death. Many still believe that the vendetta resulted from the Tewksburys bringing sheep into Pleasant Valley. However, Mormon pioneer and rancher Osmer Flake wrote, "The one point I want to emphasize is, this was not a sheep and cattle war; the trouble started years before Mr. Jacobs brought the Daggs sheep into the Valley."

Two Sheriffs, the Grahams, and the Tewksburys

Commodore Perry Owens was born on July 29, 1852—the anniversary of his namesake Commodore Perry's victory over the British fleet in the Battle of Lake Erie. Raised on a Tennessee farm, Owens escaped an abusive father and arrived in Arizona around 1881. He worked on various ranches and guarded the Army Cavalry horses at Navajo Springs. He stood five feet, nine inches, had a deceptively soft face, and sported long blond hair. He carried a late-model Winchester repeating rifle and wore his long-barrel Colt revolvers butt-forward, forcing him to cross-draw with "wonderful speed."

Billy Mulvenon was born October 28, 1851, to Irish immigrants in Massachusetts. By age seventeen he was working as a government contractor at Fort Harker, Kansas. With the restlessness of youth, Mulvenon left his job and followed the Santa Fe Trail on horseback, arriving in Prescott in 1876. He mined in the Bradshaw Mountains and served four years as a deputy sheriff before being elected Yavapai County sheriff on the Democratic ticket in 1884. Two years later voters gave him a second term. Yavapai County jurisdiction at that time included all of present-day Coconino County and parts of Mohave and Gila Counties, as well as present-day Yavapai County.

Participants in the feud lined up with one or the other of two prominent Pleasant Valley pioneer families: the Tewksburys and the Grahams. John Dunning Tewksbury Sr. had sailed from Boston to California during the Gold Rush days. He married an

Indian woman from California, who bore him four sons, Edwin, John Jr., James, and Frank. After her death in 1878, John Sr. moved his family to Globe, Arizona, where he married a well-to-do widow, Lydia Ann Shultes, a native of Wales. The Tewksbury men bred fine horses and established their headquarters on Cherry Creek. Good pasture and year-round water, along with abundant game such as deer, antelope, and half-wild hogs, assured a good life.

The Tewksbury brothers enjoyed frequenting the bars in neighboring towns, where in the summer of 1882, they met Tom and John Graham. The Grahams had left Boone, Iowa, for California, but stopped in Arizona when they heard about Globe's silver strike. They told the Tewksburys that they had gambled and won some cows, but didn't know what to do with them. Ed Tewksbury said, "You come and go with us and we'll go up to Pleasant Valley and we'll make cattle kings out of you." The Grahams accepted the invitation and drove their cattle into Pleasant Valley.

No Honor Among Thieves

James Stinson, a Virginian, had brought cattle into Pleasant Valley in 1873 and established a second ranch in the Salt River Valley. He hired John Gilleland, a tough Texan, as foreman of his Pleasant Valley enterprise and John Paine as a cowboy. Paine's camp would become a haven for thieves, and he would count the Grahams among his friends. Stinson promised to pay the Grahams "fifty head of good American cattle" in exchange for any evidence of depredation against him—instead, the Grahams helped themselves to his herd.

Graham cattle herds continued to increase, while those of their neighbors decreased. They needed cowboys, so a younger brother, William Graham, joined them, and they hired Jim Tewksbury as a cowpuncher for $50 a month. The Grahams bought two hundred two-year-old heifers from William J. Flake. Jim Tewksbury accompanied the Grahams to Snowflake, where the Grahams took possession of their new herd. Before beginning the ride home, the Grahams produced two running irons, and told Jim Tewksbury that they intended to do some "mavericking." (A maverick is an unbranded range animal, especially a calf that has become separated from its mother, traditionally considered the property of the first person to brand it. Cowboys often used this as an excuse to steal cattle they knew belonged to someone else.) Jim agreed to help so long as he got his fair share of the profits.

Flake did not trust the Grahams, so he sent Chris Nielsen (one of his cowboys) to make sure none of his cattle got in their herd. When Nielsen rode up, one of the Grahams said, "We have some of Flake's cows in the herd; they got in and when we cut them out they followed up." Jim told his family what had really happened along the trail, and his father insisted that he leave the Graham's employ.

John Graham registered the cattle he had purchased from Flake—and the cattle they had rustled along the Flake drive. When Ed Tewksbury learned that the Grahams had sold the rustled cattle, he demanded half of the money for which the rustled cattle had been sold (since his son had helped with the mavericking). Tom Graham told him, "Ed, hit the trail!" Because of Jim's earlier involvement in the Grahams' rustling, the Tewksburys could hardly ask the law for assistance with their own stolen cattle. Before long, the Tewksburys and the Grahams were saying harsh things about each other.

Every rancher within a sixty-mile radius of the Grahams lost cattle, and all tracks pointed to the Graham corrals, though many still suspected the Tewksburys. Stinson, who suffered depredations at his Pleasant Valley ranch, charged both the Grahams and the Tewksburys with cattle rustling. Then he promised the Grahams that if they would turn state's evidence against the Tewksburys, he would give them fifty cows and calves each and see to it that they didn't do any time. The Grahams cooperated but muddled their testimony so badly that the judge threw the case out of court.

When Ed Tewksbury found two Stinson heifers in his herd, he offered to vent his brand (scratching lines through the brand to void it) and return them to Stinson. Stinson's foreman, John Gilleland, refused to take the cattle and filed charges of rustling against the Tewksburys. But Stinson told his foreman to accept the cattle and leave the Tewksburys alone.

Gilleland smarted from Stinson's reproach. On January 11, 1883, fortified with whiskey and a bruised ego, Gilleland, his fifteen-year-old nephew, Elisha, and a Stinson cowboy, Epitacio "Potash" Ruiz, visited the Tewksbury ranch. Gilleland hoped to find rustled cattle so he could bring new charges against the Tewksburys. At the Tewksbury house, Gilleland said, "Good morning."

Ed Tewksbury asked, "You are hunting somebody?"

Gilleland said, "I am hunting no one. I have lost no one," scanning the brands on the cattle in the Tewksbury corrals.

Ed fired his pistol and said, "Well I have, you thieving son of a bitch."

With the first gunshot, Ruiz disappeared. Gilleland whirled and returned the fire. Elisha fell, wounded, from his horse. Gilleland deserted the boy, but he stopped at the Grahams', where he said that Ed Tewksbury had fired on him for no good reason and that Elisha was probably dead. The Tewksburys tended to Elisha, who was actually just more scared than hurt.

After this incident, the Grahams brought charges against all the male Tewksburys. Frank Tewksbury joined his brothers in Arizona some time between the Gilleland shoot-out and the Prescott trial. Although this youth knew nothing about the shooting, he still had to travel to Prescott, because the charges included "all male Tewksburys." During the return ride, Frank contracted measles, and back home he came down with pneumonia and died around the middle of January 1883. This first death in the Pleasant Valley War had nothing to do with guns, but the Tewksburys blamed Frank's death on the Grahams.

"CLEAN-OUT" TIME: EASIER SAID THAN DONE

On March 29, 1884, Tom and John Graham charged Edwin, John, and James Tewksbury with altering brands on Stinson's cattle. The grand jury expanded the charges to include Tewksbury friends George Blaine, William Richards, and H. H. Bishop. All of the defendants were peaceably arrested and made bond in Prescott. Then all indictments were dropped for lack of evidence. Before Blaine left Prescott, he purchased ammunition and said he would "clean out some of that damn Stinson gang."

The attempted "clean-out" occurred in July 1884, when the Tewksburys stationed themselves around Stinson's cabin. Blaine hollered, "You have had the run of this country long enough, you damned son of a bitch." John Tewksbury opened fire. Both Blaine and a young Stinson cowboy, Jefferson Davis Adams, were wounded. Complaints were filed, but none of the participants were indicted.

To compound law-enforcement problems, the Aztec Land and Cattle Company established itself in Pleasant Valley; most of the Aztec cowboys were cattle rustlers and were often on the wrong side of the law. With the completion of the Atlantic and Pacific Railroad in Arizona (and because of a drought in Texas), Arizona's cattle industry boomed in the 1880s; the Aztec Land and Cattle Company, created by the Atlantic and Pacific Railroad executives in 1884, claimed more than a million acres in the state. Although not large by Western standards, its lands were advantageously laid out in alternate one-mile squares, in such a way that no one else could really set up a ranch on the remaining square miles. The railroad company purchased most of the odd-numbered sections of lands extending twenty miles on either side of its railroad tracks between New Mexico and California for 50 cents an acre. The railroad company then developed the Aztec Land and Cattle Company, better known as the Hashknife, and went into the ranching business.

The brand, modeled after the hashknife that cowboys used to chop beef and potatoes, had been officially registered in Texas, but the Aztec Land and Cattle Company acquired it from a struggling Texas cattle company. The Aztec then bought 30,000

Texas longhorns, branded them with the hashknife, and shipped the cattle to Holbrook, Arizona. Henry Warren, vice president and general manager of the Hashknife, registered the brand in Apache County on June 2, 1885.

The Aztec Land and Cattle Company needed cowboys, and they paid well. Osmer Flake wrote that the Hashknife had some real fine men—and "some of the worst that ever left Texas." Flagstaff's *Arizona Champion* warned that trouble was brewing between the sheep raisers and the Aztec. The Aztec Land and Cattle Company ruthlessly ran off sheepherders, horse breeders, small ranchers, and Mormon colonizers, who felt they also had a right to public lands.

Pleasant Valley had long been and still is a land of open range, where cattle from different owners grazed together, and the rancher had to constantly work his herd to make certain someone else's brand did not appear on his calves. Cattle kept disappearing, and in 1885 the Yavapai Livestock Association hired one Robert Carr Blassingame to spy for them. William S. Atchison filed charges against the Grahams after Blassingame found Atchison's cattle among the Graham herds. Once again the defendants were discharged.

In February 1887, word spread throughout Pleasant Valley that the Tewksburys intended to bring sheep over the Mogollon Rim for the Daggs brothers, who had a sheep ranch north of Pleasant Valley. For several days, cattlemen watched as the line of "white woolly maggots" snaked their way along the Rim to the "dead line," commonly agreed on as the line over which no sheep were supposed to move.

Realizing that their range was in danger (because sheep pull grass out by the roots while grazing), many ranchers who had no personal quarrel with either the Grahams or the Tewksburys now sided with the Grahams. P. P. Daggs, who had hired the Tewksburys to bring in the sheep, wrote, "It cost me enough, ninety thousand dollars."

As the sheep crossed over the "dead line," several cowboys ambushed the shepherds and shot and beheaded a Basque sheepherder. The cowboys drove the sheep over the cliffs and dashed them to death on the rocks. The Basque sheepherder was a

John Tewksbury Jr.

brother-in-law of Apache County Deputy Sheriff James D. Houck, and the tracks of his murderers led straight to the Graham corrals.

WHOSE SIDE ARE YOU ON, BOYS?

Although Aztec Land and Cattle Company executives never sullied their hands in the feud, they and their cowboys were definitely Graham partisans. The most prominent Hashknife cowboys included John Paine, Thomas Tucker, and Robert Glasspie. Other Graham ranchers and supporters included the brothers Al and Ed Rose, Charley Duchet, Mose Roberts, the Blevins family, Joseph Underwood, Harry Middleton from the Defiance Cattle Company, Miguel Apodaca, and Robert Carrington.

The worst shoot-out of the feud might have been prevented if the Blevins clan had not moved from Texas into Pleasant Valley. The Blevins family did not actively seek gunfights, but their outlaw son, Andy Blevins, aka Andy Blevins Cooper, was a troublesome, desperate character. His escape from the Texas Rangers drove him into remote Arizona lands. The Blevins family established a ranch near the Grahams, and the two families shared grazing land.

The Tewksburys counted among their friends many who had lost cattle to the Grahams. They included P. P. and A. A. Daggs, James F. Roberts, George A. Newton, William Jacobs, John Rhodes, Jacob Lauffer, George Blaine, William Richards, W. H. Bishop, Joseph Boyer, George Wagner, Apache County Deputy Sheriff James D. Houck, and William Colcord.

In early August 1887, Martin Blevins disappeared when he went to look for stray horses. His son Hampton, along with some Hashknife cowboys—Tom Tucker, Bob Glasspie, Bob Carrington, Jim Roberts, and John Paine—went looking for him. Ed Rogers, the Hashknife foreman, threatened to "start a little war of our own."

On August 9, the Hashknifers rode up to George Newton's Middleton Ranch, where the Tewksburys were staying. When Paine asked if they could get dinner, Ed Tewksbury replied, "No, we do not keep a hotel here." Paine called Ed a "black son of a bitch" and reached for his gun. Before he could draw, Ed shot him out of the saddle. A slug from Jim Roberts's gun clipped Paine's ear and when he ran for cover, Jim Tewksbury finished him off with a bullet. Hampton Blevins wheeled his horse and fell when a bullet crashed through his skull. Carrington fled when a bullet tore through his clothing. A rifle slug hit Glasspie in his leg and passed through his horse. After painfully making his way for two days on foot with nothing to eat, he arrived at the Blevins ranch.

When a bullet ripped through both of Tucker's lungs, he hunkered down behind his horse. To kill Tucker, Ed would have to kill the horse, and he was "kind of squeamish about killing horses." During Tucker's flight, an angry mother bear with her two cubs also confronted him. By the time he got to the Flying V Ranch his wound had become infested with blowflies and maggots.

The Law Steps In

When he got word of the fight, Yavapai County Sheriff Mulvenon mounted a posse and headed for the Middleton Ranch. At Payson, he picked up four more deputies. Mulvenon set up his camp near Charles Perkins's new store, about ninety miles north of Globe, and met with the Graham partisans. Perkins had somehow managed not to take sides during the Pleasant Valley conflict, so Sheriff Mulvenon chose this site as a neutral meeting place. However, Mulvenon saw that he faced overwhelming numbers of heavily armed men, and later said, "They came right into my camp and made their big talks of what they would do and what they wouldn't do and I saw right then that I had the worst of it and I denied having any warrants for them."

Tom Graham threatened that if the sheriff did not arrest the Tewksburys then the Grahams would fight them into extermination. When Mulvenon and his posse went to saddle up, all their horses had been stolen. Mulvenon got his Irish up and cursed every man in Pleasant Valley. Within a few hours the horses were returned.

At the Middleton Ranch, Mulvenon and his posse found two dead horses and the shallow graves of Hampton Blevins and Paine. The house and barn had been burned to the ground. Newton told Mulvenon, if he obtained warrants for the Grahams, the Tewksburys would turn themselves in voluntarily. (No sooner had Sheriff Mulvenon left Pleasant Valley than another herd of horses disappeared, this time from the Graham corral.)

On the evening of August 17, young Billy Graham rode home after a futile search for the horses. Deputy Sheriff Houck claimed to carry a warrant for John Graham. Houck had stopped at the Haigler ranch, where Haigler fed him, but told him to move on because he did not want trouble with the Grahams. At dawn, Houck rode on down the trail to wait for John Graham. Instead Billy appeared. Both men drew their guns, but before Billy could get off a shot, Houck fired and mortally wounded Billy, who died two days later.

The Grahams and their friend Andy Blevins Cooper did not go after Houck, but set out to eradicate the Tewksburys on September 2, 1887. During the crisp early-morning hours, the avenging party made its way down a trail and cautiously entrenched themselves behind the boulders around the Tewksbury house. John D. Tewksbury Sr., his sons Ed and Jim, Jim Roberts, and John Tewksbury Jr.'s pregnant wife, Mary, were inside their cabin. John Tewksbury Jr. and William Jacobs were outside working their horses.

Graham's party unleashed a volley of rifle shots that killed John Jr. and Jacobs. For a number of days, anyone attempting to leave the cabin faced a barrage of bullets. Those inside the cabin watched in horror as a herd of wild hogs began devouring the bodies over the next few days. Charles Perkins, who later helped bury the dead, said, "It was not possible to move them. They were badly torn by the hogs, and decomposition had gone so far that burying them was a most disagreeable task. All we did was to dig two very shallow graves and rolled the swollen mutilated bodies into them with our shovels."

When word of the fight got back to Prescott, Justice of the Peace John Meadows rode out with "gravel in his gizzard" to convene a coroner's jury. Jim Tewksbury said, "No damned man can kill a brother of mine and stand guard over him for the hogs to eat him and live within a mile and a half of me."

Shortly after Martin Blevins's disappearance, the Blevins family moved to Holbrook, about seventy-five miles northeast of Pleasant Valley. Cattle depredations around Holbrook and nearby St. Johns worsened, about the same time that Andy Blevins Cooper arrived in town to visit his family.

Apache County Sheriff Owens had won his election with the backing of the Apache County Cattlemen's Association. The *St. Johns Herald* berated Cooper and his friends who "openly boasted that the officers of the law were afraid of them." In late August, the Apache County Board of Supervisors ordered Owens to arrest Cooper within the next ten days or else they would initiate removal proceedings against him. Owens, tired of insinuations that he was afraid, went after Cooper on September 4, 1887.

When Sheriff Owens rode into Holbrook, John Blevins was at the livery stable. Although John did not know Owens, he suspected that this stranger might be the new sheriff, so he warned his brother, Andy, who told him to bring a horse around to the house. While Owens stopped to clean his six-shooter, Sam Brown (chairman of the Democratic Party) advised him that Andy Cooper planned to make a getaway. Owens quickly reassembled his gun, took his Winchester, and walked toward the Blevins cottage.

Andy Cooper, John and Eva Blevins (and their baby son), Mose Roberts, Sam Houston Blevins, Martin Blevins's widow Mary, her daughter Artemisia, and a friend, Amanda Gladden (with her baby), were inside. Owens knocked and Cooper cautiously opened the door a crack. When he saw the sheriff, he slammed the door, but the sheriff got his foot in the door and told Cooper that he had a warrant for horse stealing.

Cooper asked Owens to wait, but Owens went ahead and shot him dead. John Blevins fired and missed the sheriff, but his bullet passed through a wall and killed a horse. Owens hit John with a shot from his Winchester. The sheriff then dashed across the street so he could cover two sides of the house. He fired another shot, mortally wounding Roberts, who was armed with a six-shooter, when he jumped through a window. Mose Roberts shortly thereafter had a privilege accorded few men: on the verge of death, he testified at his own inquest on September 6, 1887. Roberts insisted that Owens never called for him to surrender.

Fifteen-year-old Sam Houston Blevins grabbed Cooper's weapon over his mother's protests. He

Apache County Sheriff Commodore Perry Owens, circa 1884.

hollered, "Where is that blankety-blank so-and-so? I'll git him." As he stepped onto the porch, Owens put a bullet through Sam's heart before the boy had a chance to cock the trigger. With four shots, Owens had killed three men and wounded a fourth. Without a word to the bystanders, Owens rode out of town. A grand jury exonerated Owens, and the newspapers heaped praise on him.

John Blevins survived the shoot-out, only to be accused of attempting to murder Owens. When the grand jury questioned him about a spent shell from his gun, he explained, "Yesterday I shot it off once at rabbits as I was coming in with Andy." Blevins languished in the Apache County Jail for almost a year before his trial came up. He was found guilty of assault with the intent to commit murder. On September 20, 1888, Judge James H. Wright sentenced him to five years in the Yuma Territorial Prison. On November 1, Owens and his prisoner, John Blevins, boarded the train for Yuma.

On board the train, the conductor gave Owens a telegram signed by Territorial Governor Conrad M. Zulick, ordering him to release the prisoner. Owens ignored it. Later another telegram ordering Owens to release Blevins arrived, along with instructions for the conductor to read it to Owens. Owens put Blevins off the train, and Blevins walked back to Holbrook and his surprised wife. Why Zulick pardoned Blevins is unclear. Perhaps he thought Blevins had spent enough time in jail for his part in a shoot-out that he could not have avoided.

The *Apache County Critic* (out of Holbrook) aptly predicted, "All of this is simply a chapter of the Tonto Basin history, and no man can foretell the end." The Holbrook shoot-out did not end the Pleasant Valley War. Cabins and corrals mysteriously burned to the ground, and sheepherders were ambushed. Horses and cattle kept right on disappearing. Both Ed Tewksbury and Tom Graham fanned the fires of hatred by spewing their propaganda onto newspaper pages.

Governor Zulick, Yavapai District Attorney John C. Herndon, and Sheriff Mulvenon met in early September of 1887 to find ways to stop the violence. When the *Prescott Journal-Miner* learned of the meeting, it published their plans in detail. Zulick had told Mulvenon, "Kill them, and no one will be hurt for it." They decided that Yavapai County Sheriff Mulvenon, Apache County Sheriff Owens, Gila County Sheriff Ed Hodgson, and Maricopa County Sheriff Andrew Jackson Halbert, each with a posse of ten men from their respective counties, would "scour the country until every man for whom there was an outstanding warrant is arrested."

The multi-force posse action never came about, because Maricopa County did not care for the idea. However, Mulvenon raised a posse of twenty men from Yavapai County and swept through the valley. He intended first to arrest the Graham partisans, and then send an emissary to the Tewksburys to notify them of the capture and that the lawmen were coming for them as well.

Yavapai County Sheriff John Mulvenon.

Deputy Sheriff Dan Francis, with a posse from Flagstaff, rendezvoused with Mulvenon at Payson. The lawmen then rode to the Haigler ranch, which provided an excellent lookout of the trail leading to the Graham ranch. At Haigler's, deputies Joe McKinney and Glenn Reynolds, each with four more men, joined Mulvenon. The next day Deputy Sheriff Houck, with several more men, arrived. Mulvenon arrested every suspect along the way, to preserve the secrecy of his mission to apprehend the Grahams and the Tewksburys.

During the night of September 21, all the posse members except McKinney and his men hid their horses and took up positions behind the partially constructed walls of Perkins's store. McKinney's posse had the dangerous job of serving as decoys; Mulvenon detailed McKinney to take his men and approach the store by passing the Graham and Rose ranches in broad daylight. When they passed Al Rose's place, Rose fired off warning shots. The Grahams fired in response and sent John Graham and Charlie Blevins to investigate McKinney's presence.

When Graham and Blevins came within fifteen steps of Perkins's store, Mulvenon stepped out and said, "Put up your hands, boys, I want you." The riders spurred their mounts. Graham pulled his pistol, but buckshot from Mulvenon's shotgun brought his horse down. A rifle ball tore into Graham's left arm above the elbow and passed through his body. Mulvenon finished Blevins off with his next barrel of buckshot.

The posse moved the dying Blevins to the shade of a tree and gave him a drink of water. Mulvenon asked Graham, "Johnny, why didn't you put your hands up when I told you to? Didn't you know me?" Graham shook his head. Mulvenon said, "He knows he is a damn liar, he knew me." Graham died an hour later. Mulvenon and his men rode to the Tewksbury place, where they found Ed and Jim Tewksbury, Jim Roberts, George Newton, and Jake Lauffer ready to surrender. McKinney heard a participant mutter, "There will be a quiet assassination going on here for some time to come."

Vigilante Justice Is Served

Autumn in Pleasant Valley is beautiful, with the brilliantly colored leaves and the crisp cool mountain air, but nothing cooled the Pleasant Valley War. Mulvenon deputized extra men in case violence erupted in Prescott during the trial. Yavapai County voters criticized Mulvenon for the high costs of his posses, which by now amounted to over $3,000.

In mid-October of 1887, Ed and James Tewksbury, with their partisans, were indicted for the murder of Hampton Blevins. All of the men made bond and were released. When their cases came up for trial no one would testify and everyone went free. Cattle rustling and horse stealing continued to plague even the non-participants in the feud.

Tough, taciturn Jesse Ellison, with his family and two thousand head of cattle, had moved into Arizona in 1885. According to Bob Voris (whose memoirs on this dark history were not unsealed until many years after his death), Ellison led the Vigilante Committee of Fifty. This group, Voris recalled, which was "fast, grim, and deadly, soon became feared in Pleasant Valley as no other body was ever feared."

This vigilante committee hanged Al Rose at the Houdon Ranch in early November 1887. Rose, a Graham partisan, had been ordered by the committee to leave the valley, because they knew he rustled horses, and he talked too much. He decided to round up his cattle and horses first. On the morning that the vigilantes hanged Rose, Louis Naegle had stopped by to visit him and was almost hanged, too, "for being in bad company."

James Stott, a newcomer from Massachusetts, stopped first in Texas to learn the ranching business and then went to work for the Hashknife. Stott picked up the bad habit of rustling cattle to stock his own homestead about forty miles south. Other Hashknife rustlers also used Stott's place to hide their stolen cattle, and Jim Scott and Billy Wilson, Hashknife cowboys, spent their last night on earth at Stott's ranch.

Motte Clymer, a young tubercular, was working during this time at Stott's ranch for his room and board.

On the morning of August 11, 1888, six to eleven men, including Deputy Sheriff Houck, rode up to Stott's cabin. In the Western tradition of hospitality, Stott invited them to come in and eat breakfast. Afterwards, the vigilantes "invited" all but Clymer to take a short ride. Encouraged to leave the area immediately, Clymer boarded the next train out of Holbrook. The vigilantes and their prisoners rode down the Verde road. Scott and Wilson pleaded for their lives, but Stott faced his assailants with curses and called each man by name. After putting the nooses around their necks, the vigilantes switched their victim's horses across their rumps, leaving each prisoner to dance the dead man's jig.

Hashknife cowboys Billy Wilson (left) and Tom Tucker (right).

On December 3, 1888, James Tewksbury, the deadliest gun of Pleasant Valley, died of tuberculosis while visiting a friend in Phoenix. Still, the war would continue. On April 10, 1892, George Newton, a Tewksbury partisan, disappeared. Several friends had unsuccessfully attempted to dissuade Newton from making the dangerous trip from Globe to his Pleasant Valley ranch that night. His wife's $10,000 reward attracted many searchers, including Ed Tewksbury, who discovered Newton's pack-horse on a Salt River sandbar, with its load still in place. Newton's other horse was found shot between the eyes. No one ever found Newton.

The Death of Tom Graham

Meanwhile, Tom Graham had moved to Tempe, where he fell in love with Annie Melton, daughter of a Tempe Baptist minister. On October 8, 1887, Tom and Annie were married in her parents' home with her father, the Reverend William Jasper Melton, officiating. Four days after the wedding, Tom presented himself to Maricopa County Sheriff Halbert, who contacted Sheriff Mulvenon in Yavapai County. Tom Graham and Tom's attorney, Albert Baker, rode to Prescott. Tom appeared in court, posted bail, and was ordered to face the grand jury in December, on the same day that the Tewksburys were to appear in court. The Tewksburys charged Tom Graham with the murder of the Basque sheepherder who had first brought sheep into Pleasant Valley. When no one would testify, Tom walked out of court a free man.

Tom returned to Pleasant Valley for one day, and hired Silas Young and a few more cowboys to round up his cattle. Bill Colcord rode out to meet Tom Graham's party and asked, "Well, boys, is it peace or war?" Graham said he preferred peace. He drove his cattle to Tempe without incident. Silas Young agreed to manage Graham's seven hundred head of cattle on shares. Tom heard rumors that the Tewksburys began a week-long bacchanal the day he left the valley. He, in turn, spread the story the Tewksburys were afraid to hurt him while he was in the valley.

On August 2, 1892, Tom Graham passed a wooded area while riding to Tempe with a wagonload of barley. Mollie Cummings and Grace Griffith, on a morning buggy ride, saw two men with guns hiding in the brush. The men fired, and a rifle ball severed Tom Graham's spinal cord. In those brief moments just before he collapsed from being shot, he turned to see his old adversaries, Ed Tewksbury and John Rhodes, leveling their Winchesters at him. The horses spooked and galloped, with the dying Tom and the wagon, to the house of W. T. Cummings. During his final hours, Graham spoke with visitors and with his wife, Annie, at the Cummings home.

Dr. Scott Helm tactlessly said, "They have got you this time, Tom." Graham admitted that he was "done for." A coroner's jury ruled that Tom Graham came to his death from a gunshot wound caused by John Rhodes and Ed Tewksbury. The newspaper headline read, "Murdered: A Culmination of the Bloodiest and Most Savage Feud That Ever Cursed the Territory." After Tom Graham died at age thirty-eight, Ed Tewksbury became the "last man."

The Trial

That same morning, Tempe constable Manuel Gallardo arrested Rhodes about ten miles from Phoenix. The unarmed Rhodes, who probably had given his gun to Tewksbury, did not resist and professed innocence. Samuel W. Finley, a Phoenix bartender, knew Tewksbury and was a good friend of Rhodes, so Maricopa County Sheriff John Montgomery deputized him to bring in Tewksbury. Finley left for Pleasant Valley on the evening of Tom's murder to arrest Tewksbury, who agreed to surrender to Gila County Sheriff John H. Thompson in Globe.

ARIZONA FEUD IN NATIONAL HEADLINES

By now the Graham-Tewksbury Feud was making national headlines. *The Los Angeles Times* sneered that "If Arizona should have a few more feuds like that out in Tonto Basin it would be difficult to get enough people together there ever to admit her as a state."

Exhibited like an animal in a zoo, Rhodes snapped at a reporter, "I haven't got a God damn thing to say about this affair." Charlie Duchet, a loyal Graham partisan, tried to shoot Rhodes, but the quick action of Deputy Tom Elder deflected his aim. The bullet ended up in the *Tempe Daily News* door.

Rhodes appeared for his hearing on August 9 before Judge W. O. Huson. (This was summer in Phoenix, Arizona, with no air conditioning in the courtroom.) On the second day, Mollie Cummings and Grace Griffith both identified Rhodes as one of the men they saw shoot Tom Graham.

In the afternoon, after asserting her right to sit at the front of the courtroom near Rhodes, Annie Melton Graham threw back her black widow's veil, and "her eyes glittered with a deadly purpose." She asked for a glass of water and stood up to drink it, while glaring at Rhodes. No one knew that she had smuggled Tom's gun into the courtroom. Suddenly she sprang forward and placed the muzzle of her cocked Colt .45 revolver against Rhodes's back. She tried to pull the trigger, but the hammer caught in her handkerchief. Everyone in the courtroom dashed for the exit. Sheriff

Montgomery seized Annie, and with help of several bystanders took the gun away from her. Annie screamed, "Oh, my God! Let me shoot! Oh, do let me shoot! Oh, God, he killed my husband!"

The next day the courtroom filled to capacity to hear Annie's testimony. The composed twenty-four-year-old widow testified calmly regarding the events on the day of Tom's murder. Judge Huson ruled that the defense had so conclusively proved their alibi that he had to release the prisoner. After spending the night of August 19 in jail, Rhodes left for Pleasant Valley the next morning with a troop of heavily armed friends. The press scorched Huson for what it perceived as a miscarriage of justice.

People lost interest in Rhodes when Ed Tewksbury came before Judge Harry L. Wharton for his hearing on the charge of murdering Tom Graham. Mollie Cummings provided a moment of high drama, when she pointed to Tewksbury and said, "That is the man." On December 5, Tewksbury was arraigned on a charge of murder. His attorneys moved for a change of venue.

On September 10, 1893, Judge Richard E. Sloan ordered the trial moved to Tucson. On December 14, Tewksbury's trial opened under District Judge J. D. Bethune. Within a week the jury received the case, and after two days of deliberation it brought a guilty verdict. Tewksbury's attorneys knew that even if they did not win the case, they could not lose. Before the judge pronounced sentence, the attorneys informed the court that Tewksbury had not been allowed to plead either innocent or guilty. When his plea could not be found, Judge Bethune had no choice but to grant Tewksbury a new trial.

Tewksbury appeared before Judge Richard Sloan in Tucson on January 2, 1895. This time the prosecution lacked an important witness. Annie Graham had remarried and moved to California. Sympathy shifted to Tewksbury, who had spent almost three years in the Pima County Jail. After a long deliberation, the jury found itself hopelessly deadlocked. A new trial might result in another hung jury or acquittal for Tewksbury. In case of a conviction, Tewksbury would certainly appeal.

Thomas Graham, 1882.

Then the territory would face the problem of securing a supreme court quorum. Three judges constituted a quorum for the Arizona Territorial Supreme Court. However, Chief Justice Albert Baker could not rule on the case because he had been Tewksbury's attorney. Judge Bethune could not act, because Tewksbury's case had been tried before him in the lower court. This left only two supreme court judges with the right to act on a Tewksbury appeal, so the Maricopa County district attorney felt he had no choice but to drop the Tewksbury case.

On February 6, 1895, while waiting for approval on the paperwork to drop the case, Judge Bethune set Tewksbury's bail at $10,000. Within a week, Tewksbury posted bond and walked out of jail a free man. He returned to Globe, where he served as a constable and as Gila County deputy sheriff. On April 4, 1904, Ed Tewksbury lost his last fight when he died of tuberculosis.

The Sequel: Lawless Become Lawmen

William Mulvenon, after serving two terms as Yavapai County sheriff, went on to represent Yavapai County in the Territorial legislature. Mulvenon died at age eighty-eight in 1915 in Prescott.

Jefferson Davis Adams, Maricopa County Sheriff several years after the events of this chapter took place.

Jefferson Davis Adams, the young cowboy who had been seriously wounded in the July 1884 shoot-out at Stinson's cabin, served as a Maricopa County deputy sheriff under Sheriff Carl Hayden. When Hayden became the first United States senator from Arizona, Adams succeeded him as sheriff.

After serving as Apache County sheriff, Commodore Perry Owens applied for the sheriff's position of the newly created Navajo County, where he served a relatively quiet term. After losing the next election, Owens went to work as a special agent for the Atchison, Topeka and Santa Fe Railroad, and for Wells, Fargo and Company, and served as a deputy U.S. marshal. In 1900, he married Elizabeth Barrett and opened a mercantile in Seligman. Owens died on May 10, 1919.

Glenn Reynolds, alleged to have been a member of the vigilantes, was killed while transferring the Apache Kid and other Apache prisoners to the Yuma Territorial Prison in his capacity as Gila County sheriff. Samuel W. Finley, the deputy who had brought in Ed Tewksbury, was shot and killed in the spring of 1902 near Tonopah, Nevada. While trying to arrest four outlaws, Finley killed three of them before the fourth one murdered him.

John C. Gilleland, wounded in the Pleasant Valley War, went on to become a Gila County deputy sheriff. Gilleland, who homesteaded near Buckeye, died at his Phoenix home on January 3, 1936. Tom Tucker, the Hashknife cowboy, later became a lawman in New Mexico; in 1905, Tucker served as a cattle inspector at Socorro, New Mexico. When the sheriff of Santa Fe County, New Mexico, asked Tucker to serve as his under-sheriff, the former outlaw embarked on a long law-enforcement career wherein he shot nine men "who disputed his authority to arrest them." In 1929, Tom Tucker died in his seventies of natural causes.

James D. Houck, a sheep man and Apache County deputy sheriff, suffered business reverses toward the end of his life. One day after feeding the chickens he told his family that he had just taken strychnine because he was "tired of living." He lay down on his bed and asked that his shoes be removed.

Besides serving as an Apache County deputy sheriff during the Pleasant Valley War, Joseph McKinney was appointed constable at Winslow in 1887. He joined the Arizona Rangers in 1905. McKinney died in Mesa on October 2, 1948.

John Blevins became a prosperous rancher and homesteaded land southeast of Heber on the Mogollon Rim, and served as Arizona cattle inspector in 1928. On May 23, 1929, he was killed near Buckeye by a hit-and-run driver.

John Rhodes married Mary, the widow of John Tewksbury Jr. On August 1, 1906, Rhodes at age fifty-five became the oldest man ever to serve in the Arizona Rangers. His superiors rated him "excellent." John Rhodes died in 1918 of tuberculosis.

Many who started on the wrong side of the law ended up being Arizona officers of the law. One must remember that in the 1880s in Arizona, the law was bought with guns, and no one questioned too carefully where the experience came from.

CHAPTER 2.
The Power Shoot-out

John and Tom Power (left to right), later in life.

On the cold, crisp morning of February 10, 1918, gunshots rang out in Arizona's Galiuro Mountains. Graham County Sheriff Robert Franklin "Frank" McBride and his deputies, Thomas Kane Wootan and Martin Kempton, died in a hail of gunfire, and Thomas Jefferson Power Sr. collapsed in a pool of blood, mortally wounded. Those who knew the true motives for the shoot-out and who drew first have long since gone to their graves. The gunfight left three dead lawmen, three widows, and twenty-one fatherless children. In the movies, peace officers either kill or capture the desperados. In real life, lawmen often die in shoot-outs and their families suffer grief and hardship.

Sheriff McBride and the Power Family

Sheriff McBride, born January 4, 1875, in Eden, Utah, came with his Mormon family to southeastern Arizona as a child. The McBride family settled in Smithville, now

Pima, on February 10, 1880. They lived in a two-room log house until Peter McBride (Frank's father) finished their adobe farmhouse. For three years, young Frank attended the Mormon Church school, and a year at the St. Joseph Stake Academy in Thatcher completed his formal education. Frank's mother ran a boardinghouse for the students while his father taught at the academy.

Frank excelled in athletics and enjoyed acting in church-theater presentations. For several years he courted Clara Sims, a member of another pioneer Mormon family. Finally she accepted his proposal and on August 16, 1899, they were married. Two years later, Frank received a call to fill a mission for the Mormon Church. He left by train for Salt Lake City, where he underwent a couple of weeks of training at the temple before serving the church in Texas.

Upon his return, Frank helped on his father's farm and worked as a carpenter. In January 1915, Graham County Sheriff Tom Alger appointed McBride as a deputy sheriff. However, Alger fired McBride when McBride ran against him on the Democratic ticket; McBride subsequently defeated the sheriff after a bitter campaign.

About the same time that the Mormons settled in southeastern Arizona, many Texans—who were running from either the law or the severe droughts—settled along the Arizona-New Mexico border. They included the Thomas Jefferson Power family. Tragedy had stalked the Power family. In 1890, Tom Power, his mother, Janie, his wife, Martha, and their son Charlie moved their herd of cattle from Texas to a ranch near Cliff, New Mexico. Here, two more sons—John Grant and Thomas Jefferson Jr.—and a daughter, Ola May, were born. While the father was helping a friend build a house near Silver City, a beam fell and killed the pregnant Martha. After her death, Tom Sr. rambled and worked at menial jobs throughout the West. Finally, the family settled in Arizona in 1909 in remote Kielburg Canyon in the Galiuro Mountains, where the Power men established the Power Mine.

Janie helped her son rear the children after Martha's death. The Power children received two or three years of formal education. Ola May attended the Willcox public school until she beat up a teacher. One day Janie and Ola May brought the men their lunch at a roundup near Cedar Spring. On their way home, a horse spooked, throwing both women out of the buggy. Ola May got help from a nearby ranch, but it came too late for Janie, who had suffered a broken hip and head injuries.

To supplement their income, the Power brothers hired out on roundups and made moonshine whiskey. They ran their own cattle and were no better or worse than average when it came to rustling their neighbors' beef. Tom Jr. once claimed that Frank

McBride once asked him to serve as his undersheriff so that he (McBride) could "run the office, drink good whiskey, smoke cigars, and prop his feet on the desk." Evidently, the families knew each other fairly well.

In 1917, Tom Sr. hired Thomas Sisson to help build a road to the mine in exchange for room and board. Sisson had learned the blacksmith and wheelwright trades while serving in the cavalry. After his discharge, he was convicted of stealing cattle, but Governor G. W. P. Hunt paroled Sisson after he served only a few months of a five-year sentence at the Arizona State Prison.

The Power men and Sisson lived in one shack, while Ola May had her own cabin. On December 6, 1917, her father found Ola May collapsed across her bed in convulsions. She

Graham County Sheriff Frank McBride.

allegedly sat up and said "poison" just before she died. The coroner, Dr. W. E. Platt, discovered two broken neck vertebrae, but her death certificate stated that Ola May Power died of an unknown cause.

Mrs. Boscoe, who had dressed Ola May's body, recalled that when Tom Jr. commented on her death, their father said, "It don't do no good to grieve about it now. What's done is done." Gossip implied that Ola May's brothers may have accidentally broken her neck. Others said that when Ola May tried to elope with a serviceman, John threw her down and cracked her head.

Tom Power Sr., along with many others, believed that American boys should not be shipped overseas to fight. On May 18, 1917, President Woodrow Wilson signed the Selective Military Conscription Act (later called the Selective Service Act), requiring registration of all men between the ages of twenty-one and thirty for military service. The Power brothers—Thomas and John, ages twenty-four and twenty-six respectively—were eligible for military service. Whenever strangers approached the Power place, Tom and John hid out in caves. Tom Sr. told his neighbors that his boys would go to war "over my dead body."

Around the middle of January 1918, Sheriff McBride asked the Powers' neighbor Jay Murdock to deliver a letter to the Power family, explaining the seriousness of the boys' refusal to register for the draft. Murdock, who had already argued with Tom Jr. and John over property right-of-way and knew how the family felt about the draft, expressed reluctance to deliver the letter.

Murdock told McBride that on the night of Ola May's death, he had asked her father what he would do if the authorities came for his sons. Tom Jr. interrupted with prophetic words. "Let them come. I'd just as soon die now as any time, and while they're getting us, we'll get some of them, maybe more than they get of us."

McBride's letter explained that the boys were traitors to their country if they failed to register. The sheriff assured them that they would not be prosecuted if they came in immediately. He pointed out that ultimately the U.S. government would arrest them if they refused to come in. Ending on a curious note, McBride commented, "Ola May would not approve of her brothers' stand against the war."

When Murdock saw that the sheriff was trying to avoid trouble, he agreed to deliver the letter. Much to his surprise, the father acted as though the letter was unimportant. After receiving no response, McBride brought the situation to the attention of County Attorney W. R. Chambers, who asked Justice of the Peace U. I. Paxton to issue warrants for the apprehension of all the Power men and Sisson.

McBride formed a posse and deputized Martin R. Kempton, Thomas Kane Wootan, and Frank Haynes, all of whom had extensive law-enforcement experience. During his brief term as sheriff, McBride had already earned respect from the outlaw element. Both Kempton and Wootan came from pioneer Mormon families. Kempton, born in Brigham City, from time to time served as a deputy sheriff. However, his real interest was in his farm, and he used his law-enforcement wages to develop it. Wootan worked as a rancher and served part-time as a peace officer.

On February 9, 1918, U.S. Deputy Marshal Haynes, Graham County Sheriff McBride, and Deputy Sheriffs Kempton and Wootan set out on their fateful journey. Haynes carried a federal warrant to bring in Tom Jr. and John for draft evasion, and McBride had a warrant to bring in Tom Sr. and Sisson for questioning in Ola May's death.

At Al Upchurch's ranch near Klondyke, the lawmen enjoyed a hot

John Power.

supper, and borrowed horses and guns from Upchurch. Carefully the posse picked its way through treacherous mountain passes, so rugged that even today the Power cabin is inaccessible by automobile. Late that first evening, they stopped for coffee at Merle Haby's ranch, where Wootan got into an argument with McBride. Wootan said, "If you will just wait until daylight and let me go up there all by myself, just let me go alone in broad open daylight; I will bring them boys and that old man out and there will be no trouble." The sheriff refused and insisted that the posse go in together.

TROUBLE BREWING FOUR YEARS EARLIER?

Difficulties between the Power and Wootan families had started four years earlier, when Tom Jr. and John caught the Wootans roping and driving their cattle off the forest reserve. After warning them to stop, the Power boys held them at gunpoint while they cut their stock out of the herd. A year later Wootan swore out a warrant for the Power brothers, charging them with stealing his cattle. Rancher Lee Solomon would later testify that Wootan planned "to shoot the hell out of the Powers and get elected sheriff himself."

Early the next morning, the posse started over a trail that led to a deserted ranch house. The lawmen built a campfire and discussed their strategy, and around 4:30 a.m., they proceeded on horseback toward the Power cabin. At dawn, Wootan and Haynes, armed with rifles and six-shooters, approached the south end of the cabin while McBride and Kempton went to the north corner. Tom Sr., wearing a flour-sack apron over his long johns, was preparing breakfast when he heard someone holler, "Throw up your hands." Then a horse whinnied. With his .30-30 Winchester rifle, he went outside to investigate the commotion. By now, the two brothers and Sisson were awake and had grabbed guns. Shots rang out, and the father fell.

McBride got off a snap shot from his rifle and hit the door. Splinters sprayed into John's eye. He fired off three shots and hit McBride in the neck. Haynes watched McBride go down, but he could not see what had happened to Wootan or Kempton. Sisson hit Kempton in the knee, and then got off another shot that killed the deputy. Wootan's shots crashed through the window, filling Tom Jr.'s eye with glass. Tom then punched out the window and shot and killed Wootan when the deputy tried to drag Kempton out of the way.

Haynes rode seventy miles back to Safford. Along the way he stopped at ranches and gave his account of the gunfight. Several ranchers gathered at Upchurch's place to wait for additional instructions. Haynes interrupted a church service to call out the sheriff's brother, Howard McBride. Haynes said that Frank was probably dead but he did not know what happened to the other two deputies.

After they were convinced that no more lawmen remained in the area, Tom and John moved their father to the mine-tunnel entrance. Then they took the posse's remaining horses, money, guns, and cartridge belts, and began their flight. Sisson, who had scouted in his cavalry days, would attempt to guide them into Mexico. They stopped at Murdock's camp, where a neighbor, young Henry Allen, asked, "What is the matter?"

John replied, "The matter is laying there over in the yard."

Allen asked, "Any of you boys hurt?"

John replied, "No more than what you can see."

Murdock, who had heard the gunshots, asked, "It has happened?"

One of the brothers said, "You're damned right, it has happened."

Murdock asked, "Where is your father?"

"They shot him. He is wounded."

Murdock asked, "Is he dead?"

"No."

John, his face streaked with blood and pierced with splinters, said, "I killed McBride."

The brothers claimed that Wootan shot their father after he dropped his gun and threw up his hands. The bullet that mortally wounded Thomas Jefferson Power Sr. pierced his left breast and came out between the shoulder blades. When Dr. Platt (the coroner) lifted his arm, Power bled from the chest, indicating that he had been shot while he had his hands up. Murdock's descendant Russell Murdock still contends, "Power was shot with his hands up, no question about it."

After the trio left, Jay Murdock and his uncle rode over to the Power cabin, where they covered the dead lawmen with blankets and attended to the father. Barely alive, he said, "This is Dad," mistaking Murdock for one of his sons. He asked for a drink of water and kept repeating, "I am cold, so cold."

Before his death, he told Murdock, "I stepped out in the yard. They hailed me and hollered 'throw up your hands' and I dropped my gun and throwed [sic] up my hands. I says, 'We give up,' and then Kane shot me." Thomas Jefferson Power Sr. lapsed into unconsciousness and died at about four o'clock that afternoon.

Pursuit of the Fugitives

After McBride's death, the Graham County Board of Supervisors immediately named Brig Stewart as sheriff. Deputy Sheriff Dave Skaggs, Dr. Platt, Graham County Attorney W. R.

Sheriff J. D. Skaggs.

Chambers, Frank McBride's brother, Howard, and Martin Kempton's brother, Nate, along with the ranchers who had gathered at Al Upchurch's place, rode out to bring in the fallen lawmen. Not knowing if the Power brothers and Sisson were still in the vicinity, the posse took extreme care upon approaching the cabin. Howard McBride and Nate Kempton broke down and wept when they saw their dead brothers' faces, mutilated with heel marks.

Angry posse members pillaged the cabin and appropriated the family's Model T Ford. (The court later ordered that the vehicle be sold and the proceeds given to the widows of the lawmen.) Dave Wilson and Upchurch, experienced ranchers and packers, wrapped the bodies in quilts and tied them facedown with diamond hitches on individual horses. Upchurch claimed that this was the only way a horse could be made to pack out a dead man. Murdock buried Power near his mine.

Andrew Kimball, president of the St. Joseph Stake of the Mormon Church, officiated at the single funeral service of McBride, Wootan, and Kempton in the Safford community hall. Afterwards, many organizations and individuals came forward with rewards. Governor Hunt offered $1,000 for the capture and conviction of the missing men. Hunt evidently hoped to avert a lynching by adding the conviction stipulation. The Graham County Board of Supervisors and other groups offered rewards for capture "dead or alive." The Power shoot-out precipitated one of the largest manhunts in Arizona history, which included over three thousand men from Arizona and New Mexico.

Tom and John Power and Tom Sisson were tough, desperate men, but during the winter, Arizona mountain nights are very cold, with snow at the upper elevations. At their first stop, the fugitives arrived at Redington, where a friend informed them that Pima County Sheriff Rye Miles and Cochise County Sheriff Harry Wheeler were forming posses. At that time, the Posse Comitatus law, or "power of the county," applied to all male residents fifteen and older who might be summoned by the sheriff.

After a brief rest and some food, the fugitives continued their flight along a railroad track that led them to Cochise Stronghold. That night they took turns sleeping and keeping watch. Just before dawn they rode out toward Pearce, where they stopped at a house and bought food. Before long they saw two cars full of armed men, including Deputy Wootan's brother Frank. Sisson had gotten lost, and they had turned north instead of south. That evening a patrol vehicle passed within two hundred yards of the fugitives. Tom, who had field glasses, claimed that most of the time they had the posses in their sight line. They cooked their food and watered and grazed their horses, before resting themselves. The next morning they were awakened by a covey of cooing doves. Because the outlaws found it easier to cover their footprints than horse tracks, they turned the weary horses loose in a canyon.

Continuing their flight on foot through rain and snow into the Chiricahua Mountains, they went without food for two days. The hungry fugitives rustled and killed a yearling calf near Rodeo, New Mexico. A log-and-grass lean-to provided some protection, but the next morning they woke up in ten inches of snow, hearing voices from a nearby posse.

Silently they made their way through the mountains for another twenty-four hours until they reached the TM Ranch in New Mexico. They bought food at the ranch and for three more days and nights they plodded across New Mexico's Peloncillo Mountains, stopping only for brief rests. Finally they crossed the international border and walked another ten miles into Mexico.

Military units from Fort Huachuca, Arizona; Fort Bliss, Texas; Camp Harry Jones, Arizona; and Hachita, New Mexico, had all established patrols along the U.S.–Mexico border. In Mexico, Lieutenant Colonel Agustín Camou of Agua Prieta, Sonora, commander of the military forces of northeastern Sonora, ordered his troops to capture and turn over the Power brothers and Sisson to Arizona authorities if they crossed over into Mexico. In addition, Graham County Deputy Sheriff David Skaggs, Cochise County Sheriff Harry Wheeler, Gila County Sheriff Thomas Armer, Greenlee County Sheriff Arthur H. Slaughter, and Pima County Sheriff Rye Miles all rounded up posses to track down the fugitives. None of these colorful Arizona lawmen lacked in either courage or experience.

Wheeler almost got killed when his posse came within rock-throwing distance of the Power brothers and Sisson in Rucker Canyon. The trio drew a bead on him, but let him pass when they realized that he had not seen them.

Each day brought news that arrest of the fugitives was imminent. But days passed into weeks and still they remained at large. Dust and snowstorms followed by cold rains obliterated their tracks. On March 8, Captain Hugh Mitchell of I Troop, United States 12th Cavalry in Hachita, New Mexico, with a detachment of six soldiers, trailed the outlaws into Mexico. About ten miles across the border, Mitchell found himself looking down three gun barrels. John and Tom Power and Tom Sisson were hiding behind mesquite brush.

Mitchell courageously dismounted. The trio dropped their guns and surrendered, almost a month after the original gunfight. The outlaws felt that they had a better chance with the military than with a posse, which might lynch them on the spot. The Power brothers needed immediate medical attention. John experienced excruciating pain from the wooden splinters and maggots in his eye. Tom's eye was still full of glass. Famished and thirsty, they had survived with no water for twenty-four hours and nothing to eat for three days, except two raw rabbits. Each man had bits of dirty, raw rabbit meat in his pockets. The fugitives carried strychnine, presumably to poison water holes where their pursuers and their horses might drink.

FURTHER EXPLOITS OF THESE ARIZONA LAWMEN

Cochise County Sheriff Harry Wheeler, a diminutive man of only five feet, four inches, is best remembered for the infamous Bisbee Deportation, when on July 12, 1917, he ordered more than one thousand striking miners deported by train to Columbus, New Mexico.

Gila County Sheriff Thomas Armer prevented violence in the Globe-Miami area when the Industrial Workers of the World (IWW) endeavored to get union recognition in 1918. Armer and his posse raided an IWW dance and seized their literature.

In 1917, Greenlee County Sheriff Arthur H. Slaughter had met with three hundred strikers, who made threats about what they would do to the "scabs." He stationed his men behind barricaded cars and pretended he had more deputies behind nearby mesquite trees. After he called for a surrender, a few men attempted to flee. Slaughter fired at their feet, and that night seventy of the strikers enjoyed the hospitality of the Clifton jail.

When Pima County Sheriff Rye Miles visited in Casa Grande, a murder occurred near the train station. Miles chased the murderer and killed him on his third shot. He later recounted that the man "committed suicide, because any fool that runs from a man armed with a rifle surely isn't doing anything else."

After giving them water and dry crackers, Mitchell fired rifle shots in the air to alert the rest of his detachment. His men arrived with New Mexico's Hidalgo County Sheriff Frank Shriver, who insisted on taking the fugitives into custody. Mitchell, who insisted that they were his military prisoners, telegraphed Graham County's Sheriff Stewart that he had captured the Power brothers and Sisson. Stewart, with Deputy Sheriff Karl Foster and Safford Town Marshal Oscar Lancaster, drove to Duncan. At Duncan they picked up handcuffs and leg irons, and were joined by Slaughter and his deputy, Roy Kelly. The five lawmen traveled to Hachita, where Mitchell turned the outlaws over to Stewart.

Shriver, who wanted the reward money, still insisted that the prisoners were his responsibility. After the Graham County sheriff did some "plain talking," the New Mexico sheriff left empty-handed. Ultimately the reward money went into the I Troop fund of the 12th Cavalry. On the return trip, the prisoners were jailed at Duncan while the officers ate dinner.

Frank Wootan, with several of the dead lawmen's friends, planned to intercept the sheriff and lynch the fugitives. However, Stewart took a roundabout way to the Graham County jail in Safford. After the Power brothers and Sisson were safely in jail, they received haircuts, shaves, baths, clean clothes, and medical attention for their infected eyes (each brother eventually lost one eye). Stewart had his hands full with squelching lynch-party talk and coping with the curiosity-seekers who paraded in and out of the Graham County Courthouse.

Sisson talked freely. He said that he "felt right at home behind bars." He suggested that the sheriff charge 5 cents admission and that "the women are having a fine time."

Frank Wootan visited the prisoners, but before he went in, Stewart confiscated his car keys, knife, and anything else that might be used as a weapon. Tom and John refused to speak to him. Wootan finally asked Sisson what happened. Sisson replied, "Just what do you think happened?"

Charlie, the older brother of Tom and John, hired New Mexico attorney James S. Fielder for $100 to defend them. For Charlie, who had moved to New Mexico in 1915, this was the last contact with his family. He did not attend the trial and refused to give interviews.

Fielder secured a change of venue from Safford to Clifton. He advised the men to waive their right to a preliminary hearing, and their trial opened on May 13, 1918. Tom and John and Sisson were tried together for the murder of Frank McBride. Prosecutors contended that if they beat this case, then they could be tried separately for the murders of Wootan and Kempton.

Judge Laine ruled that the deathbed statement made by the father, Tom Power Sr., to John Murdock, reflecting his confusion as to why he had been shot when he had his hands up, was inadmissible. In an attempt to absolve their friend, John insisted Sisson had not taken part in the shooting. However, the bullet that killed McBride came from Sisson's .303 rifle, the only one of its kind in the cabin. John made such a poor showing that Fielder opted not to put Tom Jr. on the stand.

Tom Sisson.

Tom Power.

The only survivor of the shoot-out, Frank Haynes, testified that when Tom Sr. appeared at the cabin door, Wootan called out twice, "Throw up your hands." Instead he shot at the lawmen. Dr. Platt suggested that the Power brothers probably stomped on the faces of the dead lawmen in anger, leaving their heel marks. Will Mangum, a Pima store-keeper, gave the most damaging testimony, when he said the father had told him, "If Uncle Sam takes my boys, they'll do it over my dead body."

The jury deliberated just thirty-five minutes before finding Tom and John Power and Tom Sisson guilty of murder in the first degree. On May 20, 1918, Judge Laine sentenced them to be imprisoned at the state prison in Florence, Arizona, for the rest of their natural lives.

The Powers bothers always contended that the lawmen intended to kill them just to get the mine. In August 1918, the superior court gave the Power Mine, valued at $10,000, to the widows of McBride, Wootan, and Kempton.

Fielder chose not to appeal their case, even though he could have done so at the expense of the state. During their incarceration, Tom Power escaped from prison twice. On December 16, 1923, Tom, who had achieved trusty status, escaped with Willis Woods. Woods had told Tom that he knew where gold bullion had been hidden after a pack-train robbery in Mexico. Tom planned to find the gold and go to South America to purchase a cattle ranch, but he was recaptured a few months later when he tried to cross back into the United States at Juárez–El Paso.

Justice Served but Lives Wasted

On December 28, 1939, Tom and John Power, along with William Faltin, another lifer, escaped from prison together. Tom claimed that W. L. "Braz" Wootan, a new guard and a brother of the murdered Thomas K. Wootan, was looking for an opportunity to kill them. Graham County Sheriff Emert Kempton, brother of slain deputy Martin Kempton, led a posse into the Galiuros in search of the Power brothers and their accomplice.

The brothers made it across the border, where they claimed that Mexican authorities helped them get to Mexico City. When their money ran out, they returned to Texas. On April 20, 1940, Tom and John Power walked into the arms of U.S. Customs officials while wading across the Rio Grande.

In 1926, 1952, and 1954, the Power brothers made unsuccessful bids for parole. They showed no remorse for their deeds and continued to deny knowledge of the requirements for the World War I draft registration. Moreover, they could not provide the parole board with viable plans for their life outside the prison walls. The families of the murdered lawmen provided strenuous objections to their bids for freedom.

For Thomas Sisson, who died in prison on January 23, 1957, at the age of eighty-six, it was truly a life sentence. The $10,000, which he had accrued in savings from his military pension, he bequeathed to John Power. In 1960, the Power brothers made their final bid for freedom before the parole board. Attorney W. W. Richardson, representing the families of the slain men, insisted they exhibited antisocial attitudes and that the McBride and Kempton widows still feared for their lives.

Lorenzo Wright, former prison warden and president of the Maricopa Stake of the Mormon Church, in a shouting voice, demanded that the brothers ask for forgiveness. The men faced eighty-three-year-old Frank Wootan, brother of the slain deputy, and Leonard McBride, son of the slain sheriff.

Tom said, "We would like to be forgiven. We are sorry for whatever happened."

John said, "We beg their forgiveness."

The parole board unanimously approved their petition, and Governor Paul J. Fannin signed their parole and commutation-of-sentence papers. When Tom and John Power left the prison on April 27, 1960, they had served longer sentences than anyone else in the history of the Arizona State Prison before receiving a parole. John, age seventy, took his grinding stones, blacksmith equipment, and clothes. Tom, age sixty-eight, took only a cardboard box and an iron suitcase that he had made. Each man received $12.50 mustering-out pay. Tom had saved over $1,000, and John had over $12,000, including the money that Sisson left him.

Two years later, after considerable public pressure and sympathy for the brothers, Governor Jack Williams signed their full pardon and restored their citizens' rights. The men worked at various odd jobs and attempted to operate their old mine, which had been abandoned. Tom cast his first vote a few days before he died on September 11, 1970. Six years later, John died in his trailer behind the Klondyke store on April 5.

Justice was served. However, senseless murders and wasted lives are reflected in the violent tragedy of the shoot-out at the Power Mine. Graham County Sheriff Robert Franklin McBride and deputies Thomas Kane Wootan and Martin Kempton became part of a long list of peace officers who gave their last full measure. The Power brothers, along with Tom Sisson, wasted their lives in prison, after their father died in a pool of blood.

CHAPTER 3.
The Sheriff as Executioner

Yavapai County Sheriff George C. Ruffner.

The benefit of capital punishment, or legal administration of the death penalty, continues to be debated in Arizona as well as the rest of the nation. Proponents defend capital punishment on the basis of the Old Testament precept of "an eye for an eye" and the increase of public safety through the elimination of a murderer. Opponents contend that execution of the guilty does not deter murder, and that "an eye for an eye" is not civilized justice.

Over the ages, the methods of inflicting the death penalty have been many and varied. In early England, the condemned were pressed to death. In Japan, executioners shoved people into vats of hot ashes. During the Inquisition heretics were burned at the stake. France guillotined its royal prisoners, and the Spanish invented the spiked collar or garrote.

The first recorded Tucson murder trial took place near the San Xavier del Bac Mission in 1813, under Spanish rule. Lieutenant Manuel de León, acting military commander and civil judge of Tucson, found Francisco Xavier Díaz guilty of murdering his wife, María Ignacio Castellano, on July 6. Díaz accused María of infidelity with a Pima Indian man named Juan. The record of his execution has been lost, but Díaz was probably garroted toward the end of 1814.

Executing criminals by hanging them by the neck from a noose is one of the oldest methods of capital punishment. Traditionally the hanged died of slow strangulation, but in the late nineteenth century, an English executioner, William Marwood, discovered the "long drop." Marwood's technique consisted of dropping a body six to eight feet through a trapdoor. The neck is dislocated, the spinal column snaps, and the condemned dies instantly.

Prescribed By Law

In 1846, Arizona received its first U.S. code of laws while it was still a part of the New Mexico Territory. That year, General Stephen Watts Kearny proclaimed American civil government in the New Mexico Territory. Kearny derived his code of laws from Missouri and Texas laws. When a prisoner was scheduled for a hanging, the sheriff removed him to an isolated cell, where the condemned was kept under a watch. Kearny's code also prescribed fees for each of the services performed by a sheriff. The highest fee, $15, was paid for the execution of a prisoner.

During Territorial days, several crimes were punishable by execution: murder, train robbery, treason to the United States, bombing a building that resulted in a human injury, perjury during a trial that resulted in the execution of an innocent person, kidnapping and harming a hostage, and assault with a deadly weapon while on parole. In 1973, the Arizona legislature did away with the death penalty for assault, kidnapping, train robbery, and bombing a building. For first-degree murder, the legislature changed the law so that the trial judge rather than the jurors imposed the sentence. The legislature retained the death penalty as a possible sentence for treason, perjury resulting in the death of a human, and first-degree murder. Today the death penalty in Arizona is reserved only for first-degree murder.

Arizona Territorial law allowed the prisoner to have the services of no more than two ministers of the gospel, and he might choose up to five male witnesses to attend the execution. Women and children were not allowed to witness an execution, although sometimes children and a few women found vantage points for viewing the proceedings.

After an execution, the hangman pulled the legs of the condemned to prove that he had earned his fee. This act gave rise to the expression, "You're pulling my leg." After extensive experimentation, hangmen discovered in the mid-nineteenth century that an Italian hemp rope did not break easily. This five-stranded rope measured 1¼ inch in diameter. The hangman calculated the length of the rope from the height and weight of the condemned, and tied the knot at a spot where it fit under a man's ear.

Despite the comparatively high pay, most sheriffs detested the job of executioner and preferred to hire a hangman. When Cochise County Sheriff Stewart Hunt ordered his jailor, Joseph Axford, to hang a man, Axford resigned. One juror in 1912, knowing how much Maricopa County Sheriff Carl Hayden loathed hangings, voted "not guilty," even though he believed that Louis Eytinge had murdered John Leicht. As Arizona's first congressman, Hayden initiated state legislation to transfer executions from the county to the state prison.

Pima County Sheriff Peter Rainsford Brady, an Annapolis graduate, arrived in the Arizona Territory in 1853 with the Andrew B. Gray survey team. After serving as a midshipman, he resigned his commission to join the Texas Rangers in San Antonio. In 1855, Brady served as a Spanish translator for the Boundary Commission. When Civil War troops arrived in Tucson in 1862, Brady went to Mexico rather than swear allegiance to the Confederacy. In 1868, during his second term as Pima County sheriff, Brady faced the unpleasant possibility of having to hang a woman, Dolores Moore, who had been convicted of the murder of her husband, Mahlon Moore.

Mahlon Moore, a military express courier, was found shot to death in his Tucson home on October 4, 1868. That same day a coroner's jury indicted his wife, Dolores. When Brady arrested her, she told the sheriff that she did not know the location of her husband's pistol or who killed him. She insisted that an American who rode in with Mahlon from Camp Grant had killed her husband. She did not know the American's name, but thought he had also stolen Mahlon's pistol and pocketbook. Brady never found anyone fitting her description of the American. And Dolores Moore had, in fact, given the pocketbook to a neighbor for safekeeping.

Moore's trial began on December 17, 1868, under Judge Henry T. Backus. District Attorney Granville Oury served as prosecutor, and James McCaffry defended her. John Willis testified that Dolores had told him, "It was a *desgracia* that it happened in my house. Mr. Moore is dead." C. G. Jones testified that when Mahlon caught Dolores in a room with another man, Dolores's relations with her husband became "hostile." The star witness, eight-year-old Agustín Gallego, had passed by the Moore house during the shooting. He testified, "I saw the killing. Lola [Dolores] did it. The prisoner at the bar is the person. She did it with a pistol. I saw Moore fall when he was shot."

After almost eighteen hours of deliberation, Sheriff Brady accompanied the jury to the scene of the crime. The jury deliberated for several more hours and returned the verdict of "Guilty!" The jury recommended mercy, but Judge Backus sentenced Dolores Moore to be hanged by the neck until dead on February 26, 1869. Many Tucsonans, including Sheriff Brady, felt that hanging a woman would bring shame on the community. However, many more prominent citizens felt she should not be allowed to "commence anew her blood and violence."

While her appeals went through the court system, workmen constructed a special gallows for Dolores. Even a murderess could not be expected to go to her hanging in anything but her best dress. Dolores's gallows had to protect her from being viewed from underneath. While her

The 1905 hanging of Martin Ubillos.

gallows went up in the courthouse yard, a citizens' group, including Sheriff Brady, petitioned acting governor James P. T. Carter for clemency. The day before her execution, Carter commuted her sentence to life imprisonment.

For three years, Dolores Moore occupied one of the two cells at the Pima County Jail, while any number of men were incarcerated in the adjoining cell. On February 20, 1872, Governor A. P. K. Safford pardoned Dolores Moore on condition that she leave the United States within twenty days and never return. Her mother and sister took Dolores, who was in bad health, back to Mexico.

Throughout his life Peter Brady participated in public service. After two terms as Pima County sheriff, he ran unsuccessfully in 1870 for the Territorial legislature. He opened a flour mill in Florence and served a term as Pinal County sheriff. Brady successfully won election to the Territorial legislature in 1874. Three years later, he was appointed chairman of the Territorial prison board. Peter Rainsford Brady died quietly at his Tucson home on May 2, 1902, and he is buried in Tucson's Holy Hope Cemetery.

Did the Wrong Man Die In the First Legal Hanging?

From time to time, Arizonans, believing that the wheels of justice ground too slowly, decided to take the law into their own hands and lynched the criminals themselves. One objection to lynching is that an angry mob may execute the wrong man. Yet, the law may have hanged the wrong man during the Arizona Territory's first legal hanging.

Yavapai County Sheriff Edward F. Bowers, born in New Hampshire, worked as a miner in Colorado and California before settling on a ranch in Skull Valley. The Yavapai County voters elected Bowers as sheriff on the Independent ticket in 1874, and he had the dubious honor of becoming the first Arizona sheriff to legally hang a prisoner. A jury tried and found Manuel Aviles, about thirty years old, guilty of the murder of a Verde Valley ranch hand known only as Gregorio. Aviles failed to convince the jury that he had just found the victim, with his skull slashed and a bloodstained shovel lying nearby, when two men rode up and arrested him.

Bowers accompanied Aviles to the gallows on August 5, 1875. In his last words, Aviles told the crowd that his father had been shot by a firing squad for supporting a rebellion in Mexico, and that they both had bad luck in this life. When he asked for a cigarette, a flurry of cigarettes cascaded over him. The priest put one between his lips and lit it. After taking a puff, Aviles nodded to Bowers, indicating that he was ready. Sixty years later Gregorio's neighbor is alleged to have made a deathbed confession, stating that he had killed Gregorio over water rights.

FLOOR-SWEEPING EARNS HIGH PRAISE

The *Arizona Miner* (published in Prescott) complimented the big, good-natured sheriff for operating a well regulated jail and for sweeping the floor every day. When he came under criticism for not collecting taxes in Clifton in a remote far-eastern part of Arizona, Ed Bowers responded, "I shall not go to Clifton, as I cannot find anyone who has been there or knows the trail." On January 5, 1879, five days after completing his second term as Yavapai County sheriff, Edward Franklin Bowers, at age thirty-nine, died of pneumonia.

Frontier Justice

Arizona sheriffs have executed prisoners under other than legally sanctioned conditions. Pima County Sheriff Charles Shibell arrived in Tucson in 1862 as a teamster with Colonel James Carleton's California Column. After his discharge from the Union

Army, Shibell worked as a merchant, rancher, and miner, and actively participated in Pima County's public life. Shibell, a slightly built man with a pleasant demeanor, seemed more gentleman than gunfighter. Nevertheless, in August 1878 he led the posse that gunned down William Whitney Brazelton, a highway robber.

Brazelton, one of the few highwaymen who operated alone, had begun his robbery career in New Mexico. When New Mexico lawmen got too close for comfort, he moved to Tucson, where he found a job at Bob Leatherwood's livery stable. He bullied another livery employee, David Nemitz, into supplying him with food and ammunition. Brazelton held up the Tucson–Florence stage about twenty miles north of Tucson in early August 1878. Although the driver,

Manuel Aviles, the first man hanged for murder in Arizona.

Art Hill, was armed, he was no match for Brazelton's Spencer carbine and pistol. On August 8, the same masked man hit the same stage, now accompanied by Undersheriff John Miller, on the same spot. Hill yelled, "There he is again!" Brazelton replied, "Yes, and here I am again. Now throw up your hands!"

Newspapers took Shibell to task for losing the robber's trail both times. However, a posse member, Juan Elías, noted that the robber's horse had a crooked hoof, which he tracked to Nemitz's place. Nemitz, with a little persuasion, confessed to what he knew about Brazelton. Nemitz, fearing revenge, agreed to set up a rendezvous with the outlaw only if the posse agreed to kill Brazelton and not to take him prisoner.

Nemitz sent word to Brazelton to meet him near Point of Mountain (about eighteen miles west of present-day Tucson), where their signal would be a cough. On the evening of August 19, 1878, Shibell and his deputies took up concealed positions near the meeting place. Within an hour, the posse saw a shadowy figure approach. Brazelton gave the prearranged signal, a cough. Without warning, shots cracked the air. William Brazelton, swearing, "You son of a bitch I die brave, my God, I'll pray till I die," crumpled to the ground.

The posse took Brazelton's body back to Tucson, where they propped him against a Main Street wall for a couple of days, as a warning to anyone considering robbery as a career. When the corpse began to stink, he was buried in Potter's Field.

Shibell was reelected in 1880, tallying more than 60 percent of the votes. After he left the sheriff's office in a scandal of ballot-box stuffing, he operated the Palace Hotel and a Tucson mercantile. He served as Eugene Shaw's undersheriff in 1887, and two

Dennis Dilda.

years later he won the election for Pima County recorder. Shibell held this position for twenty years until his death on October 21, 1908, from "writer's palsy" (probably Parkinson's disease).

Last Requests

As if Yavapai County Sheriff William Mulvenon did not have enough to do with the Tewksbury-Graham Feud, he also had to hang Dennis Dilda for the murder of Yavapai County Deputy Sheriff John H. Murphy. In the autumn of 1885, Dennis Dilda, a swarthy, sullen loner, complained that he could not operate William H. Williscraft's ranch alone. Williscraft hired James Jenkins to help him. Jenkins arrived at the ranch with home passage funds for England. When Williscraft returned a few days later, his pocket watch and Jenkins were missing. Dilda explained that Jenkins had taken ill and gone to the Prescott hospital.

Williscraft soon learned that Dilda had been seen flashing a new pocket watch, and Jenkins never went to the hospital. Williscraft and Deputy Sheriff John H. Murphy rode out to serve Dilda with a warrant for petty larceny. At the ranch, they found Mrs. Dilda with her two children. She told Murphy that Dilda had gone hunting. Later that evening, Murphy decided to serve the warrant alone, despite warnings from neighbors that Dilda was dangerous. Murphy never returned.

On December 21, 1885, a posse found the bodies of Murphy and Jenkins buried in a cellar at Dilda's home. Murphy had been shot in the back. Mrs. Dilda admitted that she had helped bury the bodies, but insisted that she had not committed the murders. She professed not to know where Dilda had gone. In the meantime, Sheriff Mulvenon learned that Dilda was wanted for murders in Texas and New Mexico. His brother-in-law had disappeared, and the family believed that Dilda had killed him. The posse arrested Dilda at Ash Fork, where he was sleeping off a drunk in a ditch. He had Murphy's hat and handcuffs.

When a lynch mob met Mulvenon's posse outside of Prescott, the sheriff promised them a public hanging if they let justice take its course. A jury convicted Dilda and sentenced him to hang on February 5, 1886. On the morning of his hanging, Mulvenon provided him with a bath, a haircut, and a new suit of clothes. Dilda ordered a breakfast of chicken, lamb chops, steak, and oysters with peas, potatoes, bread, jelly, coffee, and cake. At 11:00 a.m. he ate another huge meal, probably consuming the Yavapai County budget.

The manacled Dilda sat on his coffin on a wagon during his ride to the hanging site at Willow and Gurley Streets in Prescott. He requested and received a drink of whiskey. The Prescott Grays, a local militia group, were assigned as guards at the scaffold. Just as Dilda dropped into eternity, the captain of the Grays and a future Yavapai County sheriff, William "Buckey" O'Neill, fainted. Fortunately Buckey—who later served as a Rough Rider in the Spanish-American War—never had to execute a prisoner during his term as sheriff. (Today, a heroic-sized bronze of Rough Rider O'Neill is prominently displayed on the Yavapai County Courthouse Plaza.)

Most sheriffs attempted to accommodate a condemned prisoner's last wishes. Pima County Sheriff Matthew Shaw heard one of the more unusual requests from a young Tohono O'odham (Papago) prisoner, Firimino, condemned to hang for the murder of J. D. Ford. Because he was an Indian, Governor Conrad M. Zulick stayed the execution so the U.S. Supreme Court could determine whether the Arizona Territory had the right to hang an Indian.

After a final thirty-day reprieve, time ran out for sixteen-year-old Firimino in mid-April 1889, when the U.S. Supreme Court upheld Arizona Territory's right to try and execute Indians who committed crimes within its jurisdiction. For

The execution of Firimino, Tucson, Arizona.

several days, Firimino refused food. When Sheriff Shaw asked if he had any special wishes for a last meal, he said no, but he would like to appear on the scaffold wearing a pair of red cowboy boots. Deputy Jeff Milton and Shaw scouted Tucson for red boots and finally found them at Zeckendorf's store.

On May 25, 1889, precisely at 12:30 p.m. Deputy Sheriff Charles Kresham unlocked Firimino's cell and read the death warrant. At 1:00 p.m. the jail's iron door swung open and Sheriff Shaw arrived to escort Firimino to the gallows. The prisoner walked calmly up the scaffold steps and turned to face the crowd. According to the *Tucson Weekly Citizen*, "He could not refrain from casting admiring glances at his new boots." Flanked by Sheriff Shaw, Kresham, and jailor William Moore, Firimino faintly smiled for the photographer.

Deputies placed the black hood over his head, and Shaw put the noose around his neck. The trap was sprung and the prisoner dropped to his death. Five minutes later, the doctor pronounced Firimino dead and Sheriff Shaw handed his body over to tribal members and returned the boots to Louis Zeckendorf.

After leaving the Pima County sheriff's office, Shaw worked for the Cananea Consolidated Copper Company in northern Mexico; he also served as assistant superintendent of the Yuma Territorial Prison, special agent to the Southern Pacific Railroad, assistant chief of the Tucson Police, Tucson town constable, and night watchman for the University of Arizona. He spent his last days as a night watchman at the Pima County Courthouse. Matthew F. Shaw died in Tucson on June 23, 1935.

Fatal Mistake Leads to a Pair of Murders

In 1889, an Apache named Nah-Diez-Az was hanged for the murder of Gila County Sheriff Glenn Reynolds and his deputy W. A. "Hunkydory" Holmes. Reynolds had arrived in Arizona in 1885 from Albany, Texas, where he had served as Throckmorton County sheriff. Reynolds survived the Pleasant Valley War, but he lost his life on November 2, 1889, while transferring Apache prisoners (including Nah-Diez-Az) to the Yuma Territorial Prison.

Because Indian tribes were considered wards of the federal government, tribal members were tried in federal court and incarcerated in federal prisons in Ohio and Illinois. On April 15, 1889, the U.S. Supreme Court ruled that these trials were illegal, and ten Apaches (among them Nah-Diez-Az and the Apache Kid) were set free and returned to Arizona.

The Apache Kid earlier had proved himself a loyal scout and an excellent tracker. However, on one occasion he got roaring drunk with his friends. After their arrest, Army scout Al Sieber disarmed and humiliated the Apaches. Because the Apache Kid had sworn revenge, Sieber pressured Reynolds into reopening the cases against the freed Apaches. Reynolds arrested the fugitives, who were charged with crimes ranging from horse stealing to murder.

Ten prisoners appeared for trial before Judge Joseph H. Kibbey in Globe on October 23, 1889. One prisoner went free, and eight received prison sentences. To the astonishment of the court and Sheriff Reynolds, a jury found Nah-Diez-Az guilty of the murder of Lieutenant Seward Mott and sentenced him to death.

Sheriff Reynolds chose Eugene Middleton's stagecoach line to transfer the prisoners to Yuma. Middleton had just purchased a heavy-duty Concord coach with a forest-green paint job and bright yellow wheels. On February 1, 1889, Reynolds and his deputy, Hunkydory Holmes, boarded the nine Apaches and an embezzler, Jesus Avott, on the Concord and set out for the Yuma penitentiary.

The next morning they approached a steep grade and Reynolds ordered several prisoners to get out and walk so that the coach could make it through the sand. Middleton went on ahead to check out the road. Reynolds made a fatal mistake by allowing the prisoners to get behind him.

The Apaches waited until Middleton disappeared from sight, then they ambushed Holmes and Reynolds. The lawmen struggled desperately with their assailants, who

Jack Caruth—hangman, prospector, and miner from La Paz and Parker, Arizona.

took the keys and unlocked their manacles. When Reynolds tried to get up, one of the Apaches, named El-Cahns, fired into the sheriff's face with his own shotgun. Middleton heard shots, but thought the lawmen were shooting rabbits. Avott called out a warning just as a rifle bullet cut through Middleton's neck. An instant later an Apache named Pash-Ten-Tah wounded the fleeing Avott. Middleton feigned death until the Apaches left. Avott, who later received a pardon, rode a stagecoach horse for help. (Unfortunately, he picked the only horse not broken to the saddle.) Middleton walked four miles to Riverside and reported the crime.

The Gila County Board of Supervisors immediately appointed Deputy Sheriff Jerry Ryan as Gila County sheriff at a salary of $300 per year. The supervisors also offered a $50 reward for the capture of the Apaches or authentic evidence that they had been killed. Ryan assembled a posse and offered a personal reward for the return of Sheriff Glenn Reynolds's watch. Ultimately, all of the prisoners except the Apache Kid were either captured and given life sentences or killed. They were all found guilty of participating in Reynolds's murder, but only Nah-Diez-Az was hanged for the crime.

On December 27, 1889, Ryan read the death warrant, which the Apache scout Constant Bread translated into Apache. Nah-Diez-Az rejected religious consolation from either Father J. Monfort or Reverend N. F. Norton. Ryan adjusted the noose and said, "Good-bye." Nah-Diez-Az responded, "Good-bye, Hell!" Unlike the conventional method of hanging, where the condemned drops through a trapdoor, Nah-Diez-Az was sentenced to stand on the ground and be pulled upward by a bar of copper bullion weighing about three hundred pounds. This method gave rise to the macabre expression "jerked to Jesus." The executioner swung his axe, which severed the rope controlling the weight. However, because of a miscalculation in the rope slack, Nah-Diez-Az's body crashed into the crossbar at the top of the scaffold. As for the Apache Kid, legends grew up around sightings of this fugitive, but he was never captured. Any commentary on the fate of the Apache Kid must be pure speculation, as we simply do not know what happened to him. One account even has him killed by an Indian scout, Walapai Clark, in the Santa Catalina Mountains north of Tucson around 1894.

About six months later Gila County Sheriff Jerry Ryan, who had just gotten married, drowned in a small lake, near where the present-day Inspiration Copper Company is located, during an unsuccessful attempt to rescue Mary Frush, who had fallen out of a capsized canoe while picnicking on June 1, 1890.

Sheriff Leatherwood

Robert Leatherwood, born in North Carolina in June 1844, served with the Confederate forces during the Civil War. Leatherwood, who stood five feet, five inches tall and

"BUT WHERE THE HELL IS TUCSON?"

During his term as mayor of Tucson, Robert Leatherwood deluged government officials with telegrams proudly announcing the arrival of the railroad in Tucson on March 20, 1880. Recipients included the president of the Southern Pacific Railroad, the mayor of Yuma, the mayors of Los Angeles and San Francisco, the president of the United States, Arizona's governor, John Fremont, and the Pope. Leatherwood's telegram to the Pope announced that Tucson was now connected with the Christian world. After a few potations, Leatherwood's friends composed an eloquent reply, stating that the Pope "sends his benediction but for his own satisfaction would ask, where in hell is Tucson?"

weighed 130 pounds, was known as the "Little Giant." This man of valor and grit arrived in Tucson in 1869, whereupon he opened a livery stable and engaged in mining and ranching in the Santa Catalina Mountains. Eventually he became Pima County sheriff. Frontier U.S. marshals worked with small budgets, large districts, an abundance of lawbreakers, and a scarcity of competent peace officers. Consequently, they often cross-deputized Arizona sheriffs as deputy U.S. marshals.

In 1897, Sheriff Leatherwood hanged Philip Lashley, a black soldier, in his capacity as deputy U.S. marshal. The federal government funded Lashley's execution because he held Danish citizenship. On April 9, 1896, while serving his third tour of duty with the all-black 24th Infantry at Fort Huachuca, Lashley had murdered another black soldier, John Sanders. Lashley, born in Denmark, spoke and wrote fluent Danish. Prior to joining the U.S. Army, he worked his way to the United States as a sailor. At the time of his execution, his mother resided in Copenhagen and his father was dead.

After Lashley exhausted all his appeals, Territorial Governor Benjamin J. Franklin ordered a stay of execution at the request of the Danish prime minister. Although Franklin requested a commutation to life imprisonment, President William McKinley declined to intervene. During his deathwatch, several Tucson ministers offered their services, but Lashley refused their visits, saying he had no belief in the hereafter. On July 9, 1897, at 3:00 p.m. Leatherwood escorted Lashley to the gallows.

Tucsonans congregated in the courtyard and spilled out onto the sidewalk. U.S. Deputy Marshal J. P. Welles read the death warrant. Leatherwood asked Lashley if he wanted to make a last statement. The condemned man rambled on for about twenty minutes about the unfairness of his trial. Then the deputies pulled the black cap over his head. At 3:43 p.m. the trapdoor was sprung, and a few minutes later a physician pronounced him dead. The reporter for Tucson's *Arizona Star* commented, after viewing Lashley in his coffin, that his facial expression "showed no signs of pain or suffering."

Over the course of his career, Leatherwood served three terms in the Arizona Territorial legislature. Although barely literate, in the late 1880s he served on the Tucson school board and the Tucson city council. He bought a raffled cake for $100 and the funds went toward building a new public school. On April 4, 1920, the former sheriff went to Rossi's restaurant on Congress Street, where Leatherwood, age seventy-six, told the manager, "I am not feeling very well." Before the doctor arrived, Robert N. Leatherwood died.

Invitation to a Hanging

After Frank J. Wattron's parents died in Missouri, his uncle (a priest) urged young Wattron to study for the priesthood. At age thirteen, Wattron ran away. After wandering around New Mexico and Colorado, he showed up in Holbrook, Arizona, in about 1874, with $5 and a deck of cards. Wattron served as a deputy sheriff under Commodore Perry Owens, before defeating him in 1896. The tall, handsome Wattron chomped on a long cigar, sported a huge black moustache, and exhibited a special talent for profanity.

Navajo County Sheriff Wattron treated George Smiley's execution with a macabre sense of humor. In 1899, Smiley, a railroad worker, had shot his supervisor, Thomas McSweeney, in the back during a wage dispute. McSweeney left a blind widow and three small children. A jury tried, convicted, and sentenced Smiley to hang. Under the Arizona Revised Statutes, Penal Code, Title X, 1849, Arizona sheriffs were obligated to issue invitations to executions. No guidelines existed as to the form. Wattron's first invitation to Smiley's hanging read:

> Mr. _____ You are hereby cordially invited to attend the hanging of one: GEORGE SMILEY MURDERER. His soul will be swung into eternity on December 8, 1899, at 2 o'clock p.m. sharp.
>
> The latest improved methods in the art of scientific strangulation will be employed and everything possible will be done to make the surroundings cheerful and the execution a success. F. J. Wattron Sheriff of Navajo County.

The *Holbrook Argus* editor did not have the facilities to print the invitations, so he sent the job to the *Albuquerque Citizen,* where a reporter saw the text and wired the contents to the Associated Press. Copies of the invitation went to newspapers all over the United States and Europe. An embarrassed President William McKinley complained about the incident to Arizona Governor Nathan O. Murphy. Murphy reprimanded Wattron and stayed Smiley's execution for thirty days. Wattron took care not let the second invitation get out too early. The second copy read:

> With feelings of profound sorrow and regret, I hereby invite you to attend and witness the private, decent and humane execution of a human being: name George Smiley; crime, murder. The said George Smiley will be executed on January 8, 1900 at 3 o'clock p.m.
>
> You are expected to deport yourself in a respectful manner, and any "flippant" or unseemly language will not be allowed. Conduct on anyone's part, bordering on ribaldry and tending to mar the solemnity of the occasion will not be tolerated. F. J. Wattron Sheriff of Navajo County.

Wattron suggested that the next session of legislature have a form of invitation to executions embodied in the laws. At the gallows, Smiley said, "I have nothing more to say except to thank the sheriff and deputies for courtesies, and I die a Christian." Father Dille prayed while Smiley dropped into eternity.

The hanging of Fleming Parker (face covered); also pictured (left to right): Shorty Lacey, Johnny Munds, Sheriff George Ruffner, Jeff Davis, and Morris Goldwater.

Wattron's many professions included: druggist, notary public, gambler, bartender, constable, sheriff, and justice of the peace. On August 2, 1905, at age forty-four, Wattron accidently took an overdose of laudanum, for some undisclosed ailment. Defiant to the end, he said he had a "ticket punched straight through to hell with no stopovers."

Friends on Opposite Sides of the Law

From time to time, prisoners have requested that the sheriff, himself, hang them. For example, in 1898, Fleming Parker insisted that a former friend, Yavapai County Sheriff George C. Ruffner, do the hanging himself so he could "cash in" at the hands of a real man. In 1862, Ruffner at age sixteen had run away from home in Mason, Illinois. For a while he worked as a teamster in Minnesota's tough logging camps. His uncle, who owned two Jerome mill sites, invited Ruffner to come to Arizona. Ruffner visited his uncle, but he exhibited no interest in mining. He liked ranch work and performing in rodeos. After a few years in California, Ruffner settled in Arizona and began his law-enforcement career in 1893 as a Yavapai County deputy sheriff. A year later he was elected sheriff.

Fleming Parker arrived in Arizona in the early 1880s from Bakersfield, California. Parker and Ruffner had worked together at the Double O Ranch in Chino Valley. By the time they met again in Arizona, the lives of both men had taken very opposite paths. On February 7, 1897, Parker and three accomplices robbed a train near Peach Springs in Mohave County. As far as robberies go, Parker's heist was a failure, because the robbers only got $100 in registered mail. During the chase, officers killed one outlaw, but Parker and two accomplices were captured and jailed in Prescott while awaiting trial.

On May 9, Parker and two other prisoners—L. C. Miller and Cornelio Sarata—escaped. After they knocked the jailor unconscious, the outlaws stole a shotgun from Sheriff Ruffner's office. The young deputy district attorney, Lee Norris, heard calls for help. As he walked down the stairs, Parker shot and killed him.

Parker stole Ruffner's prize white gelding, Sure Shot, out of the livery stable. He later remarked that a man hanged just as high for stealing bad horseflesh as good. Having his favorite horse stolen did nothing to improve the sheriff's temper. Ruffner lost no time in forming a posse to go after Parker. Miller quickly gave himself up, and after a long hard chase, Parker was recaptured on May 28. For the duration of his prison stay, Ruffner ordered that Parker's legs be chained with heavy manacles. A jury convicted Parker and sentenced him to hang. After several appeals, Parker's execution was scheduled for June 3, 1898.

When Ruffner asked what he would like for his last meal, Parker said he was not hungry, but that he would like to see redheaded Flossie from Whiskey Row. Ruffner brought her to Parker's cell for a one-hour visit. When Ruffner discovered that he had forgotten to send out invitations to Parker's hanging, he sent each witness a playing card. Only those with cards were permitted to enter the gallows yard where Parker was hanged.

At election time, Ruffner would press his friends into service to record the votes of illiterate citizens. "Do you want to vote for Mr. Ruffner?" the recorder would ask. If the voter answered "yes," the recorder marked the appropriate box. If the answer was "no," he would say, "Well, we'll just scratch the bastard out," after marking an X by Ruffner's name.

In 1961, Ruffner, the first cowboy chosen to represent Arizona, was elected to the Hall of Great Westerners at the National Cowboy Hall of Fame. George C. Ruffner, Arizona's oldest peace officer both in age and years of service, had died in July 1933 at the age of seventy-one.

"Oh, By the Way, I Killed Him"

Pima County's first native-born sheriff, Nabor Pacheco, also served as a Tucson policeman and constable. In 1904 the Republican Pacheco defeated the Democratic incumbent, Frank Murphy, and the Socialist Party candidate, A. C. Roswell, for the office of Pima County sheriff. Sheriff Pacheco abhorred the ghoulish publicity and the public spectacles at hangings. He performed his duty, but successfully worked to have the executions removed to the privacy of the Arizona State Prison.

During Pacheco's tenure as Pima County sheriff, the first mule-drawn streetcar appeared in Tucson, and for a nickel, a person could ride from the main gate at the University of Arizona to downtown. Until his arrest, Tucsonans knew the twenty-two-year-old Edwin W. Hawkins as a street conductor on the University line and a family man who neither smoked nor drank to excess.

But on February 29, 1908, Hawkins signed his own death warrant when he confessed to several robberies and a murder. When Hawkins tried to sell a large selection of women's gloves at a very low price, he aroused the suspicion of a Bonanza store clerk. After sheriff's deputies identified the merchandise as stolen loot, they arrested Hawkins and his wife.

Hawkins told Pacheco that he did not like the idea that his wife, Bessie, was being held in jail as an accomplice to the burglaries. In exchange for her freedom, he gave the sheriff details on over twenty robberies and petty thefts in Los Angeles, San Francisco, and Tucson. Then Hawkins startled the sheriff by saying, "I guess you want to know about the murder of Albert Leonhardt. I killed him." Pacheco had no idea that Hawkins had been involved in Leonhardt's murder.

On December 22, 1907, after Bessie had complained of a headache, her husband took her for a midnight stroll. Leonhardt stumbled out of a saloon and said, "Hello baby," to Bessie. Seconds later he lay dying on the sidewalk with bullets in his chest and brain.

Hawkins pleaded self-defense to the murder of Leonhardt, but a jury sentenced him to hang on August 15, 1908. Bessie circulated a petition asking the governor to have her husband's sentence commuted to life imprisonment, but Hawkins told the governor to ignore it. Bessie went to Chicago to live with his parents.

On August 15, 1908, the day of his hanging, Hawkins ate a hearty breakfast, read the newspaper, and gave a jailhouse interview. He spent an hour dictating a phonograph record for Bessie. At 11:00 a.m. he received a telegram from Bessie saying that she had arrived in Chicago.

He sent a wire asking her to repeat the Lord's Prayer at 1:00 p.m., the appointed hour of his death. He then asked Pacheco to wait until he received her answer. The sheriff granted his wish but no answer came. Pacheco, Undersheriff Henry Meyer, and Father Timmerman went to Hawkins's cell, where the sheriff read the death warrant. Once again Hawkins asked Pacheco to wait for Bessie's response. Pacheco agreed to wait for thirty minutes. Bessie's final message came, "Good-bye dear. I can't say any more. Bessie."

Pacheco, Timmerman, and Meyer escorted Hawkins to the scaffold. Hawkins tossed away his cigar and said "Good-bye" to the crowd. The trapdoor was sprung and Edwin Hawkins danced the dead man's jig. After the Hawkins hanging, Pacheco declared,

> It seems to me that Arizona is behind the states of the east in this respect. There they take the men to the state penitentiary and the thing is done quietly by the warden and his assistants. There is none of this disgusting and unavoidable lack of privacy which turns a hanging into a morbid holiday and kills a convict while hundreds of men and boys stare and gape at him.

After he left the sheriff's office, Pacheco served as Tucson chief of police, whereupon he announced that he would enforce city laws against spitting on sidewalks, riding a bicycle without lamps and bells, and driving automobiles without a horn and lights. Pacheco tendered his resignation in 1913 after his son shot and killed a prostitute. Six months later Pacheco was back on the job. On February 14, 1920, the fifty-seven-year-old Nabor Pacheco died suddenly of heart trouble.

Sheriffs such as Nabor Pacheco and Carl Hayden finally succeeded in having the execution of prisoners transferred to the state prison at Florence. Execution by hanging to fulfill death sentences ceased in Arizona on October 28, 1933, when the state began using lethal gas to fulfill death sentences. This change came about as a result of the bungled hanging of Eva Dugan.

Eva Dugan became the first woman to be executed for murder in Arizona on February 21, 1930. She had been convicted of killing Andrew J. Mathis, a Tucson rancher. Because of her obesity and bones wasted by a venereal disease, Dugan's head came off as she dropped through the trap.

Today, the condemned is put to death by intravenous injection of substances such as sodium pentothal in a lethal quantity. A defendant who has been sentenced to death for an offense committed before November 23, 1992, has the choice of lethal injection or lethal gas.

Witnesses at the execution of a death sentence must include the director of the state Department of Corrections, the state attorney general, and at least twelve reputable citizens of the director's selection. The condemned still has the prerogative of choosing two members of the clergy and five relatives and/or friends.

After these conditions have been met, the director selects from a pool of possible witnesses. Witnesses often come from the county where the crime was committed and may include the sheriff and county attorney from that area. Other categories of witnesses include criminal-studies people, law-enforcement personnel and county attorneys, relatives of the victim, and the media.

Between 1976 and 2006, twenty-two executions took place in Arizona. At present the death row population is 120, including two women.

CHAPTER 4.
Election Time: The Sheriff and Politics

Carl Holton, Jim Black, Buckey O'Neill, and Ed St. Clair (left to right). O'Neill was no stranger to Arizona politics, serving as Yavapai County judge, tax assessor, sheriff (three terms), and mayor of Prescott.

During Arizona's Territorial days, sheriff campaigns rarely lacked for interesting candidates. The frequency of the two-year terms of the sheriff and other officers provided for some hotly disputed races. Territorial voters, who had no voice in national affairs, took a strong interest in local politics. Before the late 1800s and early 1900s, when

Arizona introduced the Australian or secret ballot (which carries all of the candidates' names and their affiliations), political parties printed their own ballots. For those who could not read, the tickets were marked with various symbols. Republicans chose Old Glory, while the Democrats displayed an eagle or a crowing rooster. The Socialist party featured clasping hands, and the Labor party displayed a raised fist holding a hammer.

Many of Arizona's early settlers were Southerners who quickly organized the Democratic Party in the new territory. In 1880, party lines were drawn when the Arizona Republicans also organized a formal party. The gradual predominance of the two-party system started a long tradition of Republicans and Democrats baiting each other with bad names. Democrat sobriquets included the "Grab Party," the "Dishonest Party," and the "Monopoly Party," while Republicans were described as "black-hearted." Arizona politics got off to a frequently fraudulent and sometimes lethal start.

With the creation of each new Arizona county, the Territorial governor, who had been appointed by the U.S. president, made the first county office appointments. These positions included probate judge, sheriff, justice of the peace, recorder, surveyor, district attorney, and supervisors. Unfortunately, it seems that no matter what the governor did, he would be in trouble. The old county resented the creation of a new one, and the new county demanded approval of its self-government. And woe unto the governor who did not consult the new county's residents before making these appointments!

When Governor Lewis Wolfley vetoed the creation of Coconino County in 1887, George Tinker's Republican-slanted *Arizona Champion,* published in Flagstaff, carried a headline accusing the new governor of perpetrating an outrage upon the taxpayers of northern Arizona. Tinker expressed shame over the first Republican governor's actions and threatened, "Ta ta Governor, you will hear from us next week." Flagstaff citizens burned Wolfley in effigy from the cross-arms of a telegraph pole.

Because Wolfley feuded with his fellow Republicans almost as much as with the Democrats, President Benjamin Harrison replaced him with John Irwin. When Irwin nominated the first Coconino County officers (the county was finally created in 1891), he tried to appease everyone by nominating both Democrats and Republicans. Yet even then the *Arizona Champion* questioned whether a "half-breed" slate was preferable. During Coconino County's first election, the Democrats captured all of the positions except recorder, and John W. Francis defeated Ralph Cameron for Coconino County sheriff.

A candidate for sheriff had to be a male at least twenty-one years old, able to read and write the English language, and be a citizen and eligible voter of the county where he would serve if elected. The county boards of supervisors passed judgment on these qualifications. Men who aspired to be sheriff had to be good with a gun and brave. By joining a posse, a candidate could quickly gain experience and voter confidence.

HARD-EARNED DOLLARS

Upon assuming office, a Territorial sheriff had to provide bonds to protect the county coffers from being drained for the sheriff's personal use (this did happen on occasion). Usually two or three of his most enthusiastic support-ers put up the bonds for $5,000 to $10,000. The sheriff provided his own guns, ammunition, and horse. He paid his deputies out of his own pocket and then presented a bill for these expenses to the board of supervisors. While he did not receive a salary, each of his many duties provided a fee. After the sheriff performed a service, he presented his bills to the board of supervisors and hoped that they would pay him. Examples of fees recom-mended under the law code established by Coles Bashford and William T. Howell (in March 1864) are as follows:

Serving each summons in a civil case: $1.50
Summoning each witness (civil): $0.50
Levying and returning each writ of attachment of claim and delivery: $2.00
Posting the advertisement for sale under execution of any order of sale: $2.00
For executing each warrant or arrest without warrant: $2.00
For summoning each witness (criminal): $0.75
Executing a death warrant: $15.00
For duties as ex-officio tax collector and assessor: $10.00 per day and twenty cents per mile for time spent out in the field

During the 1900 election, Graham County Sheriff Ben Clark offered to assign can-didates to a posse to track down the violent murderer Agustín Chacón, which the *Lordsburg Liberal* noted "would be a first class civil service examination."

During the sheriff's campaign, buying drinks for the constituency was considered not only good form, but obligatory—until Prohibition curtailed the flow of liquor on election day. Even after repeal of the Volstead Act (Prohibition), the Arizona legislature passed a law prohibiting the sale of liquor on voting day until after the polls closed. (This law was repealed in 1993.)

Liquor did not guarantee votes, however. In 1878, Yavapai County Sheriff Ed F. Bowers and District Attorney Murat Masterson left Prescott by stage, armed with all the "modern electioneering appliances" (presumably kegs of whiskey). Still, Bowers lost the election to Joseph Walker. Louis Dupuy, a popular office worker and aspirant for the newly created Pinal County sheriff office, passed out liquor and cigars. Everyone promised to vote for him, but few thought he had the ability to handle the job. In the final tally, Dupuy got twelve out of an even seven hundred votes. His friends attempted to console him, but he said, "That's okay. I found out that there are just six hundred and eighty-eight damn liars in Pinal County."

Early-Days Election Tampering

Mention Tombstone, and universally people conjure up visions of the gunfight at the O.K. Corral, involving the Earps and Doc Holliday against the Clantons and McLaurys on October 26, 1881. Yet few realize that the seeds of hatred that resulted in this tragic event had been sown earlier, in the 1880 Pima County election scandal, which pitted the Earps against the Clantons.

In 1880, Pima County included all of present-day Cochise County, with the booming town of Tombstone. Pima County voters loved to vote, and they did it over and over again for the same candidate during the same election. Stuffing ballot boxes was a perennial Arizona sport, but rarely was it so flagrant as during the 1880 campaign, when the Republican Robert Paul opposed Democrat Charlie Shibell for Pima County sheriff.

Paul, born in Massachusetts, had attended school in New Bedford. At the age of twelve, he set sail on a whaling ship and spent the next several years traveling around the world. Paul arrived in San Francisco in 1849, just in time to participate in the Gold Rush, but his prospecting produced little success. He served as Calaveras County sheriff from 1859 to 1864 and went to work riding shotgun for Wells, Fargo in California, Nevada, and Utah.

In 1877, Wells, Fargo transferred the forty-seven-year-old Paul to Arizona, where he later made friends with Pima County Deputy Sheriff Wyatt Earp. In November of 1880, Paul complained to Earp that he had been robbed of the Pima County shrievalty by Charlie Shibell. Throughout the election day, Paul appeared to be well out in front. However, the Democrats and incumbent Sheriff Shibell kept saying, "Wait until the returns from San Simon get here." The *Arizona Citizen* (later called *Tucson Citizen*) became suspicious and commented that "a few of our New Mexico neighbors came across the line to aid their Arizona brethren."

The San Simon precinct's voting was set to be held at Joe Hill's house; Hill, aka Joe Olney, was a man of dubious character who had left Texas in the wake of murder charges. (Hill's brother, George, would serve as Graham County sheriff from 1891 to 1894; many of Arizona's early lawmen were at times on both sides of the law.) However, no one knew for certain if Hill's house was in Mexico or Arizona, so election officials moved the site to a house they knew was in the United States. Joseph Isaac "Ike"

Clanton was an election inspector for this election, and the election judges included John Ringo. A man who signed himself as "Henry Johnson" certified the votes to the Pima County Board of Supervisors—however, no one knew Henry Johnson.

Only ten or twelve registered voters resided in San Simon, but when the returns came in, election officials certified 103 Democratic votes for Shibell and one lone Republican vote for Paul. Earp and Paul decided that if they could prove that the San Simon votes were fraudulent, Paul would win the election.

The election officials—Ringo, Olney, and the Clantons—were all reputed to be members of William "Curly Bill" Brocius's gang of cowboy rustlers (although Brocius could not be blamed for the election discrepancies, because he occupied a Pima County Jail cell during the actual election). Just a few days before the election on October 27, 1880, Brocius had been arrested for the murder of Tombstone Marshal Fred White. Earp allegedly told Brocius after the election that he would testify that White's shooting was accidental if Brocius cooperated in exposing the San Simon election fraud. Brocius would go free for murder, and Earp would get credit for exposing the election fraud. But on the day before the Paul vs. Shibell hearing, the judge released Brocius on the basis that White had torn the pistol from Brocius's hand and inflicted the wound on himself.

On November 15, the Pima County Board of Supervisors certified Charles A. Shibell as sheriff. Four days later, Paul requested copies of the poll lists from the San Simon, Solomonville, Turkey Creek, and Benson precincts, so that he could compare them with the Pima County Great Register of voters. At the same time, Shibell asked for the poll lists from Tombstone, Willcox, Camp Grant, and Pajarita, insinuating that Paul partisans had perpetrated voter fraud in these precincts.

A spate of legal talent participated in the election contest. Attorneys Warner Earll, F. M. Smith, G. W. Spaulding, Alexander C. Campbell, James F. Robinson, and John Haynes appeared as counsel for Paul. Shibell secured the services of Brocius's lawyer, James C. Perry, along with Benjamin Morgan, Lyttleton Price, Charles Silent, Benjamin Hereford, and James A. Zabriskie.

On December 18, Paul's attorneys contested the election in district court on the basis that Henry Johnson was an alias, and therefore all of the San Simon votes should be declared invalid. A hearing date was set, and U.S. Deputy Marshal Joseph Evans served Shibell with the court's citation. Paul obtained subpoenas for several names that appeared on the San Simon voting list, and in his own capacity as U.S. deputy marshal, Paul served several of the subpoenas himself. One James Johnson, who had been arrested and released on the same night that White was murdered, turned out to be the "Henry Johnson" who had certified the poll lists. Shibell ordered his new Tombstone deputy, Johnny Behan, to arrest Ike Clanton. However, the armed Clanton gang refused to let Ike be taken into Tucson.

In court, Shibell denied Paul's allegation of voter fraud. On January 17, 1881, the star witness, James Johnson, admitted that he had signed his name as Henry Johnson. He said that the judges rejected one would-be voter whose name was not on the list. They did this in the presence of a Republican observer, R. B. Kelly, just to make him believe that they were honest. Johnson thought maybe three or four legal votes had been cast but not more than fifteen people appeared at the precinct. Tucson's *Arizona Star* stated that "it looks to us like a very plain case that out of the one hundred and four votes cast at San Simon, about one hundred were fraudulent ..."

Lester F. Blackburn, a Tombstone poll-observer, had watched out for Shibell's interests. Blackburn testified that when tickets were called off with Shibell's name, they were counted for Paul. Paul's attorneys pointed out that Blackburn had asked Paul for a deputy sheriff's commission, but Paul had refused to promise him one. Thus, his testimony might be a case of sour grapes. George Atwood, a Tombstone election inspector, admitted that he should not have certified the voting reports, which were full of discrepancies, such as more voters than were registered in the precinct.

Graham County Sheriff Ben Clark (right) with an unidentified companion.

When Shibell requested that the Tombstone ballot box be introduced into evidence, Paul's attorney insisted that Marshall Williams, Tombstone's Wells, Fargo agent, examine it first to find out whether the box was in the same condition as when it left his charge. Williams testified that he was positive that someone had tampered with the box. During the examination, the court turned up almost forty erasures of votes for Paul.

Shibell's attorneys called Paul to the stand, where he admitted to having loaned money to James Johnson but not "for any evil purpose." William S. Oury, later a Pima County sheriff, had neglected to serve a subpoena for Ike Clanton. When asked why, Oury replied, "That's my business."

Judge French ruled that all of the San Simon votes were fraudulent and invalid. Of the 3,312 legal votes cast in Pima County, Paul received 1,684 and Shibell, 1,628. The Pima County Board of Supervisors certified Robert H. Paul as the duly elected sheriff. Shibell appealed French's decision to the Arizona Supreme Court, and refused to give up the sheriff's office until the appeal was decided.

On March 15, 1881, Paul climbed aboard the Tombstone stagecoach. The driver, Eli "Bud" Philpott, had complained of stomach cramps, so Paul offered to drive for a while. About 10:00 p.m., they reached a rise near Contention City (now a ghost town near Tombstone). Shadowy figures hollered, "Hold!" Shots rang out, and when the bullets hit Philpott, he fell between the wheels. Paul supporters later maintained that the shots had been meant for Paul, because he would have been sitting in Philpott's place if the driver had not gotten ill.

Paul fired his shotgun and roared, "I don't hold for nobody!" The bandits fired again and wounded Peter Roering, a passenger. Paul drove hard to Benson, where he telephoned the news of the attack to Wyatt Earp over one of Arizona's earliest telephone connections. The next day Paul met Earp, Marshall Williams, and legendary frontier lawman Bat Masterson at the scene of the attack.

Earp, who hoped to win the Cochise County shrievalty in Cochise County's first election, insisted on pursuing Philpott's murderers. Democrat John Behan and Republican Wyatt Earp vied for the sheriff's appointment when they learned that Cochise County would be created. They allegedly made a deal that if Earp withdrew from the race, Behan would name him as his undersheriff. Behan joined Earp and Paul and they captured Luther King, who named Jim Crane, Harry Head, and William Leonard as accomplices to the shooting. While Earp and Paul went in search of these fugitives, Behan and Williams brought King back to jail, but King quietly stepped out the back door of the Tombstone Jail while Undersheriff Woods was otherwise occupied. When Earp returned to Tombstone, he learned that not only had King escaped, but that his friend John Henry "Doc" Holliday was rumored to be one of Philpott's murderers.

Earp could console himself that the Territorial supreme court had officially designated his friend, Robert Paul, as Pima County sheriff. After the O.K. Corral shoot-out and Wyatt Earp's subsequent indictment for murdering the man he believed had killed his brother, Morgan, the Republican Earp stood little chance of being elected sheriff himself. However, the inept handling of law enforcement by the appointed John Behan tarnished his reputation within the Democratic Party, and he stood no chance of reelection. In 1882, the Democrats put up Larkin W. Carr. Tombstone Marshal Dave Naegle ran as an Independent. Republican Jerome L. Ward, running on a law-and-order campaign, won by a plurality of 255 votes.

Jail and RR Provide Ready Voters

Pima County continued to fight election-tampering problems in the courts. Paul returned to Tucson to take over as sheriff while Shibell escorted insane patients to Stockton, California (at the time this was one of the sheriff's duties, and there were no facilities for the insane in Arizona). Shibell's deputy sheriff Henry Ward refused to surrender the sheriff's office until Shibell returned. On May 1, Shibell found Paul taking inventory of the office supplies, whereupon Shibell gave up his fight for the sheriff's office and Paul took over as Pima County sheriff.

For Paul, even jailbreaks did not escape politics. In a "wholesale delivery" (a mass break-out), seven prisoners—accused of crimes including murder, highway robbery, and U.S. mail robbery—escaped from the Pima County Jail on October 23, 1882. Tucson's *Arizona Star* reported that it had no means of knowing whether the escaped prisoners were Democrats or Republicans, nor to which party the turnkey, jailor George Cooler, belonged. However, the newspaper contended that the prisoners ought not to have been permitted to escape and Sheriff Paul should not have allowed it to happen.

The next day the *Star* accused the Democratic Party of being the real culprit, and alleged that the Democrats had released the prisoners so as to defeat Paul in his next bid for sheriff. Tucson's *Arizona Citizen* wanted to know by what "hocus-pocus arrangement" the Republicans had found out the political complexion of the prisoners. Paul arrested and charged George Cooler with malfeasance, but an investigation exonerated the jailor. In spite of this escape, Paul won the 1882 election over Eugene O. Shaw.

Paul forged strong alliances with the railroad. When he ran for a third term as Pima County sheriff in 1884, the Democrats again put up Eugene O. Shaw. Democrats complained that not only did Southern Pacific get all of its local employees to vote, but the railroad brought in many Texas employees, and all of them voted in the Pima County election as well.

The 1884 Pima County sheriff's election was riddled with fraud, with both candidates accusing each other of tampering with the ballots. Initially, Paul operated the sheriff's office, although Shaw had been declared the winner. The court ordered that the ballot box be opened and that the votes be recounted. The ballots had been wrapped and sealed three times with wax. The wax on the inside wrapper should have carried the imprint of a silver half dollar. The middle wrapper should bear the seal of the Pima County Recorder, and the outside wrapper seal should bear the insignia of Wells, Fargo and Company.

When the package was opened in court, the recorder's seal appeared on the outside wrapper and the half dollar on the middle wrapper. The Wells, Fargo seal was on the inside wrapper. Shaw partisans considered this proof that someone had tampered with the ballots. Moreover, Shaw claimed to have evidence that voter registration papers had been fraudulently drawn up in the office of the Southern Pacific Railroad division superintendent.

Investigators tracked Barry Barron, a barber, all the way to San Francisco. He confessed that Paul had furnished him and a friend with Southern Pacific Railroad passes and they were supposed to leave the Arizona Territory after the election. Barron testified that ten days before Paul filed notice contesting Shaw's election, the Southern Pacific Hotel manager had obtained a key to the building where the Tucson precinct ballots were stored.

The manager gave the key to John Muir, division superintendent of Arizona's Southern Pacific Railroad, who in turn gave the key to Barron. Barron and his friend entered the building at midnight, stole the ballot package, and delivered it to Sheriff Paul. Paul removed the wrappers, erased Shaw's name, and wrote his name on several ballots. The sheriff then rewrapped the package using the same wax seals, but he put them in the wrong order. Barron returned the package and the key to Muir, and left town.

A grand jury indicted Paul and three Republican confederates. The *Star* warned Paul that "for much less grievous offenses, communities have risen in their might and driven the miscreants from office." After eighteen months of legal battles, an out-of-court settlement was reached, wherein Paul turned over the office to Shaw in March 1886 in return for six months of salary. (By this time Pima County sheriffs were receiving a salary of $7,500 per year.) Shaw, in turn, allowed the case against Paul to be dismissed without prosecution.

When Paul later sought the post of U.S. marshal, his foes brought up the charges of Pima County election tampering, but Paul held the post from 1890 to 1893. In his later years, Paul unsuccessfully tried his hand at mining, then served as a Southern Pacific agent and as a Pima County undersheriff before his death in Tucson on March 26, 1901.

FAMOUS FICTIONAL AND "NEAR" ARIZONA SHERIFFS

Ask anyone who they think Arizona's most famous sheriff was, and the answer may be "Wyatt Earp." Actually, he was never a sheriff, though he did serve as a U.S marshall and as a deputy sheriff in Pima County for a time; he was an unsuccessful candidate for the office of sheriff of Cochise County.

Former U.S. Surgeon General Richard Carmona was a Pima County Sheriff's Department deputy and leader of its SWAT team from 1986 to 2002. He also served as a Green Beret in Vietnam, where he was awarded two Purple Hearts and a Bronze Star. On his return to Tucson after his term in Washington ended, he rejoined the Sheriff's Department as the agency's surgeon and a SWAT team member, and rumors circulated that he might one day try to succeed his good friend Clarence Dupnik, whose seventh term as sheriff runs through 2008.

Many Arizona sheriffs appear as characters in Western genre novels of the nineteenth and twentieth centuries, perhaps most notably in the works of Zane Grey (1872–1939). Aside from the legendary figures associated with Tombstone, the best-known fictional Arizona sheriff may be Joanna Brady, the imaginary sheriff of Cochise County and the main character of J. A. Jance's contemporary mystery series beginning with *Desert Heat* (1993).

The 1933 film *To the Last Man*, starring Randolph Scott and featuring Shirley Temple, aged five, was based on Zane Grey's novel of the same name, based on the Pleasant Valley War (see Chapter 1). Roy Rogers starred in the movie *Sheriff of Tombstone* (1941). None other than John Wayne portrayed the fictional Arizona Sheriff John T. Chance in *Rio Bravo* (1959). Robert Mitchum played the role of Sheriff J. B. Harrah in *El Dorado* (1967), a remake of *Rio Bravo* filmed in Arizona against backgrounds of saguaro cacti (although the movie is technically set in Texas, where saguaros do not grow).

One-time Pima County Sheriff's Deputy Wyatt Earp has been played by many actors, including stars like Henry Fonda in *My Darling Clementine* (1946), Burt Lancaster in *Gunfight at the O.K. Corral* (1957), James Garner in *Hour of the Gun* (1967), Kurt Russell in *Tombstone* (1993), and Kevin Costner in *Wyatt Earp* (1994). On television, Hugh O'Brian starred in the series *The Life and Legend of Wyatt Earp* (1955–1961).

The Shaw Brothers

Eugene O. Shaw had arrived in Arizona in 1873 from North Carolina. His brother, Matthew, who would also serve as a Pima County sheriff, came to Tucson a little later on a vacation. Eugene founded the Old Boot Mine at Silverbell, which he later sold for a handsome profit. He managed the Empire Ranch and supervised the San Carlos Indian Reservation beef contract for Tully, Ochoa & Company in Tucson.

In the 1886 election, Republicans selected rancher Lewis Gormley as their choice for sheriff. The Democrats endorsed Eugene Shaw, and both sets of partisans launched a hearty battle of mudslinging. Gormley and the Republicans accused Shaw of incompetence and of overcharging the county for transportation of prisoners to the Yuma Territorial Prison. The Democrats accused Gormley of double-billing the county and insisted that Gormley was Paul's puppet. Shaw won the election with 956 votes to 615 for Gormley. Shaw rubbed salt in Republican wounds by replacing Republican deputies with Democrats, and he named Charles Shibell, who had had several court fights with Paul, as undersheriff.

Shaw's years of hard drinking eventually caught up with him, and by now he suffered from severe cirrhosis of the liver. Less than two months into his second term as Pima County sheriff, Shaw requested and received a thirty-five-day leave of absence for health reasons, and he returned to Faison, North Carolina. On April 9, 1887, the Pima County Board of Supervisors approved his request for an indefinite leave of absence "to go beyond the limits of the County of Pima and the Territory of Arizona."

On September 6, 1887, the terminally ill Shaw resigned by telegram as Pima County sheriff. He asked that his brother Matthew be named as his replacement. The next day the supervisors appointed Matthew, age twenty-nine, as Pima County sheriff. When Eugene O. Shaw died on October 11, 1887, Matthew draped the sheriff's office with black crepe and accepted the condolences of both political opponents and friends.

In the 1888 election the Republicans nominated Tucson businessman Douglass Snyder as their candidate for sheriff. Matthew Shaw's nomination was by no means secure. Undersheriff Robert Leatherwood, Fred G. Hughes, and John O'Brien had all thrown their hats in the Democratic ring. On the third ballot the Democrats were deadlocked on Hughes and Shaw. After the fourth ballot, Hughes asked the convention to declare Shaw the unanimous winner. On November 6, Pima County voters returned Matthew Shaw to the Pima County sheriff's office by a fifty-vote plurality.

Shaw decided not to run during the 1890 election, but he maintained order at the polling places. He instructed his deputies and U.S. Marshal Robert Paul that all persons were to pass in at one gate of the courthouse yard to the polling site and out at another gate. After casting their vote, they were not to return. Tucson merchant William Zeckendorf voted and left, then tried to reenter. When a deputy stopped him, Zeckendorf shoved the officer aside. Paul, a tall, large man, stepped forward and physically prevented Zeckendorf from entering the area. Zeckendorf sued Paul for $25,000 in damages allegedly sustained when Paul obstructed Zeckendorf's entrance into the polling place, but a jury upheld Paul in the performance of his duty.

After he left the sheriff's office, Shaw held a number of positions, most of them related to law enforcement, throughout southern Arizona and northern Sonora, Mexico. He held his final position as a Pima County Courthouse watchman until shortly before his death in June 1935.

Campaign-Time Shootings

Arizonans' passion for politics had turned lethal as early as 1871 with the creation of Maricopa County. But if whiskey did not buy votes, shooting another candidate did not get one elected, either. No formal political parties or election procedures existed in the new county. John Augustus Chenoweth, superintendent of the Salt River Canal, ran for Maricopa County sheriff on the Railroad ticket. James Favorite, a rancher and a candidate on the Peoples ticket, opposed Chenoweth. During the campaign, Favorite circulated a story that he had entered into an amicable agreement with Chenoweth that, if Favorite should be elected, Chenoweth would be his deputy and vice versa.

Chenoweth went to Favorite's ranch to discuss his disagreement with the rumor. Favorite denied the story but refused to make a public statement. In the ensuing quarrel, he shot at Chenoweth with a double-barrel shotgun but missed. Chenoweth chased Favorite through the corral and killed him with his revolver. After his exoneration for self-defense, Chenoweth withdrew from the sheriff's race.

Another shoot-out occurred during the 1887 Pinal County election for sheriff. In the 1870s, Josephus Phy served as a Pima County deputy sheriff and sold that precious commodity, water, to Tucsonans at 5 cents a bucket. He further supplemented his income by playing the violin at dances. When Phy moved to Florence, Pinal County Sheriff Peter Gabriel hired him as his deputy sheriff.

In 1887, Gabriel announced that he would not run for sheriff, so Phy decided to seek the office. When Jere Fryer announced his candidacy, Phy told people, "I have been sent to Casa Grande to beat a scrub [Fryer] for a sheriff." After Gabriel chided him for this comment, Phy pistol-whipped Tom Montgomery, who had spread the remark. Gabriel arrested Phy, took his guns, Bowie knife, and badge, and ordered him to vacate his room over the sheriff's office.

Thereafter, Phy nurtured a bitter resentment against Gabriel, and on May 31, 1888, he attempted to settle the score. Gabriel, back in Florence after a trip to his mines, was enjoying a drink in Keating's Tunnel Saloon. About 8:00 p.m. Phy burst into the bar and with one bullet he shot out the only light and put the establishment in total darkness. The patrons prudently left. Out on the street Phy shot and wounded Gabriel. When the wounded sheriff returned fire, Phy pitched over into the dust, shouting, "Yes, I am gone." When the doctor said Gabriel had been fatally wounded, Phy died with a smile on his face. Over the next few days, Gabriel hovered between life and death. Then he steadily improved and was up and about in about a month. However, for the rest of his life, Gabriel suffered pain from these wounds.

Special-interest groups figured prominently in early Arizona politics. The railroad bloc elected Pima County Sheriff Frank Murphy in 1900. Murphy, not inclined to work too hard at electioneering, went to Silverbell on mining business during his campaign. Before long, he received an urgent letter from his campaign manager, W. P. B. Field, who informed the sheriff that the opposition was working hard to unseat him: "The majority of the railroad boys are tied up for you … The point has been reached when you must be personally present." Murphy returned and won the race.

During Murphy's term as Pima County sheriff, he refused to hang Teodor Elías, because he believed this convicted murderer to be insane. The governor agreed and commuted Elías's sentence to life imprisonment. Tucsonans were incensed, because Elías had brutally murdered a popular young fireman, William Katzenstein. When Katzenstein turned on a fire hydrant, Elías shot him in the chest. Pima County voters believed that Sheriff Murphy did not have enough nerve to hang a man, and his act of mercy cost Murphy the next election.

Arizona voters have frequently exercised their right to selectively remember or forget mistakes when it comes time for reelection. In 1906, Deputy Sheriff Pete Pemberton shot and killed Winslow Town Marshal Joe Giles during an argument. While he awaited trial, Navajo County Sheriff Chet Houck permitted Pemberton, who had once saved his life, to run free in Holbrook during the day. The sheriff locked him up at night, and Pemberton served a short prison sentence. However, by favoring his old friend, Houck incurred the voters' wrath and lost the 1906 election by a landslide to Joseph F. Woods.

Recount and Recall in Modern Times

When the legislature amended the Arizona Constitution in 1964 to make major state offices four-year terms instead of two years, the act reduced the frequency and expense of elections. Nevertheless, ballot tampering and voter fraud have not been confined to Territorial days.

In 1960, Pinal County Sheriff Laurence White and his former deputy, Coy De-Arman, fought a bitter battle against each other for the Pinal County shrievalty. In 1929, Laurence White, born in Uvalde, Texas, homesteaded a ranch at Aravaipa Canyon in Pinal County. He was a master leather craftsman and wrote a book called *Songs of the Hills and Mesas*. Besides holding office as sheriff, White served as secretary and administrative assistant to the state prison. Coy DeArman, born in Rising Star, Texas, arrived in Arizona in 1941; he worked as chief security guard for Kennecott copper mines near Ray and served as chief deputy at Superior under Laurence White from 1952 to 1957. Both men were Democrats. During the 1960 primary campaign, DeArman accused White of incurring costs almost double those of the Arizona state average. DeArman lost to White, but ran again in the general election as an Independent under the theme "Better Law Enforcement." No Republican ran for sheriff.

The first returns showed DeArman to be the winner by more than 250 votes. Then someone discovered that 375 absentee votes had not been counted. After these absentee votes were counted, DeArman led by fifty votes. White partisans pointed out that the voters were confused when they marked their ballots: some voters marked a straight Democrat ticket and then wrote in DeArman's name. When most of these ballots were thrown out, DeArman's margin of victory diminished to three or four votes.

White filed an injunction to prohibit the Pinal County Board of Supervisors from issuing a certificate of election to DeArman. After the court ordered the supervisors to certify DeArman, White successfully sued for a recount. DeArman's counsel was a brilliant young attorney, William Rehnquist, who later sat on the U.S. Supreme Court bench and was chief justice at the time of his death in 2005.

White contested ninety-eight ballots. On December 16, a recount favored Sheriff Laurence White, giving him a sixteen-vote lead over DeArman. In the recount, White received 6,267 votes and DeArman got 6,251. A week later, superior court judge Ruskin Lines accepted thirty-two of the ninety-eight challenged ballots as valid. DeArman took the lead with 6,308 total votes against White's 6,296. The court allowed DeArman to take office on January 1, 1961, but he could not collect a salary until the state supreme court ruled on White's appeal. Rehnquist contended that the Arizona Supreme Court took a "very narrow-minded interpretation of the write-in statute."

Pinal County Sheriff Laurence White.

Pinal County Sheriff Coy DeArman, removed from office after an election recount, then legitimately elected two years later.

After DeArman had served as Pinal County sheriff for five-and-a-half months, the Arizona Supreme Court ruled that Laurence White should have been certified as the Pinal County sheriff. On June 3, the court reversed the outcome of the election by giving twenty-six votes of the thirty-two accepted votes to White and six to DeArman. The court also gave White the sheriff's pay that had been withheld from DeArman. (DeArman had to pay for the recount, but he went on to win the next election.)

White faced a recall later that same year, charged that he ignored the will of the people, spent too little time in his office, allowed his deputies to use county property for personal use, and had a violent temper. (He had shot and killed Billy Joe Williams, whom he had arrested for being drunk and disorderly. En route to jail in White's car, Williams yanked the keys out of the ignition and attacked the sheriff. White subdued his prisoner with two shots in the chest. An investigation exonerated White, and the attempted recall failed.)

Pinal County Sheriff DeArman, finally elected for real in 1963, handled the last Arizona train hijacking on August 29, 1966. Two Arizona State Prison escapees, William H. McAllister and Edward R. Schiffauer, commandeered a Southern Pacific train near Florence. The fugitives held the conductor and two brakemen hostage. Dozens of Pinal County sheriff's deputies, highway patrol, and police units waited near Hayden. The convicts ordered all law-enforcement officers to allow them one hour to escape. DeArman refused their demand, and they surrendered.

Over the years, efforts have been made to either abolish the office of sheriff or make it a political appointment. On July 1, 1969, the state legislature officially established the Arizona Department of Public Safety (DPS). In the beginning, the function of the DPS was to establish a state-level agency that would provide coordinated services and facilities for use by local law enforcement agencies. Before long, the DPS trod very heavily on county sheriffs' toes by making arrests and investigations in areas that the sheriffs considered to be under their jurisdiction.

In 1970, the Arizona state legislature attempted to wipe out eight state elective offices, including those of the sheriff and county attorney. These positions would be filled with gubernatorial appointments. The attempt to expand the state power base came in the form of six reorganization bills and four Constitutional amendments prepared by the twelve-member Council on Organization of Arizona State Government.

An editorial in Tucson's *Arizona Daily Star* favored a state police force, but only if the office of county sheriff were abolished as a criminal law-enforcement agency. The sheriffs and county attorneys saw this editorial as a vendetta against one of their own—Pima County Sheriff Waldon Burr (who would ultimately leave the office in disgrace). Phoenix newspapers favored passage of a law to allow the boards of supervisors to appoint the sheriff. For the most part, however, keeping the sheriff's office in the hands of the people has worked successfully. Only when the sheriff is a problem does the hue and cry call for a change in the election laws. Arizonans, for the most part, seem to have elected their sheriffs wisely.

CHAPTER 5.
The County Jail

Andrew James Doran, sheriff of Pinal County 1883–1884.

In medieval England, the shire-reeve kept the peace and acted in the interests of the Crown. Today, the sheriff's two primary responsibilities are keeping the peace and maintaining the county jail. Caging other human beings against their will, whether for protection of the innocent or punishment for a crime, has always been one of society's most difficult obligations, and the practice of imprisonment goes back at least as far as biblical times. In medieval times, most English jails or *gaols* belonged to the church and nobility. However, at the A.D. 1166 Assize (trial session) of Clarendon, King Henry II established a jail in each of his shires and put his reeves in charge of them.

The sheriff must protect innocent citizens from criminals, but he is also expected to protect prisoners from each other. Overcrowding violent persons is potentially dangerous for those both inside and outside the jail. During incarceration, the sheriff must supply the prisoners' material needs and, today, their educational needs. The goal is to rehabilitate prisoners so they can reenter society. While there have always been individual reformers, only in recent times have we as a society sought to educate inmates for life outside of jail.

The Sheriff's Duties

Early Arizona sheriffs served as tax collectors, assessors, and ex-officio members of the county board of supervisors. They derived part of their income from a percentage of their tax collections. In 1887, the Arizona tax-collector position became a separate office, and a year later the assessor's office became an independent office as well.

The first Territorial Assembly authorized paying the sheriff a daily rate of 75 cents per prisoner to cover all expenses—including overhead such as jail upkeep and a jailor's salary, as well as clothing, bedding, and "wholesome food" for each prisoner. Laws for the new territory had been drawn up first in New Mexico and later adopted in Arizona; the New Mexico penal code stipulated that prisoners, not taxpayers, must contribute to their upkeep. If the prisoner or his family could not pay, he performed street-cleaning and other public chores. On April 6, 1875, the supervisors ordered Pima County Sheriff William Sanders Oury to require county prisoners to clean out the old well in the jail yard or else dig a new one. Exceptions to the work rule were made in the case of a more dangerous prisoner, such as a murderer, or someone too ill to work.

In 1864, administration of the law in Tucson rested with Judge Charlie Meyer, Tucson's druggist. Everyone loved to imitate Meyer's German accent, and they recorded it as best they could. Meyer instituted the "shain" gang and threw bad men in the "yug." Meyer frequently assigned the culprit a number of lashes. The offender would be given half the sentence and told to return the next day for the rest. Most miscreants failed to show up on the second day. This strategy helped rid the town of criminals, and there is no evidence that anyone tried to chase them down.

In spite of Meyer's efforts, however, J. Ross Browne, a travel writer for *Harper's New Monthly Magazine,* wrote a series of articles in 1864 under the title "A Tour Through Arizona." He described Tucson as "a place of resort for traders, speculators, gamblers, horse thieves, murderers, and vagrant politicians." The worst criminals were hanged. For other crimes, Arizona Territorial courts, like their Colonial counterparts, meted out lesser punishments intended to shame the culprit, including fines, whipping, and banishment.

Early sheriffs had considerable freedom to exercise corporal punishment. In 1883, Pinal County Sheriff Andrew James Doran assigned his inmates the task of painting the courthouse. When they showed a disinclination to work, Doran put them on a diet of bread and water. After a few days on this fare the prisoners felt more industrious.

Often the sheriff's wife cooked the prisoners' meals and served as the matron for female prisoners. In 1871 the Pima County Board of Supervisors began securing bids for jail food from restaurant owners. J. Neugass bid $1 per prisoner per day. D. A. Bennett offered cooked provisions at the rate of 95 cents per head, and Frank S. Alling would provide two meals per day for 99.9 cents per prisoner with "two extra dishes on the Sabbath." In February 1893, the federal prisoners incarcerated in the Pima County Jail petitioned U.S. Marshal Robert H. Paul to investigate their bad provisions. They complained, "The food is too horrible for even Mexicans."

Sheriffs have always been responsible for their prisoners' health. If a contagious disease broke out in or near the jail, the sheriff, with written approval from a superior court judge, removed the prisoners. In August 1871, Dr. John Handy bid on and was awarded a contract to serve as the Pima County physician. He proposed to attend to county prisoners for $50 a month and to provide free medicines. He would also include care for indigent persons and furnish hospital accommodations for $80 per month.

THE CREATION OF ARIZONA'S COUNTIES

On April 9, 1864, the new Arizona Territory's governor, John Goodwin, created three legislative or judicial districts with three appointed sheriffs: Berry Hill De Armitt for Pima County, Isaac C. Bradshaw for Yuma County, and Van Ness C. Smith for Yavapai County. Arizona's first Territorial Assembly retained these districts and created one more; on December 15, Goodwin appointed Milton G. Moore as Mohave County sheriff (Another county, Pah-Ute, was carved from Mohave County in 1865, but within five months most of it was given to Nevada Territory. The remaining portion of the new county was reabsorbed by Mohave County in 1871.) Between 1866 and 1912, the Arizona Territorial Assembly created ten more Arizona counties: Maricopa, 1871; Pinal, 1875; Apache, 1879; Cochise, Graham, and Gila, 1881; Coconino, 1891; Navajo, 1895; Santa Cruz, 1899; and Greenlee, 1909. The state legislature approved residents' request for a fifteenth county, La Paz, in 1983.

The County Jails

The first order of business of each new county was to construct a courthouse and a jail. Early Arizona jails consisted of a few primitive cells constructed from adobe blocks. In remote areas, the prisoners were simply chained to a boulder or a tree. Whenever possible, sheriffs separated dangerous criminals from youthful offenders or the occasional town drunk. Often one windowless cell served to hold the most dangerous felons. Serious troublemakers wore the Oregon boot, a heavy metal chain attached to an ankle band and attached at the other end to a heavy iron ball.

PIMA COUNTY The guardhouse of the original Tucson presidio served as Pima County's first jail. This adobe structure was refitted with a heavy mesquite floor, iron doors, and shutters. Prisoners were shackled to a stone in the middle of the floor. In 1868, the Pima County supervisors purchased a lot at the corner of Court and Ott Streets from Mark Aldrich for $200. On this land, Charlie Meyer built the first Pima County courthouse, according to specifications that required a rock foundation and "walls of adobe made of good dirt mixed with straw."

As the Arizona Territory grew, so did its jail population. By 1888, Pima County Sheriff Matthew Shaw had 279 prisoners in the county jail. Most of them had committed misdemeanors, but thirty-eight were felons. Eighty were federal prisoners, nine were considered insane, and four awaited extradition to other counties.

In 1928, Pima County Sheriff James W. McDonald and the Pima County Jail quartered eighteen Mexican deserters from the Mexican Revolution, who had marched across the border, laid down their arms, and surrendered to the U.S. Border Patrol rather than be captured by Mexicans. After baths and food, they settled in to enjoy McDonald's hospitality. This jail, designed for eighty prisoners, now held 137—continuing the county's earlier pattern of overfilling inadequately sized jails.

ACCOMMODATING FEMALE INMATES

In the nineteenth century, women only composed about 4 percent of the United States prison population, but they still presented many problems. They had to be segregated from the male convicts and administered by matrons. As Arizona Territory grew, it became obvious that county jails needed not only separate cells for women but also separate cell blocks. Yavapai County became the first Arizona county to add a women's cell block, in 1897.

YUMA COUNTY La Paz, now a ghost town in the county of the same name, served as Yuma County's first county seat. In 1867, the Yuma County Board of Supervisors appointed A. J. Waldeman to draw up plans for a county courthouse and jail. This old jail had eighteen-inch-thick walls and a dirt floor. When the county seat moved to Yuma in

1870, the records, the furniture, the county seal, the prisoners, and the supervisors were moved along the Colorado River on the steamboat Nina Tilden. The new county jail provided two rooms—one for prisoners and the other for a guard. Prisoners were secured by ankle cuffs linked to an eight-foot chain connected to an iron bolt in the floor.

By 1872, Sheriff George Tyng considered the Yuma County Jail so unsafe that he began using the army dungeon at Fort Yuma to house the prisoners. On January 1, 1872, the supervisors ordered the construction of a new courthouse and a jail, which consisted of a large tank and four small cells. The cells and corridors were lined with thick boiler iron. Yumans bragged that the jail was escape-proof; however, Que-Cha-Co, a Yuma-Mojave Indian who had killed Yuma County Sheriff James T. Dana in September of 1871, escaped on October 28, 1873, and was never seen again. In 1927, a fire destroyed this structure, and Yuma County Sheriff James Chappell accepted a new jail with two rolled-steel cells for maximum-security prisoners on April 7, 1928.

YAVAPAI COUNTY In 1864, the supervisors bought Yavapai County Sheriff Jerome B. Calkins a desk and a set of Arizona law books. Until a jail could be built, all prisoners were boarded with the army, for a fee. On the first floor of the first Yavapai courthouse, four jail cells accommodated "vicious and obstreperous customers." Large floor logs ran the full length of the building, which also had heavy cell doors made of timber. The jailor secured the doors with two heavy iron straps and two large padlocks. Three cells were lighted by small barred windows, but the fourth cell remained dark. In 1891, the supervisors issued contracts for a new jail, and prisoners graded the area in preparation. After a low bidder failed to post bond, the supervisors granted the $4,870 contract to the Pauley Jail Building Company of St. Louis, Missouri, which constructed jails all over the country. The new jail accepted its first prisoners in mid-January 1892.

MOHAVE COUNTY Mohave County had a wandering county seat, starting with Mohave City in 1865, Hardyville in 1868, Cerbat in 1873, and four years later, Mineral Park. In 1877, the supervisors authorized $8,000 in bonds for the courthouse and jail construction at Mineral Park. When the county seat moved to Kingman ten years later, the first Mohave County Jail in Kingman was a wooden structure with a stockade of planks enclosing the back yard.

In March 1910, while a new jail was being constructed, three prisoners broke out of a holding shack. In April the supervisors approved the new jail and turned it over to Mohave County Sheriff Walter Brown. This two-story structure, now a historic monument, came to be known as the "old lie detector" and the "hot box." The jail's ground floor had an office for the jailor and four cells, two of which were reserved for city offenders. The second floor had three cells, including the felony tank, which was a cell within a cell. Prisoners were conducted through a tunnel to the courthouse.

FRONTIER JAILS: STEEL CAGES ON FLAT WAGONS

Starting as steamboat blacksmiths on the Mississippi River, members of the German-American P. J. Pauley family founded the Pauley Jail Building and Manufacturing Co. in St. Louis, Missouri, in 1856. Their timing was right: heavy river traffic, accompanied by gambling and assorted criminal behavior, generated a flourishing business.

After the Civil War, as America pushed its western frontier toward the Pacific Ocean, P. J. Pauley Sr., then 33, envisioned an enormous expansion opportunity. His company would wheel its small steel cages, anchored to flat wagons, to Texas, New Mexico, and no doubt Arizona, where counties in emerging territories and states were charged with housing prisoners until they could be transferred to a state prison.

The Pauley Jail Building Co.'s involvement in the detention business has thrived into this century, with great-great grandsons now running the show. Along the way, the firm has pioneered everything from double-ribbed bar and tool-resisting steel to special plumbing fixtures that would not clog (Noverflo) and a line of security windows (Invisiguard) that replaced the old, exposed guards.

PINAL COUNTY Pinal County—created on February 1, 1875, from portions of Pima and Maricopa Counties—chose Florence as the county seat. County officers served without pay the first year so that Pinal could be kept debt-free. (Unfortunately, the first Pinal County sheriff, M. Rogers, disappeared with the tax money sometime during his first year of office.) In July, the supervisors instructed Sheriff Rogers to rent a house for use as a jail, with rent not to exceed $5 per month. Jailors slept in front of the burlap-draped doorway of this small, windowless, adobe jail. Prisoners were chained to a large boulder in the center of the room. A Chinese man, Jim Sam, fed the prisoners for 62.5 cents per day per prisoner. In 1950, Pinal County replaced the anti-quated old jail, which had been set up to accommodate twenty-five prisoners but often held as many as seventy. In 1991, Pinal County Sheriff Frank Reyes warned his con-stituency about the overcrowding and abuse of guards in the 1950 facility, which has since been completely renovated, with additional beds added.

APACHE COUNTY The Tenth Territorial Legislative Assembly created Apache County, with St. Johns as the county seat, entirely from part of Yavapai County on

February 24, 1879. The first Apache County Jail has been described as a "relic of Hell." A new facility, built some time in the 1890s, served Apache County for about twenty years. Edwin Whiting, the local blacksmith, riveted shackles onto the prisoners' ankles.

COCHISE COUNTY The Eleventh Territorial Assembly carved Cochise County from a part of Pima County on February 1, 1881. Three years later, residents pointed with pride to the two-story courthouse, which contained the county jail, county offices, and a handsome courtroom. (Today this Tombstone courthouse is a museum and is listed on the National Register of Historic Places.) In 1884, the supervisors ordered Cochise County Sheriff Robert Hatch to "get a janitor to keep order in the county building for $50 a month." He hired Florence Hamseth as "janitrex." Hatch also purchased five dozen hand grenades for protection of the county buildings.

Often the prisoners had too much idle time. Cochise County jailor Mack Axford allowed Chicago Whitey to purchase a cook stove and sell his Mexican pies (empanadas). Axford also acquired boxing gloves, checkerboards, and harmonicas for his prisoners, and he also let one inmate with barber skills set up shop in the jail courtyard and charge for his haircuts.

During Cochise County Sheriff Del Lewis's term in 1903, his prisoners held a daily kangaroo court in the county jail, which they dubbed "Hotel Lewis." Their bailiff called out, "Hear ye! Hear ye! The kangaroo court of the Cochise County Jail, having jurisdiction over all persons within its confines, is now in session." The prisoners somberly removed their hats and arranged themselves around their "judge." Their "sheriff" marched a new arrival before the judge to be read the rules. He always found the new prisoner guilty of Rule No. 1 which read, "All persons entering this jail are subject to a fine of not less than $1; persons not able to pay their fine must work one week or more scrubbing the jail, washing clothes, etc. according to the sentence." The judge pointed out that Rules 5 and 6 stipulated "that any person paying a fine is exempt from work; any person having money and does not pay a fine is subject to ten lashes well laid on." If the prisoner pleaded financial embarrassment, the court sentenced him to one bath and a week's labor.

With the decline of silver mining in Tombstone and the rise of copper mining in Bisbee, the county seat moved in 1929 to Bisbee, where a new courthouse and jail were built. In 1985, Cochise County prisoners were transferred from the old facility to a new modern jail, also in Bisbee.

GILA COUNTY The Eleventh Territorial Legislature created Gila County from portions of Maricopa and Pinal Counties on February 8, 1881, with Globe designated as the Gila County seat. In May, the Gila County Board of Supervisors bought property on the corner of Broad and Oak Streets for $900 for the first courthouses and jail.

These buildings were razed in 1887 to make way for a new courthouse with a jail inside it. Every office in the new courthouse had a stove and electric lights.

In 1910, another new jail was constructed, serving Gila County until 1981. Portions of the site, enclosed by a wooden fence, provided a prisoner exercise yard and housed temporary structures, such as the gallows. In 1981 Sheriff Lyman Peace closed this old county jail when he accepted a new facility.

GRAHAM COUNTY On March 10, 1881, the residents of this newly created county, formed out of portions of Navajo and Pima Counties, broke with the prior tradition of using Indian names for Arizona counties; the county's namesake, William A. Graham, was admired because he had served as secretary of the Navy under Millard Fillmore from 1850 to 1852. The Arizona Territorial legislature approved the residents' choice of Safford as the county seat, and in April, A. M. Franklin offered the supervisors the use of three rooms in his general office building for two years, rent-free. The supervisors ordered that the rooms, which would serve as both court and jail, be "fit up in a fair, habitable condition." They authorized Sheriff George Stevens to purchase two iron cells measuring six by eight feet and six pairs of handcuffs and shackles. Two years later residents voted to move the county seat to Solomonville.

On April 16, 1883, J. E. Solomon and his wife, Anna, deeded to Graham County 462 square feet of land—small by today's standards—to be used for construction of a courthouse and a jail. A year later the supervisors approved the courthouse and called for bids on the outhouses and a jail wall. Prisoners dug a town well on the courthouse square. During the great flood of 1906, prisoners had to be removed by ropes through a small window high up in the roof. In 1915, the county seat returned permanently to Safford, with a new courthouse and jail financed with $50,000 in bonds.

COCONINO COUNTY In 1887, the state legislature created Coconino County, with Flagstaff as its county seat. Because Flagstaff already had a jail, the supervisors approved a monthly allotment of $60 for its upkeep until a new county jail could be built. In September of that same year the Atlantic and Pacific Railroad offered land for the courthouse and jail site, and the Pauley Jail Building Company erected a new jail with steel cells for $4,870. By 1895 the courthouse had electric lights, and the supervisors gave permission to the Western Union Telegraph Company and to Postal Telegraph and Cable Company to place telephones in the new building for public use. These expenses were borne by the telegraph companies.

In 1891 the *Arizona Champion* in Flagstaff called upon the Coconino County Board of Supervisors to do something about the county jail, which it described as "little better than a dog house, and to confine human beings in such a place bordered on barbarism." A year later Coconino County Sheriff John W. Francis took over a new county jail. He removed the prisoners from "the old rookery," and before putting them in the new facility he "treated them all to a bath and new clothing, which the prisoners fully appreciated."

In May 1899, the supervisors removed Coconino County Sheriff Fletcher Fairchild from office for reason of insanity, and shortly after being declared insane, he died. During his brief term two locals, Casey and Brannen, "celebrated the Fourth of July" in November by becoming very drunk and getting thrown in jail. In the early morning, they broke open the jail door and swiped as much jail bedding as they could carry. After selling it to a secondhand dealer, G. W. Morris, they got drunk again, and when the money and booze ran out, they made another raid on the jail clothes. This time Morris refused to buy, so the miscreants sold the second batch to railroad-section hands. Casey was caught, but Brannen "hopped the twig."

NAVAJO COUNTY On March 21, 1895, Navajo County was carved out of a portion of Yavapai County, with Holbrook as the county seat. The Navajo County Board of Supervisors issued bonds for construction of a courthouse on land provided by F. A. and J. C. Zuck, in return for having their 1897 taxes cancelled, and the Pauley Jail Building Company installed the new jail.

SANTA CRUZ COUNTY The Twentieth Territorial Assembly created Santa Cruz County on March 15, 1899, with Nogales as the county seat. Ten days later, the board of supervisors leased twelve rooms for offices and space for a jail from George B. Marsh at $100 per month. Until a courthouse could be constructed, district-court sessions were held in a theater. In 1902, the county issued bonds for $35,000 to build a courthouse and a four-cell jail.

GREENLEE COUNTY By the early 1900s, electric lights flickered in all but the poorest homes all over the Arizona Territory, and the copper-mining towns boomed. Mining officials, although rarely interested in seeking political office for themselves, sought to consolidate their base of power in the Clifton-Morenci District with a new county. Carved from the eastern part of Graham County, the fourteenth county, Greenlee, came into being on March 10, 1909. For two years, residents disputed the new county boundaries. Finally they agreed that Greenlee would be smaller than originally anticipated, and that the new county would absorb all of Graham County's indebtedness. After arguments over the location of the county seat, the residents settled on Clifton.

With a hard-drinking, rough mining population, Clifton had needed a jail as early as 1878. A local miner—Margarito Barela—picked, drilled, and blasted a hole in the side of a rock cliff until he had dug one cell for dangerous criminals and a larger room to hold other lawbreakers. The cells were fitted with massive iron doors, which pivoted on solid iron rods. Light streamed through two iron-barred windows about ten feet above the ground. After Barela collected his pay, he celebrated in John Hovey's saloon. When he fired off his gun, Hovey, also a Graham County deputy sheriff, arrested him, and Barela became the first inmate of his own jail.

LA PAZ COUNTY Residents created the last Arizona county, La Paz, on January 1, 1983, from the northern portion of Yuma County. La Paz County residents felt they shared more common interests with each other than with the Yuma County seat, 120 miles to the south, and they had resented their taxes going to care for indigent aliens who crossed the Mexico border. At that time, Arizona law provided that "a split can be approved with 66.6 percent support from the voters in the proposed new county and 15 percent from the remainder of the county." At midnight, December 31, 1982, La Paz County Sheriff Rayburn Evans and Yuma County Sheriff John Phipps met at the new county line, where Evans received keys to the sheriff's facilities in La Paz County.

La Paz used a holding tank that had been built in 1946 as a temporary county jail. When La Paz County Sheriff Marvin Hare took over the facility in 1989, this jail, originally designed to hold fourteen prisoners in four cells, housed forty to fifty prisoners each day. The supervisors expanded this jail, but it never met American Correctional Association standards. In 1992, a new facility costing approximately $4.2 million was constructed.

Jailbreaks Run the Gamut

Once a sheriff takes custody of a prisoner, he must keep him in jail until he comes up for trial, is released on bail, is transferred to another facility, or serves out his sentence. But boredom and idleness have driven prisoners to attempt escapes, and nothing gets public attention so quickly as a jailbreak. Arizona inmates have used a number of escape methods, including: resorting to trickery or force to get the keys to their cells, setting fire to their cells and fleeing during the ensuing chaos, and—the least successful (but most often tried) escape method—digging or breaking out of the facility.

In 1870, Pima County Sheriff Peter Brady turned stray dogs loose in the jail yards and in the jail aisles to prevent escapes. After a jailbreak on New Year's Eve in 1875, Tucsonans registered their displeasure with Pima County Sheriff William Sanders Oury, who had lost twenty-five prisoners in four years, seventeen of them in one mass escape. He replied, "Well, damn it, let the bastards go. It saves the county money to get rid of them." When the supervisors conducted an investigation into the escapes, they discovered that jailor Ad Linn frequently left his post to drink and gamble in the local saloons.

In 1877, Yavapai County Sheriff Edward F. Bowers caught J. A. Lewis trying to saw out the logs in his cell floor. Lewis, under a death sentence for murdering his wife, had constructed three saws out of pieces of tin and iron. In another cell, John Davis served time for trying to steal a horse from Sheriff Bowers's ranch. During a check, Bowers found Davis muddy from head to foot. While trying to dig a log out of the floor, he had become mired in mud and water under the floor. Bowers manacled Davis's ankles and installed a boulder in the hole.

Shortly after his appointment in 1890 as Coconino County sheriff, James A. Johnson discovered that eight prisoners had broken out of jail by cutting the bolts in the cell bars that had been installed during a previous repair. Then they cut a hole in the ceiling and in the steel roof. The prisoners reached the ground by climbing down blankets tied together, but they were recaptured within a few days. A plumber, Harry Kelley, who had a contract for the county jail, had helped the prisoners escape.

By February 1977, the corroded metal cells of Santa Cruz County's dungeon-like stone jail were so decomposed that the prisoners were able to tear off strips to make knives and daggers. Santa Cruz County Sheriff Zeke Bejarano lodged all prisoners in one tank, where hard-core felons mixed with young men who had simply overstayed their work permits from Mexico. On one occasion, after a mob of rioters set fire to the jail roof, they burned out the superintendent of education's office above it. Finally they barricaded their jail door. When Bejarano forced the door open, a spear-shaped piece of pipe narrowly missed his head. The inmates hurled chunks of metal and chains ripped from the iron cots at the deputies. Supervisor William Baffert called for more stringent measures in dealing with prisoners, but Bejarano said, "Hell, no measure will ever suffice here."

During Apache County Sheriff Commodore Perry Owens's tenure, a couple of New Mexico outlaws dug through a jail wall. When Deputy Sheriff Joe McKinney and Owens caught them, the prisoners said, "Old boy, if we ever get the drop on you, you stand and we won't hurt a hair of your head, but if we ever get a drop on that red head [Owens] down comes his meat house." Owens had to serve as jailor for a while when the aged Apache County jailor (McKinney) could no longer do his work. During this time McKinney killed one escapee and captured another a day later. When McKinney returned to St. Johns from out of town, he discovered that Owens had not only removed him as undersheriff, but accused him of letting the prisoners out. After McKinney called the sheriff "every name in the book," Owens apologized, but McKinney walked out.

Cochise County had many problems with early outlaws. In April 1899 a gang of train robbers—Billy Stiles, Burt Alvord, and Bravo Juan Yoas—broke out of the Cochise County Jail. Alvord—a short, bald-headed ruffian—generally busied himself with guns, wild women, practical jokes, drinking, and train robberies. He had also served as a Cochise County deputy sheriff and a constable in Pearce and Willcox. He used his position as a lawman to pass on details of train shipments of gold to his outlaw confederate, Billy Stiles. Near the Cochise train station on September 11, 1899, four masked men held up the train and dynamited its safe. When the news reached Tombstone, Alvord made a half-hearted, unsuccessful attempt to find the robbers.

Finally a black waiter from Schweitzer's saloon revealed to Willcox constable Bert Grover that he had heard Alvord, Stiles, Yoas, and William Downing planning the holdup. After Stiles confessed to the robberies, Sheriff Scott White made a serious mistake by letting him come and go as he pleased within the confines of the jail. On the evening of April 6, 1900, jailor George Bravin was the only officer on duty. Stiles grabbed a rifle and shot Bravin in the stomach, then freed all the prisoners. Several

Cochise County Sheriff Scott White.

inmates remained in the jail and tried to help Bravin. The escapees stole horses and fled toward Mexico. Sheriff White was not amused when he received the following letter dated April 20, 1900:

Scott White, Esq. We send you the keys to the jail. We would have given them to Sid Mullen [another outlaw] but he was too swift for us, we could not overtake him. We met the Mexicans that killed the gambler in Johnson Camp but as we had no warrants we did not arrest them—and we were afraid they would shoot, and we had no warrant and we couldn't collect mileage. Tell the boys we are all well and eating regular. Tell the man I got the Studebaker saddle and will send it home soon. Signed Bravo Juan, Stiles, and Alvord.

Stiles and Alvord were caught in 1903 and sentenced to terms in the Yuma Territorial Prison. However, while waiting for their transfer, they languished in the Cochise County Jail in Tombstone until December 20, 1903, when they dug through a wall, climbed down a rope, and rode to freedom. Deputies wounded Alvord during a recapture, but Stiles disappeared. After receiving an early release from the Yuma

Territorial Prison for good behavior, Alvord left Arizona and reputedly went to Jamaica, Canada, and South America, and he may have died in Honduras. Billy Stiles became a deputy sheriff in Nevada and died the way he had lived, by the gun. He had killed a cattle rustler, and in 1908 the rustler's brother shot Stiles in the back.

Shenanigans in Maricopa County

The first Maricopa County courthouse, in Phoenix, included a central courtroom flanked by offices. On Sundays the courtroom also served as a church. The county jail, behind the courthouse, consisted of a tier of cells set into an adobe wall. Its dirt floors were sprinkled down every morning.

The Maricopa County Jail has made continual news, from Territorial days up to recent times. While Maricopa County Sheriff Noah Broadway prepared to go home on September 16, 1885, eight prisoners broke open an iron-bar door and rushed into the jail yard, but Broadway and his deputies captured them while they tried to scale the fence. The *Phoenix Herald* called for a brick wall around the jail or else it would be safer to "herd the prisoners in the open air than to try and keep them in the county jail."

Maricopa County Sheriff Lindley Orme began his term in 1881 with an office in a new two-story brick courthouse and a new ten-cell jail. The Phoenix Light and Fuel Company furnished and installed incandescent lamps in the courthouse and jail at no charge for the first year, and charged 16 cents per kilowatt hour for the power.

Jail scandal and a bizarre set of events clouded the career of Maricopa County Sheriff John Elliott Walker, whose laxness regarding one inmate's incarceration probably cost a deputy his life savings. Deputy Sheriff W. T. Williams did not trust banks, so he carried all of his money—$1,100 in gold and $75 in silver—on his person. On November 23, 1904, on his way to visit the territorial fair, he stored his property in the sheriff's office. After he missed the train home that night, Williams bunked in the sheriff's office, using his satchel of valuables for a pillow. None of the guards knew the combination, so he could not put his money in the safe. The next morning Williams stashed his possessions in a wardrobe while he attended to personal business. When he returned, his possessions were gone.

During this period, Phoenix constable Lee Redwine had pleaded guilty to charges of extortion, and the judge sentenced him to a $30 fine and thirty days in jail, refusing to let him substitute another $30 for jail time. Redwine walked the streets, even though the district attorney had urged Sheriff Walker to keep Redwine confined. When rumors circulated that the sheriff was derelict in his duty, Walker put Redwine in jail but did not restrict him to a cell. On the evening that Williams's possessions were stolen, the guards went to sleep assuming that Redwine would do the same.

Redwine disappeared, and gossip associated his disappearance with Williams's missing money. On December 15, the *Arizona Republican* (precursor to today's *Arizona Republic*, published in Phoenix) published a letter from Redwine, postmarked in Los Angeles, denying that he had stolen Williams's money and stating that he would return if the thirty days of jail time were dropped. But Redwine never returned to Phoenix, nor did Williams get his gold and silver back. Walker's disgrace and personal debt drove him into depression. After he left office, on December 19, 1906, Sheriff Walker placed a gun to his head and committed suicide.

Wright Keeps the Pot Boiling

Maricopa County Sheriff Charles Henry Wright stands out as one of Arizona's more controversial lawmen. Born in Arkansas, he grew up in Oklahoma, then known as Indian Territory. In 1907, Wright moved to Phoenix, where he founded the Wright Land and Cattle Exchange. After serving as a Maricopa County deputy sheriff, he ran for sheriff as the lone Republican in 1928 and defeated his Democratic opponent, Dan E. Jones, by more than two thousand votes.

To his credit, as early as 1929, Wright advocated fingerprinting children. He also directed the search and capture of fugitives Irene Schroeder and Glenn Dague, who had killed a Pennsylvania policeman that same year. During their crime rampage across the nation, the pair was joined by another ex-con, Vernon Ackerman, aka Joe F. Wells. Near Chandler these fugitives killed an Arizona lawman, Maricopa County Deputy Sheriff Lee Wright (no relation to the sheriff). While Ackerman awaited trial in the Maricopa jail, another inmate warned the sheriff that Ackerman planned to kill Sheriff Wright with a homemade dagger during a trip to court. During a shakedown, deputies found a stiletto among Ackerman's possessions.

Maricopa County Sheriff Charles Wright.

Prison architecture had not yet arrived at the point where large concrete multi-storied jails with individual cells were constructed separate from the courthouses. Sheriff Wright's problems began with the operation of the new Maricopa County Jail on the fifth and sixth floors of the courthouse. On December 19, 1929, four prisoners escaped during the night.

They had hauled up piano wire and valve-grinding compound through the open barred windows. No one heard them remove the bars during the day, because there was so much noise from a nearby air compressor. The inmates wriggled out, dropped to the courthouse roof, broke through a window in the supervisors' office, and took the stairs to the second floor. There they broke another window, slid down a braided rope made from mattress covers, and fled. No one discovered their absence until a janitor reported them missing the next morning.

Fearing additional escape attempts, Wright posted extra guards around the building at night, but Deputy Sheriff Gus Dobrinsky was almost killed when an inmate tossed a copper frame from a jail window at him. When Wright went to the press with a list of urgent jail needs, the supervisors told the newspapers that they had planned to take care of these problems all along.

Wright put Tank D on bread and water for throwing soap in the courthouse pool and tin pans into the courthouse yards. The soap annoyed the fish. Then Tank A prisoners, who had been smoking marijuana pulled up from the courtyard, joined in the troublemaking. When jailor M. R. Chumbly heard a plate-glass window shatter, he put his eye to the peephole and a prisoner shoved a broom handle at him. Chumbly fired his revolver through the peephole and wounded two men.

One Sunday night the prisoners rioted, and on Monday morning the supervisors demanded a full report from the sheriff on the jailhouse troubles. Wright issued orders that prisoners could only have county food (nothing brought by relatives or other visitors), and only visitors on important business were allowed in the jail. Armed deputies patrolled the jail floors and the courthouse yard. On January 8, the prisoners hurled plates and obscenities at pedestrians on the street. That same night the inmates threw a bale of blazing mattresses onto the courthouse roof. After deputies put out that fire, the rioters dropped another flaming bundle out of the Jefferson Street window in an attempt to hit Sheriff Wright's car, although they missed their target.

Wright locked up the ringleaders in the "snakes," a totally dark cell. They got only bread and water until they promised to improve their behavior. Deputies and jailors carried tear-gas bombs and had orders to use them at the first sign of trouble. Wright commented to the press that the prisoners did not appreciate kind treatment.

However, the supervisors accused Wright of inefficiency. He responded with charges that the new jail construction was already twenty years out-of-date and that he did not have either enough money or personnel to do a good job. The supervisors hired an inspector to investigate the design defects. On his advice, they called for bids to install thick welded-steel screens on the windows, and they approved the installation of bulletproof glass in the observation panels.

On a separate front, Wright and the supervisors fought each other over the costs for accepting federal prisoners into the Maricopa County Jail. Because the new jail had cost more than the supervisors anticipated, they ordered Wright to charge the federal government $1 instead of 75 cents per day to house each federal prisoner.

U.S. Marshal George Mauk defended Wright and described the Maricopa County Jail as a "birdcage." The federal government refused to increase the allowance unless the supervisors agreed the jail would operate its own kitchen rather than contracting out for meals. So the supervisors ordered Wright to refuse custody of all new federal prisoners, claiming that the county had no money for a kitchen, and besides, the government had no business dictating to Maricopa County how it should run its jail.

Mauk insisted that no contractor could produce decent jail food on the 19.75 cents per day for two meals per prisoner currently mandated. The supervisors sampled this inexpensive jail food and announced that it was just as good as that served in the average home. Supervisor Phil Ensign suggested holding out for a $1.25 allowance, saying, "The excellent view afforded the inmates of the jail from the top of the courthouse should be worth at least another quarter."

When Wright refused to accept new prisoners, U.S. Marshal Mauk informed the sheriff that he could be held in contempt of court. By law, any sheriff who refuses to receive or arrest any person charged with a criminal offense may be punished with a fine and/or imprisonment. But when Wright began accepting federal prisoners again, the supervisors withheld his paycheck.

County Attorney George Wilson advised Wright to sue the supervisors for his salary, and finally they released his check but asked for a restraining order to prevent the sheriff from accepting federal prisoners. When Mauk began sending his prisoners to other county jails and the Phoenix City Jail, the supervisors agreed to accept the government's new offer of 95 cents per day per prisoner.

Wright's battles with the supervisors never ended. On February 19, 1930, the supervisors ordered the janitor to move Wright's office to a smaller area. Wright refused to move, and Supervisor Phil Ensign decided to settle the matter himself. That led to a heated exchange and Ensign applied an epithet, which resulted in fisticuffs.

Just why Wright decided to run for reelection is baffling, but he did. He won the primary but lost the general election to James R. McFadden, who had capitalized on Wright's problems, describing the sheriff as an unreasonable burden on the taxpayers. However, as a result of Wright's problems McFadden had a better jail and more money.

Wright then went to work for the Phoenix Police Department, where he also became involved in endless rounds of controversy with his superiors. On July 9, 1943, Wright suffered a heart attack and died at age sixty-one. He had been involved in law enforcement for over forty years. In spite of previous conflicts, the police comments described him as a "model officer and a loyal member of the department who would be missed for his ever-willing and constant offer of advice and assistance, his ready smile and gracious disposition."

A later Maricopa County Sheriff, Ernest Roach, was accused in 1945 of permitting a kangaroo court, in which inmates were fined and punished by other prisoners. Subsequently, Roach laid down twenty-three rules prohibiting gambling, wrestling, boxing, and kangaroo courts. The final rule informed prisoners that defacing the list of jail rules posted in their cells could result in prosecution for destruction of county property.

Enter Sheriff Joe Arpaio

In modern times the Maricopa County Jail has made national news under its "get tough" Republican Sheriff Joe Arpaio, who won the office in 1993 after thirty years

of experience as a decorated agent with the U.S. Drug Enforcement Administration. Arpaio frequently says, "Nobody inside jail should live better than people on the outside." Over protests from critics, Arpaio has revived the chain gang, for both male and female prisoners. Prisoners wear easily recognized black-and-white striped suits. When Arpaio faced the problem of overcrowding, he erected a tent-city jail for about sixteen hundred inmates, using military-surplus canvas tents. On top of the security-fence enclosure, a neon light announces "Vacancy." To cope with the problem of prisoners

Maricopa County Sheriff Joe Arpaio.

stealing jail-issued socks and underwear, Arpaio ordered that these items be dyed bright pink. His volunteer sheriff's posse has earned thousands of dollars for various projects by selling pink shorts autographed by Arpaio and tent-city tee-shirts to the public.

Arpaio's jail is tobacco-free, and the prisoners do not get coffee. Hair is cut short so it cannot conceal contraband. Prisoners are randomly tested for drugs. Arpaio stopped girlie magazines, and prisoners are only allowed to watch in-house cable television, which features Newt Gingrich's Renewing America college course, the Weather Channel, and the Disney Channel.

If prisoners complain about being served cold bologna sandwiches, Arpaio says that "If they do not like it, they don't have to return." When the jail received a donation of emu meat, Arpaio worked this unusual item into the menu. Maricopa County voters have continued to return Arpaio to office since 1993.

County jails have tested the ingenuity of Arizona's sheriffs since the lawmen were first saddled with the proprietorship. And perhaps the most worrisome problem has been overcrowding, which leads inevitably to a new jail or addition as well as how to pay for it and maintain it. Not only do expanding populations in the counties affect jail overcrowding, but so does the fact that convictions in the county courts aren't the only source of prisoners. For an appropriate daily fee, cities and towns within the county, and even the federal government, may incarcerate their prisoners in the county jail.

There also is a closely related issue, a more recent state-ordered mandate that each Arizona county must offer an education program to serve prisoners under eighteen years old or those with disabilities who are twenty-one or younger when confined in the county jail. The county sheriff and the county school superintendent must work together to determine the method of delivery of the education program.

CHAPTER 6.
Rodeo Breeds Many Lawmen

Arizona sheriffs at the Phoenix rodeo, 1940.

In the early days of the West, lawmen were chosen for their knowledge of the land and for their ability to handle a horse and a gun. These talents, often gained through ranching, were also frequently expressed in the rodeo. Rodeo participation not only helped the sheriffs with good publicity but provided opportunities for peace officers to exchange information and appeal to regional pride. So important were rodeos to the law that in 1892 the New York-based *National Police Gazette* reported that, at the Territorial Fair in Phoenix on October 29, Charlie Meadows's "Arizona Charlie's Wild West Show" had eclipsed all previous records with as much grace as if "he were in an armchair."

Although Charlie was not a full-time lawman, his brother, Mobley, served as the first sheriff of Imperial County, California. Mobley occasionally deputized Charlie and another brother, Jake, for work along the California-Arizona border near Yuma and along the U.S.–Mexico border. Another member of Charlie's Wild West Show, Tom Wills, would later become a Pinal County sheriff and an Arizona legislator.

While serving as Pinal County sheriff in 1906, Wills took off time to ride at the Cheyenne rodeo, and on July 4 he won the bronc-busting contest at Florence. In later years when Wills served as a state senator, old-timers refused to let him forget his days of sowing wild oats when he shot out the lights in Florence saloons during his rodeo and cowboy days. Arizona Charlie's Wild West Show performed at such unlikely places as the Yuma Territorial Prison, where Wills acted the part of a stagecoach guard, fighting off bands of robbers. In Stockton, California, Wills suffered a serious accident while roping steers. His horse slipped into a pothole concealed by grass, catapulted into the air, and landed on Wills (who eventually recovered).

Around this same time, friction developed among the show members when a performer discovered that someone had put a real bullet instead of blanks in a gun used in the shoot-outs. Charlie let loose with "trenchant rhetoric" and "quit in high dudgeon and disgust," leaving his former employees to carry on without him. The remaining performers put on such poor exhibitions that the show folded in Oakland, California, where the local sheriff sold off the show's assets at auction.

The Miller Brothers' 101 Wild West Show produced two Arizona sheriffs: Pima County's Ed Echols and Maricopa County's Joseph Lon Jordan. Two of the show's most popular entertainers were humorist Will Rogers and actor/trick rider Tom Mix. The show's trademark was the hair-raising entry of Zack Miller: on his Andalusian stallion, Ben Hur, Miller would ride into the ring at full speed and come to a complete stop with his horse erect and pawing the air. Miller would then give his famous salute by raising his hat to the crowd. Hard times eventually fell on the Miller brothers when they were brought to trial on federal charges, which resulted in a conviction and a fine for defrauding Indians of their land allotments. In 1936 the show declared bankruptcy.

The Early Days of Rodeo

Wild West shows enjoyed their peak of popularity from about 1890 to 1915, but eventually gave way to the modern rodeos that sprang up in Western towns when cowboys got together and put on the Saturday-afternoon entertainment. Early rodeos were haphazard affairs, with the livestock owners making most of the money, paying the cowboys very little, and the contestants making up rules to suit themselves. Everett Bowman, an Arizona lawman and cowboy, participated in the first cowboy strike and helped organize the first professional United States rodeo organization, the Cowboy Turtles Association. Bowman, born in Hope, New Mexico, served as a deputy sheriff in both Maricopa and Pinal Counties. After losing the race for Maricopa County sheriff in 1946, he went on to become a captain with the Arizona Highway Patrol and a Wickenburg constable.

Bowman's father had done his best to thwart his son's dreams of becoming a cowboy by exiling him to town and school. His efforts were to no avail, though, because at the age of fifteen, Bowman ran away to Arizona and landed a job with the Double Circle outfit as a horse wrangler. No one ever expected much out of any young wrangler, and Bowman tried everyone's patience because he kept falling asleep in the saddle. One day his boss asked, "Do you really want to make a hand out of yourself?" Bowman replied, "Why of course I do." Then with strained patience, the boss admonished him, "For chrissake open up your goddam eyes."

Bowman also kept getting lost. Someone would say, "See them cows on the north side of that little butte, son?" With a big smile, Bowman would say, "Sure, sure." Then the cowboys would give him detailed instructions on how to bring them back. Five hours later someone would say, "Where's the kid?" "Oh him! Well only three more to brand and then we'll fetch him home." Bowman got fired from the Double Circle after they decided that they had put in their share of his range schooling and it was time for someone else to lend a hand.

Not a bit discouraged, he got a job with the Three C outfit, where he proved himself to be a good bronc-buster and demonstrated exceptional skill with the rope. A few years later when Bowman got the itch to move on, he traveled to his first big rodeo in Salt Lake City. When asked if he wanted to enter the bulldogging event, he replied, "Sure." He spent the next morning learning what bulldogging meant. By that afternoon, he caught the steer easily enough but let go too hard. When Bowman got up, he was holding a pair of horns in his hands; they had broken clean off. The next year he competed at Tucson and ran the horn of a steer through his leg, but a week later he was competing at Wickenburg.

Bowman functioned as a guiding force in the 1936 establishment of the Cowboy Turtles Association, whose motto was "Slow but Sure." Boston might seem an unlikely place for a cowboy strike, but it was there that Bowman and sixty-one cowboys united to get a purse increase and an imposition of entrance fees for each event. They also insisted on qualified judges, because often contestants made up the rules as they went along. During the first performance, producer Colonel W. T. Johnson refused to listen to the cowboys and threatened to drown all of his stock rather than give in to their demands. He tried to fill in with amateurs, but when the Boston Garden crowd screamed to bring on the real cowboys, Thompson relented. He gave the top performers an additional $4,000 and agreed to the cowboys' demands.

Rodeo cowboys often found themselves stranded in a strange town with no money after a rodeo, so the Turtles established an emergency fund to help these cowboys. One time a cowboy approached Bowman for money to go home because his child had been

Houston "Skeet" Bowman, rodeo performer, rancher, and sheriff of Graham County 1944–1952.

hit by a car. When Bowman discovered that the man had lied about the accident, he kicked him out of the Turtles. Later when Bowman was a deputy, the two men met again in an Arizona grocery-store parking lot. Bowman pulled his gun and told the cowboy to shoot or shut up. The cowboy left town.

Everett Bowman, who became Arizona's first World Champion All-Around Cowboy, winning eight national championships between 1929 and 1938, was elected to the Cowboy Hall of Fame in 1965. Equally at home in a modern age, he handled police cruisers and airplanes as well as livestock. During World War II Bowman used his own airplane to teach low-level (low-altitude) search techniques to Air Force recruits. In October of 1971, friends and family worried when Bowman's plane disappeared. In rough cowboy humor, someone suggested that Bowman would probably walk into Kingman with the airplane on his back. Another said, "Remember when he wrestled a steer and left a hole so big that they called it Roosevelt Lake?" Unfortunately, the search ended on a sad note. On October 27, Charles Everett Bowman, age seventy-one, was found dead near his small plane, which had crashed in the mountains near Bagdad, Arizona.

As a youth, Bowman had given his ten-year-old brother, Houston "Skeet" Bowman, a heifer and told him to build a herd until he had enough money to take a course in mechanics. Skeet also became a rodeo performer and a rancher, and served two terms as Graham County sheriff. In this role, Skeet Bowman initiated a law-enforcement training school at Safford, along with a better radio communications system. In 1948, he sponsored a fingerprint school with training by Federal Bureau of Investigation instructors.

Skeet Bowman never achieved the fame of his brother, Everett, but he, too, worked the rodeo circuit and won local championships—until 1936, when he broke his neck in a competition. After the accident, Skeet showed horses and brought home ten ribbons and a silver tray from the National Livestock Show after performing with his show horse, Poco Fisty, a young paint stallion.

No Case Left Unsolved

When the Depression hit in the 1930s, Arizona suffered from hard times. Many top professional rodeo hands were holed up in Pinal County with their earnings shot. Local ranchers encouraged them to stay and work, and Florence became known as the "Cradle of the Cowboys." Pinal County Sheriff Jimmy Herron Jr.—a slender, wiry man who rolled his own cigarettes with Velvet tobacco and usually managed to talk people out of a bad temper because of his own good nature—often appeared more interested in the rodeo and ranching than in law enforcement. When asked what he was doing in the office, Jimmy replied, "I had to come in. The Board of Supervisors stopped mailing my checks." Nevertheless, Herron made it understood that criminals would go to jail, and he had the good sense to appoint excellent deputies.

Cochise County Sheriff I. V. Pruitt.

Cochise County Sheriff I. V. Pruitt grew up on a Texas ranch and moved to Bisbee, where he worked for the Arizona Edison Company. When he was first elected sheriff in 1935, Pruitt's friends presented him with a solid gold badge. Pruitt was a familiar sight at various rodeos on his horse Jelly Bean before, during, and after his tenure as sheriff. Pruitt's most famous case, known as "the corpse in the culvert," drew national attention. On August 8, 1943, two soldiers from Douglas (on the Mexico border) and their girlfriends, while on a Sunday picnic, investigated the buzzards gathering at a culvert near U.S. 80, where they found a corpse. They called the sheriff, and when Pruitt turned the body over, he discovered that the man's throat had been cut. The victim, in his 30s, wore an expensive camel-hair coat over dirty work clothes, but Pruitt could not find any identification on the body.

Pruitt checked the currency exchange on the U.S. side of the border, and he found a woman who remembered that a man in a camel-hair coat had exchanged $200 into $2 bills, evidently planning to cross the border into Mexico. (During World War II, when the Nazis brought in fake American currency, the United States destroyed its value by declaring all bills, except $2 bills, which the Germans had not counterfeited, invalid in Mexico.)

Ezra Kent, a local farmer, identified the victim as Ed Miller, a hired hand for Lee Smith, who had taken over the Bolton farm. Smith claimed that Miller had once gone

RODEO BREEDS MANY LAWMEN 99

to a doctor after a quarrel with the Jenks boys; the Jenks boys had an airtight alibi, though, since they were in jail at the time of the murder. At Smith's farm, Pruitt discovered that part of the front-seat cover from Smith's Buick had been cut out. On August 15, Pruitt arrested Lee Smith and his son, John L. Smith, for the murder of Ed Miller. John claimed that his father had committed the murder, whereas he had just watched it from the car. When Pruitt proved that no one could have seen the murder from the car, both men pleaded guilty to robbery and murder. Lee Albert Smith died in the gas chamber and his son, John, got forty years in the state prison. When Pruitt left the Cochise County sheriff's office in 1952, not a single criminal case remained unsolved.

Sheriff Jordan, Larger than Life

Joseph Lon Jordan, born in Muskogee, Oklahoma, arrived in Arizona the year it achieved statehood (1912) with the Miller Brothers' 101 Wild West Show. Early in his rodeo career, Jordan was kicked in the mouth by a horse, giving him a slack jaw. Jordan played the villain in movies, worked as a cowpuncher, acquired his own ranch, and claimed to be "on a first-name basis with every cow in Arizona." In Yavapai County, Jordan earned the title of World Champion Roper in at least two rodeos. After his marriage, he moved to Phoenix, where he worked for an oil company. When he returned home after World War I, he served for four years as a Maricopa County deputy sheriff. Jordan received minor injuries during the 1934 labor riots in Phoenix—part of the nationwide movement promoting the right of workers to organize into unions—and signed a complaint on behalf of all the injured deputies. In 1935, Jordan accepted an appointment as deputy U.S. marshal, and three years later he entered the Democratic race for Maricopa County sheriff, easily defeating incumbent Roy Merrill, whose administration had been plagued by scandal. Voters resoundingly returned Jordan to office in 1940 and 1942.

During the 1940 campaign, Dick Fountain, a former Phoenix police chief, promised the presence of a full-time sheriff (a jab at Jordan's rodeo activities). Still, Jordan won by a four-to-one margin. Some people described Jordan as a big dumb cowboy, and his wife, Jewel, as the brains of the outfit. However, in the capture of one murderer, Jordan exhibited a shrewdness that caught the criminal and got him a new hat.

Patrolman Frank Bliss had been killed during a grocery-store robbery. The murderer died at the scene of the crime, but his partner, Bill Fox, fled toward Prescott. Jordan suspected that a local rancher, who harbored a dislike for both Jordan and Yavapai County Sheriff George Ruffner, was hiding Fox. So Jordan forged a telegram to Fox, inviting the murderer to meet his girlfriend in Prescott. He enlisted a local cowboy to deliver the telegram. Ruffner bet Jordan a new Stetson that no one at the ranch would accept the telegram. But four hours later the messenger rode in with Fox, and Jordan got his new hat.

In the spring of 1943, a Phoenix crowd watched Jordan again win first place in the sheriffs' team-roping and calf-tying event. During this rodeo, Maricopa County Deputy Sheriff Everett Bowman won the calf-roping title and the Porter Saddle Award. At the same time, Jordan and Bowman raised money for the Red Cross Servicemen's Canteen in Phoenix.

Bullfrogs and Badges

In a 1943 all-points bulletin, Jordan reported that one hundred frogs had been stolen from a local Arizona hatchery, where they were being fattened for the dinner table. An Idaho sheriff responded that his prison-yard lily pool was infested with large, vicious bullfrogs with Southern accents. He offered to obtain waivers of extradition if Arizona could submit positive identification of the bullfrogs.

Jordan, the 230-pound genial giant, could be a tough lawman. Despite warnings, many people ignored his ultimatum against illegal gambling, so Jordan's initial crusade when he took office in 1939 startled Phoenicians as he raided the Junior Chamber of Commerce, even though the organization promoted local rodeos.

Jordan used his good nature to full advantage in those days when it was important to get the confession. Often in the company of a representative from the County Attorney's Office, he treated a suspect to a delicious dinner in a good restaurant. On April 29, 1939, two Phoenix car salesmen and their car disappeared; later their bodies were found. The chief suspect, a young college student, Robert M. Burgunder Jr., was arrested in Tennessee. Sheriff Jordan and Maricopa County Attorney Richard F. Harless brought the fugitive back to Arizona in the stolen vehicle. During their dinner at the Dominion Hotel in Globe, Jordan gently prodded the young man for the truth. Just as Burgunder finished a plate of vanilla ice cream, he admitted to the double murder, saying, "It was the most cowardly, the dirtiest killing I've ever known." Burgunder went to the gas chamber on August 9, 1940.

All Arizona sheriffs have been interested in keeping up with modern technology in their efforts to operate the county jail and apprehend criminals. Jordan sponsored the first Federal Bureau of Investigation (FBI) school in Maricopa County, which he opened to every commissioned Arizona peace officer. His state-of-the-art communications system hooked up with the Arizona Highway Patrol. Jordan's volunteers formed the Maricopa County Mounted Posse. His twelve-man, twelve-plane Sheriff's Air Patrol provided civil-defense protection, apprehended criminals, combed the desert for stolen vehicles, and performed acts of mercy. Initially, Jordan served as the civil-defense director for Phoenix, where he coordinated industrial-plant protection and guarded against subversive activities. As government mileage administrator, Jordan assisted the Office of Price Administration by enforcing price ceilings, rationing regulations, and black-market controls on goods of all kinds.

An increase of military personnel in the area brought both prosperity and problems. For example, when a riot broke out in the red-light district on Thanksgiving evening in 1942, military police shot and wounded a black soldier who resisted arrest. When black servicemen protested, they came under a hail of bullets. During the chaos, three men died, eleven were wounded, and 180 were arrested. Newspapers attributed the restoration of order to Jordan's competent department.

Less than a year before his death, Jordan won prizes in Arizona rodeos, and he even hosted the 1943 midwinter meeting of the Western Sheriffs Association while suffering from leukemia. Shortly after midnight on February 28, 1944, Joseph Lon Jordan died at his home in Tempe. The Maricopa County Board of Supervisors appointed Jordan's wife, Jewel, as Maricopa County sheriff to fill out his term. (Two other women served as Arizona sheriffs—Frances Porter of Mojave County, March to December 1960, and Belle Tally of Graham County, November 21 to December 31, 1936. All three women finished out their husbands' terms.) More than 2,000 people attended Jordan's funeral at the First Baptist Church, and the crowd spilled out of the church. Jordan's obituary fittingly included a rodeo tale:

Sheriff Jordan roped his calf in lightning time and was just about to take his bow in front of the grandstand when he saw the mother of the calf charging at him furiously. Unwilling to lose his first prize money and yet hesitant to face the angry mother cow, Sheriff Jordan picked up the calf in his arms and sprinted to the grandstand with all the grace of a football player about to make a touchdown. He won first place in the race and reached safety before the cow could get him.

Ed Echols: Legend in His Own Time

Jordan's good friend, five-time Pima County Sheriff Edward "Ed" Franklin Echols, born in Stockton, Texas, had little formal education. Echols, a big man with a big smile and a soft lazy drawl, personified the image of the Western sheriff. In later years when a critic described him as an "ignorant cowboy," his response was, "Sure, last year I returned $5,000 to the Pima County taxpayers. What educated man would do that?"

On February 20, 1902, Ed and his brother, Art, had left Texas in a Studebaker wagon with a team of four horses. They headed toward Arizona, but as Ed Echols later recalled, "We didn't have any idea where we was going so we took our time getting there." Art stayed in New Mexico, and Ed got a job with the Denton and Wolfe ranch in Arizona's Texas Canyon, drawing $35 a week. He practiced roping and got so good he "could just about catch his own horse most of the time." On remembering a bad fall in 1902, Echols said, "My horse turned a somersit [sic]. I landed with my face in a pile of rock and he come down on top of me. I didn't know my own name for four days and trouble was no one else did either."

In 1907, Echols joined the Miller Brothers' 101 Wild West Show and performed with it in Chicago and at the Jamestown Exposition in Virginia at the World's Fair. After coming down with typhoid fever and malaria, he got fed up and returned to Tucson, the "new cactus patch." Five years later, after learning that the Dominion Bank of Canada guaranteed payment of the prize money, Echols traveled to Calgary to do some roping. These tough cowboys chose to rope the rankest steers, in mud and rain. At this first Calgary Stampede Echols met movie actor Tom Mix. Echols also left Calgary with $1,500. In 1952 the Calgary Stampede honored Echols and all living members of

Pima County Sheriff Ed Echols.

that first Stampede with a reunion. Echols was the only original Calgary Stampede cowboy still actively engaged in the world-championship-rodeo business.

In 1924, Echols traveled to London with Tex Austin, who put on the first rodeo "them bluddy gawd-blawsted Englishmuns had ever seen," according to Echols's memoirs. The event drew 116,000 paid admissions, including royalty. Echols didn't like England much—"too far east, too much rain, too much tay [sic], and not enough coffee." When an elderly spectator asked Echols about a horse, Echols advised him that if he had any personal business to take care of, he had better do it before trying to ride that animal. The man replied, "Young man I know my business." Just out of the chute, the horse pitched, and the Englishman got his foot hooked in the stirrup. The horse dragged the helpless rider for about a quarter of a mile. Shortly after the cowboys stopped the animal, the man died.

Not all Englishmen appreciated a Western rodeo. The London Humane Society got the bobbies to throw all of the cowboys in jail when a contestant accidentally broke a steer's leg and the animal had to be put down. Echols needed money to get out of jail, so he sold his horse Ribbon. Eventually the British returned Ribbon and the cowboys to the United States.

In 1925 Echols and a few other rodeo aficionados decided to put on Tucson's first annual La Fiesta de los Vaqueros rodeo. Prohibition was in full force. Cecil B.

DeMille's *The Golden Bed* played at the Rialto Theatre. Tucson, with a population of 33,800, had about twenty miles of paved road. On Saturday, February 21, the talk of the town was Tucson's first rodeo. Echols, who came to be known as "Mr. Rodeo," spared no time or effort on the project. The Santa Rita Hotel was booked to capacity. Tucsonans opened up their homes to rodeo cowboys and spectators alike. Visiting cowboys could also bunk down in the Elks' spacious hall.

At 10:30 a.m., spectators lined the streets to watch Tucson's first rodeo parade, which still takes place in Tucson every February and is billed as the "world's longest non-mechanized parade." Mayor John E. White and the judges divided the $400 prize money between Maggie Moodle, for the most typical prospector costume, and Tex Harvey, for the most typical cowboy costume.

Bootleggers and moonshiners raked in their profits. During the rodeo, federal agents seized fifteen stills in Tucson, confiscated two hundred gallons of bootleg whiskey, and arrested forty people. Several bootleggers were caught bringing in Mexican liquor from across the border on burros. At 2:00 in the afternoon Sid Simpson blew his whistle to start the rodeo competitions and shouted, "Let 'er buck!" The only accident occurred when a drunk tried to bulldog a steer from a car. The man fell out of the car but emerged relatively unscathed.

Echols had met Will Rogers at a roping contest on the rodeo circuit in 1901, and the two men developed a lifelong friendship. When Echols ran for sheriff in 1934, Rogers agreed to stump for him. Echols's ranch straddled Pima and Cochise Counties, so Rogers's plane landed in what he thought was a likely spot. He attracted a crowd and made a speech in support of Echols. After Echols lost, he wrote Rogers saying, "The hell of it was, Will, they throwed out all them votes you corralled for me. You landed in Cochise County instead of here in Pima County. Anyway, them Cochise County folks did their damndest."

Although Echols did not win the Pima County shrievalty until 1936, the *Tucson Daily Citizen* supported his bid as early as 1930. Echols announced that he would not tolerate professional gambling. When asked how he got into politics, Echols later recalled, "I went out and drank a little white mule with the boys one night, and the next morning before I got straightened out they had me in the [sheriff's] race."

Echols ran successfully for Pima County sheriff in 1936, while working as Pima County cattle inspector. Echols named Herb Wood as undersheriff and assumed a staff of six deputies. The Pima County Jail had been removed from the U.S. government's list of approved jails because it was deemed to be not secure enough. Echols improved the filing system and the county jail to where it once again qualified as a federal jail. This added $17,000 to the Pima County coffers in 1937. During his first term, Echols also had to capture a lion that had escaped from a small menagerie owned by the University of Arizona. Echols and his deputies put their cowboy skills to the test and lassoed the animal.

Sheriff Echols possessed a very practiced eye when it came to bovines, but in one story from his memoirs, he recalls that he found his reputation as cattle inspector at stake when R. Robles from Coolidge brought in eleven head of cows to the courthouse for inspection. Robles ranted, "Look at that. I caught it for a cow and it's nothing but an old bull!" Echols looked at the animal from the front; it was a bull all right, but from the back it was definitely a cow. Back and forth they went; front, bull, back, cow. The perplexed inspector called the seller, Dale Mercer. Oh, it was a cow all right, at least it had been a cow. It started life as a perfect lady by having a calf but then it got bullish ideas. It beat up all the other bulls in the pasture and the "she-stuff" were in a perfect dither over the thing. Echols suggested that it be butchered so no one would have to prove this tall story.

In 1938, Sheriff Echols proposed an unsuccessful plan to form a bird sanctuary in the Tucson area to prevent local residents from promiscuous shooting. A year later, Echols reported that his staff had recovered $30,408 worth of stolen property and recovered 53 out of 159 stolen vehicles and processed 1,924 prisoners into the Pima County Jail. The first thing Echols did after his reelection in 1940 was to install an enclosure to separate deputies and records from the public. He told the press that "too many loafers and politicians are sitting around doing nothing. The public gets the idea that they're deputies of mine."

That year Echols hurled a challenge to all sheriffs across the United States to compete with him in a steer-roping contest during Tucson's La Fiesta de los Vaqueros rodeo. Maricopa County Sheriff Lon Jordan, the 1939 winner, immediately announced that he was "happy to oblige." The winner had to tie three steers single-handed in the fastest time. A unique rule read, "Rules may be changed as the committee sees fit."

Other Arizona sheriff contestants who accepted the invitation included Pinal County's Jimmy Herron, Cochise County's I. V. Pruitt, Yuma County's Pete Newman, Greenlee County's Harvey Grady, Graham County's Emert Kempton, and Apache County's John Nunn. Two "foreigners" who came for the rodeo were Sheriff Howell Gray from Carlsbad, New Mexico, and Sheriff Ted Schaeffer from Fort Collins, Colorado. Echols asked Mayor Fiorello La Guardia of New York to provide at least one "dude" sheriff, but no one came from outside of the eleven Western states. Sheriff Jordan retained the "super colossal trophy" as World Champion Steer Tying Sheriff for the third consecutive year by beating out Sheriff Echols by six seconds. Jordan later said he put the trophy on his "boodwar."

For five months during 1941, Echols conducted the Pima County sheriff's business from a Saint Mary's Hospital room after an automobile accident. The sheriff had suffered a double fracture of his spine when his car overturned after a collision. When the hospital "turned him out," Echols, who had always worn cowboy boots, had to wear shoes, which he described with scalding unprintable epithets. By 1944, the sheriff's staff had increased to twenty-four men. Echols also hired three new jailors, one matron, and two cooks.

After Echols's fifth term as sheriff, he lost to Jerome P. Martin. He made a gracious farewell speech, recalling that he never had a jailbreak and never had to shoot anyone. His budget always balanced and usually he returned some of the money to the taxpayers. Echols returned to ranching, the rodeo, and private life.

Echols worked for the U.S. Bureau of Animal Husbandry and was put in charge of guarding the U.S.–Mexico border against hoof-and-mouth disease. In 1948, he once again challenged Martin but lost. A year later Echols was appointed as Tucson precinct constable, a post he held for five terms until January 1, 1963, when he retired at age eighty-three. He donated his saddle, a beaver Stetson, and a piggin' string to the Arizona Historical Society, and reflected that he could still make good baking-powder bread in a Dutch oven. Governor Ernest McFarland had nominated Echols to the National Cowboy Hall of Fame in 1956.

Until 1965, Echols always rode horseback in Tucson's La Fiesta de los Vaqueros parade, but that year he began riding in a carriage. Echols finished out his last lonely days at a nursing home with plenty of good stories, but he regretted that he had no listeners. Edward Franklin Echols, working cowboy, rodeo performer, and Pima County sheriff, died on January 26, 1969, at age eighty-nine.

Throughout the 1940s and '50s Arizona peace officers continued to compete among themselves and at local rodeos. In 1951, New Mexico Sheriff Dick Richards of Hidalgo County and his deputy, Jim Brister, defeated Arizona's Gila County Sheriff Jack Jones, Graham County Sheriff Skeet Bowman, Pima County Sheriff Frank Eyman, and Cochise County's I. V. Pruitt during the sheriff's team-tying event at a local rodeo in Douglas.

In 1964, the Pinal County sheriff's posse held an all-state posses' rodeo near Florence. A year later, the Tucson and Phoenix Police Departments challenged each other to a friendly rodeo competition. The event became so popular that law enforcement personnel from other states joined in over the next few years. In 1969, the Law Enforcement Rodeo Association (LERA) incorporated. Today LERA has members from Wyoming, Utah, Arizona, New Mexico, Colorado, California, Oklahoma, and Texas. Many agencies are represented, including the state departments of public safety, sheriffs, police, Indian police, prison personnel, livestock sanitary boards, and animal control.

CHAPTER 7

The Manhunt: Then and Now

James O. McKinney, 1890.

WANTED—JAMES McKINNEY
FOR THE MURDER OF WILLIAM LYNN
AT PORTERVILLE, CALIFORNIA,
ON JULY 27, 1902.

Nativity, American: Age, 40 years; Height 5 ft., 7 in.;
Weight about 160 lbs.; Hair, light brown, generally wears a heavy light
mustache; he may grow a beard; eyes, blue; complexion, florid; broad, square
features; high, broad forehead; short thick nose; large mouth; short, square
chin; large ears, well cut; two joints off left forefinger; was shot on July 27th,
1902; ball entered left thigh in front near crotch, so there will be a plain scar
on both sides of thigh; occupation, barkeeper and gambler; may go
to work on a ranch; he drinks and smokes and is quarrelsome
when drinking and very handy with gun.

So read a wanted poster on James McKinney nearly a year after his cold-hearted murder of William "Billy" Lynn (and more recently, the murders of two Mohave County cowboys). The rewards on McKinney's head stipulated "dead or alive," and few who knew McKinney doubted that this violent fugitive would be captured dead. California Governor George Pardee and Arizona Governor Alexander O. Brodie each put up $500 rewards. Mohave County Sheriff Henry Lovin added $500 from his personal money. The Mohave County Board of Supervisors put up $250, and the Tulare County, California, Board of Supervisors put up $200 to anyone foolhardy enough to pursue and confront McKinney.

Along with Sheriff Lovin, four county sheriffs from California—Tulare County's William Collins, San Bernardino County's John Ralphs, Inyo County's C. A. Collins, and Kern County's John Kelly—all mounted posses in search of McKinney. The search also involved government officials at the federal level from the United States and Mexico.

Rough Country, Tough Characters

The word "diversity" best characterizes Mohave County's geography. Here, you can still "get your kicks" on the nation's longest maintained segment of Historic Route 66, from Peach Springs to Topock, and even today the county's remote areas provide sanctuary for those on the fringes of the law. Situated between the Hualapai and Cerbat mountain ranges, Kingman started its life as a railroad stop. By 1887, the stop had become a town, important enough to be named the county seat.

Today, the Mohave County Sheriff's Office serves an area covering 8,486,400 acres (or 13,470 square miles). The master artisan, wielding the implements of wind, water, and time, chose the top portion of Mohave County and beyond to create that spectacular masterpiece, the Grand Canyon. West of Mohave County stretches California's great Mojave Desert, an inhospitable, parched land of scorpions, deadly serpents, spiny cacti, and blazing sun.

Rich mineral resources and the railroad brought Mohave County to the attention of settlers at the turn of the century. Immigrant miners and mining supplies arrived in Kingman on the railroad, which then hauled out gold, silver, lead, zinc, copper, and molybdenum. Mohave County's mining camps and ranches provided hiding places for outlaws like James "Jim" McKinney, as well as opportunity for dreamers such as Henry Lovin.

Lovin, born in Rockingham, North Carolina, moved in the 1880s to Ocala, Florida, where he became superintendent of the Monarch orange orchard. After moving to Phoenix, Arizona, in 1887, Lovin and a partner attempted to grow oranges and lemons on thirty acres in the Salt River Valley. Lovin invested heavily in the unprofitable Commercial

Mining Company near Prescott and went broke. He moved to Prescott and opened a store that also went bankrupt. In 1890, poor but still confident, Lovin moved to Kingman, where he worked as a merchant and formed another partnership.

In 1899, Lovin grubstaked José Jerez for $12.50, and Jerez's discovery of the rich Gold Road Mine (about two miles east of Oatman and thirty miles from Kingman) paid off handsomely for both men. Lovin served as Kingman constable, and in 1900 Mohave County Sheriff Harvey Hubbs appointed him as undersheriff. In 1901, Lovin was elected Mohave County sheriff. His manhunt and the killing of James McKinney vividly illustrate how early lawmen cooperated and relentlessly pursued their prey.

After murdering his own friend, Billy Lynn, in Porterville, California, in July 1902, McKinney fled first to Mexico and then to Arizona. He rode up to Dick "Dig" Eshom's ranch sometime in mid-March of 1903. The two men had known each other in Porterville, where Eshom had a reputation as a cattle rustler. Eshom gave the outlaw shelter, out of either fear or friendship, and McKinney worked under the alias of one of his California friends, Thomas McIntyre, as a miner in the Cedar copper-mining district at the southern end of the Hualapai Mountains.

On April 11, Mohave County residents were shocked to learn that two young cowboys had been brutally murdered near Cedar. Charles Blakely, known throughout the area as the cowboy pianist and operator of Kingman's Bucket of Blood Saloon, and Leroy Winchester, an unemployed miner, were popular young men. On March 31, they left Kingman and rode into Dig Eshom's place with $500 to see if they could purchase a saloon Eshom owned. He agreed to the sale, inviting the cowboys to stay for supper and to spend the night.

After supper, Eshom told Blakely and Winchester that he had to visit "a sick miner." He promised to meet them in Cedar the next day to conclude the saloon sale. In the early morning hours, Eshom rode into the mining camp and talked to Mc Kinney. He may have told McKinney that Blakely and Winchester were deputies. They were not, but one of them may have let it slip that they carried a warrant issued by Mohave County Deputy Sheriff Jeff Templeton for a man who had stolen a watch. After his conversation with McKinney, Eshom proceeded on to Cedar. The next morning Blakely and Winchester started for Cedar and rode along the old Tresher Road, where McKinney had concealed himself in the bushes. He blasted them out of their saddles with buckshot and robbed them.

When Blakely and Winchester did not show up in Cedar, Eshom headed back toward his ranch, where he found McKinney, who claimed to have had a little trouble with a couple of men back on the trail—and he warned Eshom not to mention it to anyone for three days. Then he picked out two of Eshom's best horses and had the rancher shoe them. Eshom saddled one horse and loaded the other with provisions.

After the three-day time limit expired, Eshom rode into Kingman and told Sheriff Lovin the story of his encounter with Jim McKinney. The sheriff rode toward Cedar, where he found two horses and the bodies of Blakely and Winchester on the old Tresher road. Lovin suspected Eshom's account and arrested him as an accessory to murder, but Eshom made the $1,000 bail.

Lovin returned with the coroner, who convened a coroner's jury. The jury determined that Blakely had taken a blast of buckshot in the face, and the pellet that entered his head near his eye had probably killed him. The murderer also had shot a full blast of buckshot into Winchester's back. The two men, who had been carrying at least $500, now only had $1.60 on their bodies. The arrest warrant for the watch thief was also missing.

Mohave County Sheriff Henry Lovin.

Eshom may have told McKinney that Blakely and Winchester were deputies just to get rid of him, or—as Lovin suspected—there might have been collusion between Eshom and McKinney to split the $500. Despite the suspicious circumstances, the coroner's jury freed Eshom for lack of evidence, and because they felt that he was also McKinney's victim.

In any case, Lovin immediately sent a telegram describing the murders to Sheriff William Collins in Visalia, California, so he could be on the lookout for McKinney:

Kingman. April 5. Sheriff, Visalia, Cal. McKinney killed two men at Cedar Creek near this city. Posse after him. Henry Lovin, Sheriff.

When Collins wired back requesting more particulars, Lovin replied that he would do everything he could to apprehend the murderer. With the hot breath of the law breathing down McKinney's sunburned neck, the outlaw was forced to keep running without rest.

Tracking a True Scourge of the West

Jim McKinney was born on January 3, 1860, in Jerseyville, Illinois. In 1878, his family moved to Leadville, Colorado. Two years later the McKinneys pulled up stakes and moved to California's San Joaquin Valley, where the family enjoyed a reputation as industrious and respectable. Even Jim was well-liked, because he worked hard as a horse trainer, teamster, and laborer. All of the McKinney brothers liked to carouse and gamble from time to time, but during his drinking bouts, Jim McKinney mutated into a violent, profane sadist. In a drunken rage, he broke up a Good Templars meeting, and when member G. W. Boggan tried to reason with him, McKinney stabbed him in the arm. A judge fined him $30.50 for assaulting Boggan and $50 for disturbing the peace.

Widely regarded as a ladies' man, McKinney participated in numerous scrapes in Visalia's tenderloin districts. In September of 1886, he accidentally shot a prostitute, Kitty Davis, in the neck, while aiming for Lawrence Turner, who had struck another woman. Davis's wound was painful but not serious. A month later he picked a fight with Tulare County Undersheriff Ed Fudge, who had arrested him earlier during the Boggan fight.

In 1889, he and a friend, Robert McFarlane, escaped from the Tulare County Jail, where McKinney awaited trial for beating a gambler, Lee Wren, senseless with his pistol. They escaped through the ceiling and rode toward the Sierra Nevada foothills. Friends helped them with mounts and provisions. At Rocklin, the escapees sold their mounts and saddles and bought train tickets to Ogden, Utah. After spending three days in Utah, they bought tickets to Rawlins, Wyoming, where McKinney won $250 in a faro game. When Tulare County Sheriff Daniel G. Overall captured McKinney in Wyoming and brought him back, he incurred the desperado's eternal hatred and a threat to kill him.

Upon his return to Visalia, McKinney received a five-year sentence in San Quentin. In 1894, he was released a few months early for good behavior. Curiously, his petition had been signed by Overall. Overall never lacked in courage, nor was he intimidated by McKinney. McKinney sent him an invitation to meet him at Lemon Cove and shoot it out. Overall appeared at the appointed time and place, but McKinney did not.

McKinney kept out of trouble for a while, but then he migrated to the rough gold-mining boomtown of Randsburg in Kern County, California. After he got mixed up in various gambling altercations, he returned to his old haunts in Bakersfield, where his tough reputation secured him and his brother, Edwin, jobs as armed guards at the irrigation ditches of the Pioneer Water Company.

In 1902, McKinney worked as a bartender in the Mint Saloon in Porterville. On the evening of July 27, he drank heavily, strapped on his guns, and prowled the bars. He shot up Zalud's Saloon but did not hit anyone. In Scotty's Saloon, drinking

buddy Billy Lynn made the fatal mistake of accusing McKinney of causing him to lose a gambling pot.

McKinney invited Lynn to join him for a drink, and it seemed as though the dispute would be forgotten. After a few drinks, McKinney flew into a drunken rage and shot up the saloon. Deputy City Marshal John Willis ordered McKinney to stop shooting, but to no avail. Willis chased McKinney out of the saloon into the street and shot him through the thigh. McKinney returned fire and shot the fifty-two-year-old lawman in the mouth. Despite his serious wound, Willis kept chasing McKinney. When he caught up with him, he hit him with his cane, but still McKinney refused to go down.

In the early morning hours of July 27, Billy Lynn and another drinking buddy, Clint Kelly, thought McKinney might be seriously wounded, so they went looking for him. As McKinney approached them, he raised his gun and hollered for them to halt.

Before either man could do anything, McKinney pumped a blast of buckshot into Lynn. Lynn's final words were, "I guess I am done for. Jesus Christ, Jim! Don't shoot your friends!"

The drink-crazed McKinney screamed in rage, "The goddamned sons of bitches wounded me and I'll get anybody who tries to interfere with me." He forced frightened livery stablemen at gunpoint to prepare a rig and horses for him. Driving through Porterville, he randomly shot at anything that attracted his attention. (Fortunately, he did not hit any human targets.) Willis recovered from his painful wound, but sixteen hours later, Lynn died an agonizing death from wounds in the stomach, chest, and face.

Tulare County Sheriff William Collins, who had just taken office in 1902, mounted two unsuccessful posses to hunt for McKinney. Newspapers sarcastically chided Collins for not apprehending McKinney, even though everyone else believed that the fugitive was hiding out near Dove Springs.

In February 1903, Collins learned through an anonymous informer that McKinney had fled to Hermosillo, Mexico, probably with the help of friends and family. On February 23, the sheriff took the train to Nogales, Arizona, where he met with American and Mexican authorities to discuss the best method to capture the fugitive.

The officials decided to follow proper extradition proceedings. Tulare District Attorney Daniel McFadzean worked fast to prepare the paperwork. Extradition papers had to be routed through the California governor's office, the U.S. State Department, the Mexican federal government, and the state government offices in Hermosillo. None of these bureaucratic organizations ever moved in a timely fashion, but time for Sheriff Collins was critical, because if McKinney learned of the sheriff's presence in the city, he might disappear before extradition could be made.

Collins met with Arizona's Santa Cruz County Sheriff Tom Turner, and both men took the train to Hermosillo. (Turner was attempting to extradite another fugitive at this time.) In Hermosillo, Collins and the local authorities agreed that the Mexican police would make the arrest and then Collins would take charge of the prisoner. Collins hid out in a hotel room.

Within two hours, the Mexican police located McKinney. However, before they could make an arrest, an order came through from the Sonora governor's office, countermanding any authorization to arrest McKinney and turn him over to Collins. Mexican officials insisted that under Mexican law an official extradition request had to come from the United States government. Even then the United States would have to present evidence to justify McKinney's extradition. Meanwhile, McKinney remained under surveillance while he rode with a known cattle rustler, John Jefford.

Desperate, Sheriff Collins wired California's Governor Pardee: "My man here. I can do nothing until the governor gets instructions from the secretary of state; necessary to act quick; Answer." Collins received no answer. It did not help Collins's cause that California newspapers picked up on his activities and speculated that the sheriff was tracking McKinney in Mexico. McKinney's brothers probably read the newspapers and got word to him. During the early morning hours of March 8, McKinney and Jefford slipped across the border into Douglas, Arizona.

Luckily, the discouraged Sheriff Collins did not go back to Visalia empty-handed. He succeeded in arresting Jefford, who he had also been trailing and who argued that he had never seen McKinney in Mexico. He told the sheriff that he had intended to rustle Mexican cattle, but he had decided not to when he heard that McKinney was in the area. A judge sentenced Jefford to a two year term in San Quentin. Meanwhile, McKinney made his way to Mohave County, where he proceeded to wreak murder and mayhem.

THE MEN OF SHERIFF LOVIN'S POSSE

Not a lot is known about Wells and Piema. Templeton was remembered by Kingman children as the man who played the part of a preacher when they buried their dead pets. Asa Harris, born in Portland, Oregon, worked as a cowboy while serving as Mohave County undersheriff from 1898 to 1912. In 1940 at age seventy-one, the Mohave County Board of Supervisors charged Harris with the care of county equipment.

Charles Bly was by far the most interesting member of Lovin's posse. At the time he rode in search of McKinney, Bly himself was a fugitive from justice in New Mexico. In 1897, a man named Frank Sherlock had escaped from the New Mexico Territorial Prison, where he was serving a sentence for horse theft; he exacerbated his difficulty by stealing the warden's horse. Three years later, Sherlock appeared in Mohave County as Charles Bly, and he served for eight years as an excellent deputy sheriff while also working as a rancher and cattle inspector. On July 21, 1908, Arizona Ranger Lieutenant Billy Old stuck a pistol in his ribs and said, "I have a warrant for your arrest."

Bly had been betrayed by a former New Mexico prisoner, whom he had fired for doing unsatisfactory work. Bly asked his fellow officers to "put in a good word for me." They did, and New Mexico Governor George Curry gave Bly a full pardon.

The Search Begins

Following the murders of Blakely and Winchester, Lovin and his posse—which included Undersheriff Asa Harris, Deputy Sheriffs Charles Bly and Jeff Templeton, a man known as Wells, and an Indian tracker by the name of Piema—relentlessly tracked McKinney through the desert. The outlaw's three-day head start seriously hampered the search, but the members of Lovin's posse were tough, hard-riding, determined men.

McKinney might have had a better chance of escaping if he had ridden through Yuma and back into Mexico. But despite his violent nature, he needed to be near family and friends, so he chose to return to a part of California where he already faced the gallows. Still, he had the advantage of a three-day lead. Both McKinney and Lovin's posse rode hard. In all likelihood, Lovin knew that he would have to shoot it out with McKinney. On April 7, Lovin and his posse crossed the Colorado River and entered California at Needles. Jurisdiction boundaries did not bother the persistent Arizona sheriff. Before proceeding northwest into the Mohave Desert of San Bernardino County, Lovin purchased provisions for his posse and wired Sheriff Collins that he was on McKinney's trail. Collins forwarded this information to other California lawmen in the area.

On April 5, Lovin received word from Constable Ed Bowers from the Manvel railroad station about forty miles northwest of Needles, stating that Bowers had recognized the outlaw when he came through riding a bay and leading a gray horse. Bowers had decided that it would be foolish to try to arrest McKinney by himself. Lovin arranged for a special train to transport his horses and men from Needles to Manvel, where he would be only forty hours behind his quarry. During the ride, both men and horses rested.

At Sarasota Springs, Lovin sent Harris, Wells, and Piema back to Arizona. Harris would act as sheriff until Lovin returned. Lovin, Templeton, and Bly continued their pursuit. Former sheriff Daniel Overall, whom McKinney had threatened to kill for extraditing him from Wyoming, joined William Collins's posse, which patrolled the area north of Kramer, California. Kern County Sheriff John W. Kelly's posse consisted of Deputy Sheriffs Gus Tower and John Collins, Randsburg constable John Arnold, and Arnold's deputy, J. R. Price. Kelly's posse searched the Randsburg district, which lay ahead of McKinney. Although San Bernardino County Sheriff John Ralph resented Lovin for not notifying him of the outlaw's Arizona murders until they were well into the manhunt, his posse patrolled and sealed off all entrances to the McKinney homes. A posse under Inyo County Sheriff C. A. Collins swept the Mojave Desert from the north.

Law enforcement faced another problem. Although the Mojave Desert is dry most of the year, the 1903 spring rains had provided water and excellent forage for the horses of both the law and the outlaw, while at the same time wiping out McKinney's tracks. At Bakersfield, Sheriff Kelly coordinated the efforts of the five sheriffs. Randsburg, with its telephone line to Bakersfield, served as the focal communications point. Kelly assigned Deputy Sheriff Warren Rankin, who knew McKinney, to watch the south fork of the road east of Kernville.

Rankin had met McKinney while the outlaw was on the lam for killing Lynn. Both men were riding the same trail, when McKinney raised his rifle and pointed it at Rankin, who just looked the other way. McKinney had decided that Rankin posed no threat. However, Rankin had guessed McKinney's identity. The two men rode together for a while, but McKinney always kept his hand on his rifle, and Rankin never got a chance to arrest him.

About 2:00 p.m. on April 12, Rankin watched as McKinney rode up to a store in Onyx, where he purchased and leisurely drank a beer. Rankin cautiously followed McKinney, and at a ranch just outside of Isabella, Rankin called Kernville constable Frederick McCracken. McCracken had just captured a horse thief in the mountains and returned the fugitive to the Kernville Jail. Now he turned around and rode out to help Rankin.

McCracken, famous for his hot temper, had survived a gunfight in a Cripple Creek, Colorado, mining camp. In his later years, he would go on to work as a professional gambler in Reno, Nevada, where on June 4, 1931, he would shoot William Graham, a Nevada kingpin—killing him with a single bullet. On the afternoon of April 12, near the Onyx store, McCracken and Rankin watched as McKinney approached them with a rifle slung over his shoulder. McCracken fired but apparently missed. He got off several shots, but McKinney disappeared into the brush. The men decided not to continue the search after dark because they did not know McKinney's condition. He might be lying in ambush.

Kern County (California) Sheriff John Kelly.

About midnight on April 12, two men named Johnny Shoemate and E. L. Ellison came face to face with McKinney while walking along the Kern River bridge in Isabella. Suddenly, the outlaw stepped out of the shadows and pointed a shotgun at them. Shoemate recognized McKinney even though he was dirty, unkempt, and covered with blood from a wound he had received from McCracken. McKinney asked where he could find his friend, Dave Ingram, a member of the outlaw fraternity and an Isabella saloonkeeper. After their conversation, McKinney ordered Ellison to move away because he wanted to speak to Shoemate privately. After a few minutes of conversation, McKinney invited Ellison to join them. Then he ordered both men to move on.

McKinney did not find Ingram during the night. However, Ingram must have gotten the word, because the next morning, he borrowed a pair of binoculars to hunt for his friend in the hills. On April 14, rumors circulated that McKinney had holed up in Linn's Valley. Kern County Deputy Sheriff Will Tibbet (whose bother Bert was also deputized for this posse) and Bakersfield City Marshal Jeff Packard hired a buggy and went looking for the outlaw. They thought they knew where he was hiding, but they could not flush him into the open.

The next day several lawmen returned to Bakersfield, including the recently reelected Bakersfield City Marshal Thomas "Jeff" Packard. Sheriff Kelly found it difficult to direct the hunt with so many lawmen from different jurisdictions crossing and recrossing the area. Communications improved when the power company offered extended use of its power line for telegraph and telephone contact into Caliente. The Southern Pacific Railroad agent at Bakersfield kept one line open at all times for the sheriffs and relayed all messages.

At the same time, lawmen kept a close eye on McKinney's brothers, in case they should lead them to the fugitive. Jim McKinney's brother Jacob met with Sheriff Kelly and insisted he had no knowledge that Jim was even in California. With all the tension and excitement of the possibility of capturing McKinney, ace reporters from California newspapers poured into Bakersfield. Both of Jim's brothers, Edwin and Jacob, announced to the press that they had proof that Jim was not responsible for the murders of either Blakely or Winchester. Through the press they requested a meeting with Lovin. The brothers claimed to have positive proof that Dig Eshom had killed and robbed Blakely and Winchester, and then blamed Jim McKinney. The officers ignored these claims, however, as ploys to throw them off McKinney's track.

Showdown in Bakersfield

Around April 17, an informant whispered to Bakersfield constable James McKamy that Jim had arrived in town. He did not tell him, though, that the fugitive was staying at a "joss house" on L Street in Bakersfield's red-light district. This building, constructed in the 1880s, provided a meeting place for a fraternal organization of Chinese

The Chinese joss house where the final shoot-out occurred.

merchants—the Suey On Association, which protected its members and cared for Chinese widows, orphans, and the elderly. A Chinese shrine and a meeting room on the second floor were the only entities providing the structure with its status as a Chinese temple.

The building's main function during McKinney's time was as an opium den and brothel. Behind the building a narrow enclosed back yard provided gate access to China Alley. A two-seat outhouse stood against the south fence. Alfred Hulse, an old friend of McKinney and an alumnus of Folsom Prison, lived together with Jennie Fox, an aging prostitute, at the joss house. Both were opium addicts. Hulse, who had once been dismissed from the Bakersfield police force because of his vicious temper, supplemented his income as a bartender by pimping and gambling. Jennie Fox, who had worked as a prostitute in California and Arizona, was no stranger to Sheriff Lovin. Born in France, she had worked in Kingman as a prostitute but now listed her occupation as dressmaker. Lovin later informed the press that Jennie Fox had been run out of Kingman.

On the night of April 17, Hulse went for a walk and Jennie went down to the basement to smoke opium. While Hulse conversed with a woman, a voice from the dark shadows called him. Hulse said, "Wait," and continued talking to the woman. Again the voice urged, "Al, come here. I want to see you." It was McKinney. Hulse agreed to take the desperate, exhausted fugitive to his place, but McKinney insisted that they first hire a carriage and a horse to retrieve the rifle and shotgun he had left under some shrubbery near the cemetery.

Next the men enjoyed a good restaurant dinner. Then they returned to the joss house, where Hulse, McKinney, and Jennie decided that McKinney should rest for a few days and then the trio would "live the life of outlaws" in the mountains. The next day Hulse informed several of McKinney's old friends that he was in town. While Hulse purchased ammunition, a horse, and a saddle for the outlaw, John Caldwell, Fritz Stumpf, Ed Potter, and Charles Davis dropped by to visit their old confederate. They plied him with liquor, and before long the word got out on the street that McKinney was hiding in the joss house.

The next night, Hulse made the rounds of the bars and even tried to pick a fight with Marshal Packard and Constable McKamy at the Arlington Saloon. Then he went to the Exchange Saloon and whispered to bartender William Fugget that McKinney was in the vicinity. Fugget passed the information on to Deputy Sheriff Bert Tibbet, who alerted Marshal Packard.

Kelly invited Sheriff Lovin and Sheriff William Collins to join his posse in Bakersfield. Lovin boarded a train from Randsburg. Early on Sunday morning, April 19, while Deputy Sheriff Bert Tibbet made his rounds, Packard caught up with him and said, "The information you gave me last night is good. We are going to take him. Will [Bert Tibbet's brother] wants you to go with us." Bert was anxious to go along, but first he had to go home and get his shotgun. In the meantime, Kelly, William Collins, and Dan Overall assembled at the sheriff's office. Overall did not believe that McKinney was in Bakersfield, so he left town to continue his search in the Visalia area. Packard drove to the train depot to pick up Lovin.

At Sheriff Kelly's office they were joined by Will and Bert Tibbet, Thomas Baker, Gus Tower, James Quinn, and Felix Etter. The lawmen knew by now that McKinney was in the joss house, but they did not know exactly where, nor did they know who might be with him. Around 10:00 a.m. they all approached the building from different directions. Will Tibbet and Jeff Packard went in Packard's buggy. Lovin and Kelly rode in Kelly's buggy. Collins, Baker, Tower, Quinn, Bert Tibbet, and Etter all took the city bus. Upon arrival on L Street, they stationed themselves around the joss house.

Packard and Will Tibbet entered the house and searched the basement rooms but found no one. On the first floor they knocked on a locked door. McKinney heard a voice in the passageway call out, "Whose room is this? Open the door." He grabbed his gun and said, "We're in for it, I guess." Hulse said, "Let's go to it." When they did not receive an answer, Tibbet and Packard secured a pass key. Before Tibbet could turn the key, McKinney unlatched it from the inside. McKinney, standing in the center of the room, hesitated before firing and wounding both officers.

Packard could see McKinney, and he hollered at Tibbet, "Look out, Bill! He has got you!" Packard fired his rifle at McKinney but missed. When Tibbet wheeled in retreat, Hulse drilled him through his right side with a rifle shot. Again McKinney

Sheriff Lovin (right) in his office with two deputies, including Walter Brown (middle).

blasted Packard and Tibbet with his shotgun. Tibbet lurched out the back door and collapsed. As Packard backed out of the rear door, McKinney blasted him again. The officer managed to take refuge behind the privy door.

Jennie Fox hid between the bed and the wall until the shooting stopped. Hulse pushed her into a closet and locked the door. Then he walked out the front door into an empty street. After they heard the shots, all of the other officers converged on the back door. Packard called to Bert Tibbet, Kelly, and Lovin to "come on in." In the few seconds that it took them to cross the street, most of the shooting was over.

Bert Tibbet thought McKinney was hiding in the other privy stall. Packard yelled, "No, he is behind you in the door!" Tibbet fired, and a load of shot hit McKinney in the neck, knocking him to the floor. McKinney got up and staggered to a window, where Tower took aim but missed. Bert ran to help his wounded brother, who was lying in the back yard, where he got a full view of McKinney and quickly shot and killed the outlaw. The shot's momentum propelled McKinney backward through the kitchen and over the stair railing.

When the posse approached the wounded officers, Will Tibbet said, "Al Hulse shot me." Packard said, "Al Hulse shot me, too." Tower pulled McKinney's body off the railing and stretched it on the floor before accompanying the outlaw's remains to the morgue in a wagon. Lovin picked up the outlaw's shotgun and unexpended cartridges, and claimed the horses that McKinney had stolen from Dig Eshom. The officers reassembled in the back yard, where they debated whether they should flood the joss house, blow it up, or set it on fire. (They did none of these things, however.)

Deputy Marshal Etter helped Packard into his buggy and drove him into town, where Dr. J. L. Carson examined the wounds and told Etter to take Packard home. Dr. A. F. Schafer, also present during his exam, asked Packard if he was certain that Hulse had shot him. The irritated lawman replied, "God damn it, I ain't no fool. I have been in this business a long time and I ain't badly fooled about anything. He was there and Hulse shot me and that is enough." The doctors treated Packard's wounds and his prognosis appeared to be quite good, but then he took a turn for the worse. Thomas Jefferson Packard died at daybreak on April 20, 1903.

Officers transported Will Tibbet to Baer's Drug Store, where Dr. C. W. Kellogg examined him. The doctor had Tibbet removed to the hospital, but then he decided that surgery would be useless. Kellogg made the dying lawman's last moments as comfortable as possible. Will Tibbet died about 1:00 p.m.

Later in the afternoon, Kelly and Tower returned to the joss house, where they were met by Al Hulse, who said, "I understand you fellows are looking for me?" The lawmen arrested Hulse and took him to jail, but he insisted that he had not even known McKinney had been in his room. That evening, the lawmen returned to search the joss house, where they found Jennie Fox still cowering in a closet. They arrested and charged her as an accessory to the crime. Jennie testified as to Hulse's presence at the shooting and was released from jail on December 1, 1903.

A grand jury indicted Alfred Hulse for the murder of William Tibbet. Hulse, an opium addict, went through hellish withdrawal stages while in the Kern County Jail. While screaming for the guards to keep the monsters away, he threw his slop jar at the jailor. He broke off a piece of iron from his cot and tried to cut his wrist, but the doctor treated his resulting superficial wounds. Even in the torment of withdrawal, Hulse refused to admit that McKinney had been in his room. Five days later, Hulse regained some semblance of composure.

Hulse's attorney presented a petition asking for a change of venue, claiming that he could not get a fair trial in Kern County. Judge Mahon ruled that a change of venue was not necessary. On November 7, Hulse's trial began. Mohave County Sheriff Lovin testified and basically described his posse chase across the desert. Hulse's attorney planted sufficient seeds of reasonable doubt in the minds of jurors. The jury became hopelessly deadlocked and the judge declared a mistrial. During a second trial on May 4, 1904, the second jury said that they too were deadlocked. This time the judge refused to see them until they reached a verdict. On June 17, they reached a verdict of murder in the second degree. On July 14 the judge sentenced Alfred Hulse to life in Folsom Prison. Hulse remained in the Kern County Jail while his attorneys went through various motions and appeals. On October 14, 1906, he borrowed a razor from the jailor, and under the guise of shaving, he slit his throat and bled to death before help arrived.

The killing of James McKinney made front-page headlines around the nation. His funeral was a simple service at his mother's home, attended by a few friends and family. The two lawmen, Jeff Packard and Will Tibbet, were given large funerals and eulogized for their bravery. But the *Merced County Sun* editorialized that it hoped that such acts of daring would not be repeated by other officers, because the acts were more foolish than brave:

> They knew he would shoot them if he got the chance. They knew that he was a good marksman, and that he would shoot to kill. They also knew that in attacking the house the bandit inside had every advantage over the officers outside, yet they made the attack. The wonder is that more of the officers were not killed.

Frontier lawmen cannot be faulted for lack of courage. The men who served on these posses were not trained gunmen. They were civic-minded and highly respected members of their communities. However, they were not as well-prepared as our modern peace officers. Today's Special Weapons and Tactics Team (SWAT) wear bulletproof clothing and have received special training for handling dangerous criminals. In the case of apprehending McKinney, modern officers might have suffered a similar encounter, but they would have had a better chance of survival.

After serving as Mohave County sheriff, Lovin remained active in the Democratic Party. He was chosen as a delegate to the 1910 state Constitutional Convention. After Arizona achieved statehood, Lovin served as senator in Arizona's first and second state legislatures. In 1925, the Mohave County constituency elected him to the Mohave County Board of Supervisors, a position he held until his death on December 24, 1931. A bronze memorial tablet for Henry Lovin was erected in the rotunda of the state capitol.

The Mohave County Board of Supervisors adopted a resolution honoring Lovin, which read:

> Henry Lovin, until the day of his death, was an indefatigable worker for the advancement and improvement of our community, an ever faithful and trusted official and one who honorably and efficiently discharged every public trust reposed in him, who always enjoyed the respect and confidence of his constituents.

CHAPTER 8.
Tolerated Vices and Tarnished Badges

Greenlee County law officers destroying liquor found in a raid of a saloon in Metcalf.

Many people look upon prostitution, gambling, alcohol consumption, and even drug use as vices, but not necessarily crimes. Yet powerful and vociferous groups have always wanted these practices banned, and when laws are passed to prohibit them, the sheriff is charged with enforcing these laws. At midnight of January 16, 1920, the Eighteenth Amendment, which prohibited the manufacture, sale, or transportation of intoxicating liquors and their importation and exportation, became law throughout the United States. Arizona had already voted to go dry six years before the rest of the nation. (Maine, along with several other states, had taken that action as early as 1852.)

Evidently most citizens were not interested in stamping out tolerated vices such as bootlegging, moonshining, gambling, and prostitution, no matter what the law stated—and it would have been naive to think that a mere law could eliminate these practices. In fact, these offenses continued and were simply driven underground, where they could be exploited by underworld mobs.

Perhaps the most sinister repercussion of Prohibition was a spawning of contempt for the law by Americans. This would be felt on some level for several decades in Arizona and the rest of the nation. Prohibition encouraged otherwise law-abiding people to become scofflaws, and typically good sheriffs began to tolerate bootlegging and moonshining—in fact, some officers even accepted bribes for looking the other way. Breaking this law carried punishment ranging from $300 fines to sentences of up to two years in jail. On the other hand, lawmen who enforced Prohibition not only faced danger from violent gangsters, they also faced ridicule and anger from members of their electorate who openly opposed the law.

Arizona's conflict with Prohibition began on December 31, 1914. A few people gave thanks for the dry vote in Tucson churches, but many Tucsonans were in the bars on Meyer Street enjoying a final phantasmagoria of merrymaking. Arizona went dry largely through the determined efforts of Tucsonans such as Louis Hughes, editor of the *Arizona Daily Star,* and his wife, Josephine, a staunch member of the Women's Christian Temperance Union (WCTU). As early as 1883, Josephine Hughes and the national WCTU leader, Frances E. Willard, traveled throughout the Arizona Territory denouncing "demon rum," administering abstinence oaths, and pinning white ribbons on their converts. Louis Hughes and Eugene Chafin, the perennial Prohibition presidential candidate, even fought the druggists who insisted upon their right to sell liquor on prescription.

The fight for Prohibition was often described as the "women's war." Weary of seeing their husbands running off to the tavern every night, where men under the influence of liquor made political choices in a haze of smoke, women organized the anti-saloon leagues and Women's Christian Temperance Union chapters. Denied the vote, they found their power in these causes. Ministers supported these women on this issue. In Ohio, Reverend Sam Small preached, "American people are crucifying that beastly, bloated bastard of Beelzebub, the liquor traffic … Yet a few months more, and we will bury the putrid corpse of John Barleycorn."

Also at the national level, the onset of Prohibition coincided with Warren G. Harding's presidency. The United States has perhaps never seen a more incompetent, unprincipled president. While paying lip service to the drys, he was known to be a heavy drinker. His tolerance for corruption and cronyism infiltrated every level of government, from the national to the local.

During Arizona's early dry years, bootleggers brought in illegal liquor from wet states such as New Mexico, and from Mexico. With national Prohibition, moonshiners—who made a variety of liquors ranging from smooth blended whiskey to poisonous rotgut—appeared on the Arizona scene. During the first two years of

Prohibition, Cochise County Deputy Sheriff Percy Bowden made 1,366 alcohol-related arrests, most of which resulted in convictions. He estimated that he had apprehended only about half of the lawbreakers in his jurisdiction.

The new liquor "brands" included Red Eye, Cherry Dynamite, Scat Whiskey, Soda Pop Moon, Jackass Brandy, and Yack-Yack Bourbon. Various manufacturers in Mexico (some legal and some not) produced a concoction distilled from potatoes, cacti, and burnt sugar, known simply as American Whiskey. From the Caribbean came Jamaica Ginger or Jake, a vile booze that paralyzed its victims. Wine bricks (blocks of dried grape juice to which you would add water, complete with instructions for how to "avoid" fermentation into wine) materialized in grocery stores. Although national statistics were not kept, deaths from rotgut liquor probably went well over fifty thousand, and thousands more suffered from blindness and paralysis.

Many an Arizona sheriff enjoyed a nip or two. Before Arizona went dry, Mohave County Sheriff Henry Lovin put a sign over his mercantile that read, "All Nations Welcome Except Carrie." He referred, of course, to Carrie Nation, the one-woman tornado who waged her own war against liquor by chopping up Kansas saloons. Former Coconino County Sheriff Sandy Donahue hung a black-bordered sign outside his saloon during Prohibition that read, "Closed on account of death."

Nevertheless, Cochise County Sheriff Harry Wheeler traveled all over his county in an effort to stop bootlegging. Along with apprehended lawbreakers, confiscated booze piled up in his courthouse. A judge even had to suspend a Cochise County trial temporarily when the fumes of whiskey wafted through the windows. The judge discovered Sheriff Wheeler breaking up fifty-quart bottles of Sunny Brook, which had been confiscated from one George F. Taylor.

The Automobile Age

During Prohibition, lawmen had a powerful new tool—the automobile—to help them enforce this law. Not everyone appreciated this tool, however. Cochise County Sheriff George Henshaw contended that it put added strain on lawmen, because criminals got away faster and farther. He dreaded seeing the day when outlaws took to the air. Despite such reluctance, though, the automobile became one of the sheriff's best tools for chasing down criminals and ferreting out moonshiners.

The last Territorial sheriff of Maricopa County, Carl T. Hayden, also became the first Arizona sheriff to participate in an automobile posse. When his friend J. F. McCarthy offered Hayden his Stoddard-Dayton vehicle to chase down a couple of young train robbers, Mrs. McCarthy was not worried that her husband would be killed by bandits, but she feared that he would kill himself and his companions by reckless driving. And in fact, Hayden later confessed to feeling apprehension during the chase. His posse easily caught the two robbers when they approached McCarthy's car and asked for water.

During this era, the most important car for the Arizona sheriffs was the seven-passenger Studebaker Big Six Duplex Phaeton. In 1925, twelve of the fourteen Arizona counties furnished their sheriffs with this car. (Graham and Santa Cruz County sheriffs still had to provide their own personal vehicles.) When Pima County Sheriff Walter Bailey left the sheriff's office, he bought the department's Studebaker and later donated the vehicle to the Arizona Historical Society. This vehicle, which had the same engine as Studebaker's twenty-one-passenger bus, carried a list price of $1,575 and possessed "a wealth of excess power." It featured deep, soft cushions, full-size balloon tires, and curtains, which provided open-car freedom or closed-car protection in less than thirty seconds. While one officer drove, another sat in the back seat and guarded the prisoner.

When Studebaker decided to document the Arizona sheriffs' preference for the Duplex Phaeton, the company commissioned Grover F. Sexton to interview all of the Arizona sheriffs who drove Studebakers. The sheriffs even deputized Sexton for this project. After Sexton presented his stories to Studebaker, the company renamed the model "The Sheriff," in honor of the Arizona lawmen who made the Studebaker a vibrant symbol of law and order. The vehicle's 1926 race from New York to San Francisco, documented in a book entitled *The Dash of the Sheriff,* offered a tribute to those "soft-spoken, hard-driving men who keep the highways and byways of Arizona safe by the swift capture of wrongdoers."

Sexton traveled with Coconino County Sheriff John Parsons and a deputy when they captured two horse thieves near the Grand Canyon. He helped Greenlee County Sheriff Skeets Witt break up an illegal gambling operation. For eleven days and nights he rode with Apache County Deputy Sheriff Tom Jones until they captured an Apache, Red Sleeve, who had stolen $1,000 from a road crew. Sexton helped Pinal County Deputy Sheriff Chester McGee return a wayward daughter to her father. He learned how Yuma County Sheriff Jim Chapell used his Studebaker to outrun a lynch mob. Sexton described Pima County Sheriff Walter Bailey as the "typical Western sheriff." For five days, Sexton accompanied Bailey on the search and ultimate capture of a murderer.

Yavapai County Sheriff Ed G. Weil, prominent in Republican politics, also ran a dairy business in the late 1800s. He had the distinction of being the first volunteer from Pasadena, California, to serve in the Spanish-American War. Sexton photographed Weil arresting H. M. "Tex" Elliott, a moonshiner, who had shot and killed I. P. McKelvie (who had operated a still in a Santa Maria Mountain canyon in Yavapai County).

For $5 a day, Elliott had agreed to operate a still for Dick Taylor, owner of a Prescott pool hall. When McKelvie, a customer, complained that Elliott made bad corn liquor, Taylor stopped paying his moonshiner. Elliott demanded his money or he would dump all the liquor into the canyon. Because McKelvie was angry and Elliott's liquor was bad, Taylor saw his chance to get rid of a troublemaker. So Taylor drove

McKelvie out to the still and left him there with a shotgun, presumably to take care of Elliott. Neighbors heard McKelvie mutter that he was going to "wrap his shotgun around that son-of-a-bitch's [Elliott's] neck." When Elliott arrived, McKelvie pulled his gun, but Elliott deflected the shotgun barrel and drew his six-shooter. He fired two shots into McKelvie's throat and chest.

Elliott called Sheriff Weil to turn himself in. When Weil and Deputy Bill Poulson arrived six hours later, they arrested Elliott and dug up twelve barrels of mash. At the same time, the officers found fifty gallons of warm, poisonous "white mule." Weil took McKelvie's body and Elliott back to Prescott in his Studebaker. A coroner's jury agreed that Elliott had killed McKelvie in self-defense.

THE LIGHT SIDE OF PROHIBITION

Prohibition was not without its humorous side. Will Rogers quipped, "Prohibition is better than no liquor at all." During the 1930s, the most prosperous moonshiners in Apache County were the Stuart brothers: Basil, Matt, Charles, Thurl, John, Tim, and Pruitt. The excellent quality of their whiskey contributed to their success. To eliminate car tracks at their stills, they trained their cows to work as pack animals.

One evening, Apache County Sheriff M. L. "Roy" Hall followed three of the brothers to a remote spot in the woods where they had cached their whiskey. Tim and John were in a hole "pinting" it out and passing it up to Charles, who crated the bottles. When Charles saw the sheriff, he fled and yelled, but his brothers did not hear him. Sheriff Hall took over Charles's job. When Tim and John came out of the dugout, they exclaimed, "Holy cow, Roy! That can't be you!" "You're right, old friend, it's me," remarked the sheriff.

Bribes and Corrupt Officials

On December 5, 1933, Congress repealed the Eighteenth Amendment. Between 1920 and 1933, over a half million people had been incarcerated for offenses such as making moonshine and bootlegging. During Prohibition, more than eleven thousand out of a force of seventeen thousand government agents of the various liquor investigatory agencies were dismissed for criminal involvement. But the corruption didn't end with Prohibition; public officials have continued to accept payoffs to overlook illegal gambling and prostitution.

Arizona officers such as Maricopa County Sheriff Roy Merrill and Pima County Sheriffs Jerome Martin and Waldon Burr took bribes. Curiously, these sheriffs with tarnished badges also did much good for their counties, yet their positive contributions often contrasted strongly with their willingness to conspire with the criminal element and to line their pockets with bribes derived from gambling and prostitution.

In 1907, at the urging of Governor Joseph H. Kibbey, the Arizona legislature had outlawed gambling in Arizona. Allegations that his predecessor, J. R. McFadden, had violated the anti-gambling laws allowed Roy Merrill to win the office of Maricopa County sheriff in 1937 by a margin of six thousand votes. Merrill had never lacked courage when it came to a fight. As a Maricopa County deputy sheriff, he had been stabbed while arresting rioters, leaving permanent damage to his left arm. Merrill's priorities as sheriff included the abolishment of liquor sales to children and the serving of long-overdue warrants for a variety of misdemeanors. A cadre of dedicated volunteers helped investigate automobile accidents. He introduced a unique car, equipped with a shortwave radio, that rendered first aid and provided water and gasoline to stranded motorists. In 1937, the Arizona Peace Officers Association elected Merrill as their president, and he received a 37 percent budget increase. However, during Merrill's turbulent two-year term, his opponents complained that he also accepted bribes from the gambling interests.

Maricopa County Sheriff Roy Merrill.

In July of 1937, Maricopa County Attorney Harry Johnson resigned by letter, citing ill health. The Maricopa County Board of Supervisors withheld announcing Johnson's resignation until they had chosen his successor, Assistant Maricopa County Attorney John Corbin. Rumors immediately surfaced that with Corbin in office, two of the supervisors saw an opportunity to get rid of both a corrupt sheriff (Merrill) and a corrupt judge (Phoenix Justice of the Peace Harry E. Westfall). Allegedly the supervisors offered Corbin the position on the premise that he agree to trap Merrill and Westfall for bribery and conspiracy.

Although the rumor was never proven, Corbin immediately began cracking down on gambling operations. He claimed that Merrill approached him with a plan for both of them to make money from gambling establishments outside of the Phoenix city limits. Merrill allegedly said he intended to make money off the gambling operations, and he suggested that Corbin also collect a percentage from these establishments. Corbin hired the Los Angeles-based Dunn Bureau of Investigation and assigned J. G. Handy, under the name of John Wilson, to pose as the county attorney's bucketman (someone who transfers illegal money). Before long, the new county attorney felt that he had enough evidence to arrest a number of slot-machine operators, along with Merrill and Westfall.

On November 18, thirty specially deputized officers, including highway patrolmen, deputy sheriffs, police officers, and a few private citizens, under Maricopa County's chief investigator, George Ash, participated in a massive sting operation. They served arrest warrants for bribery and conspiracy to obstruct justice on Sheriff Merrill, Judge Westfall, and more than twenty slot-machine operators. The sting operation came shortly

Maricopa County Attorney John Corbin.

after Merrill had announced that Phoenix should be allowed to manage its own gambling problems without sheriff interference. In yet another twist to this tale, the city of Phoenix had licensed games such as Bingo and Skill Dart. When Corbin's sting operation seized these machines, Mayor Nicholas Udall complained, because the city had collected $4,500 in much-needed revenue from them during these difficult Depression years.

Before Merrill came to trial, he was summoned to appear in court on a separate charge of overlooking gambling operations. Since slot machines were not illegal in private residences, many merchants distributed a few pieces of household furniture in their places of business, and thus deputies could not obtain search warrants for these "residences." Superior Court Judge Howard Speakman reprimanded Merrill for using this technicality to avoid enforcing the law. The sheriff made a weak excuse that he could not find these gambling operations, but Speakman questioned why the sheriff could not find these places, when the public found them easily.

As a result of the sting operation, Merrill faced separate trials for bribery and conspiracy. In March 1938, he appeared before Judge Speakman, who, in order to avoid accusations of a biased jury, had ordered that a new panel be drawn. Jury panels are drawn up in the presence of the sheriff or his representative, and therefore Merrill had theoretically participated in his own jury selection earlier.

Before Merrill's trial even began, Judge Speakman announced a mistrial. He had heard of an attempt to buy off five or six jurors, though he quickly absolved Merrill of any blame in this incident. Two women who were unintentionally included on the new panel had to be set aside, because at that time only men were allowed to serve on an Arizona jury.

Merrill's trial opened on April 13. Lynn Laney was appointed as special prosecutor, because Corbin had to serve as a witness. Corbin testified that Merrill had offered him a $250 bribe in return for not prosecuting A. L. Cowan, a slot-machine operator. According to Corbin, the sheriff had said, "I don't know what you'll do about it [gambling], but I'm going to make some money out of it." Merrill suggested that Corbin issue an arrest warrant only when citizens were willing to sign a complaint. Corbin would then refer the complaints to Judge Westfall, who would temporarily impound the gambling devices before returning them to the owners. The defense countered with a claim that Merrill, by offering this plan, was trying to trap Corbin. Merrill's defense also accused the county attorney of entrapment, betrayal of friendship, and the amount of liquor consumed during the meeting.

When Merrill took the stand, he testified that the transcript of the alleged meeting had been doctored and that some items had been added while others were deleted. The sheriff claimed that Corbin initiated the gambling payoff scheme, but then changed his mind and decided not to carry it out. Laney produced telephone records showing that Merrill had made calls from his private phone to three slot-machine operators. Merrill denied making the calls, and his defense summoned Maricopa County Deputy Sheriff Porter Northroup, who backed up Merrill's testimony. When both Merrill and Northroup denied knowing anything about local gambling, Laney asked incredulously, "How did you keep from knowing?"

After nine days the State rested its case. The prosecution had presented an array of witnesses and strong evidence, including charges that a Chicago gangster had contributed to the sheriff's campaign. Merrill's conviction seemed to be a sure thing. On the other hand, Gene Cunningham, who defended Merrill, portrayed the sheriff as an ignorant country boy who trusted Corbin and his advice.

The test for entrapment depended upon whether the offense first originated in the mind of Merrill or of Corbin. If the unlawful act had originated in the mind of Corbin, then Merrill's defense of entrapment was complete and the jury would have to find him not guilty. With the two politicians accusing each other of proposing to take bribes, the jury had difficulty determining just who had originated the bribery plan. On April 23, the jury acquitted Merrill of the bribery charges. Judge Speakman angrily silenced the cheering crowd.

This verdict presented a serious setback for the Maricopa County Attorney's war on crime. Now Corbin would find it difficult to conduct sting operations, because he would be accused by defendants of initiating payoff schemes. Nevertheless, the indictment for conspiracy to obstruct justice against Merrill, Undersheriff Porter Northroup, and thirteen others went forward. Each defendant would be tried individually, with Merrill scheduled first.

Merrill's conspiracy trial opened on May 9. Gene Cunningham had resigned, citing health problems, so Frank Beer and James A. Walsh took over the sheriff's defense and successfully filed a motion to have Judge Speakman disqualified on the basis of prejudice. Pinal County Superior Court Judge Ernest McFarland replaced Speakman. Special prosecutors, including Lynn Laney and Maricopa Deputy County Attorney John A. Murphy, introduced into evidence receipts for twenty-five bribery payments totaling $2,897.

Although women did not serve on juries at this time, racially mixed juries were not unusual—but many whites did not like to serve with blacks. Shortly after Merrill's trial started, several white jurors protested that they would not walk down the street or eat their meals in the company of the two black jurors. So Judge McFarland appointed an additional bailiff and segregated the black men during the trial in an effort to avoid a mistrial.

Witnesses repeated the same testimony that they had given in the bribery trial. Beer characterized the Maricopa County Attorney's staff as "fat slick city spiders" who caught a country fly in a game that they had started. Countering with Merrill's acceptance of $4,500 for his election campaign from a gambler, prosecutor Laney snarled, "He got his snoot dirty and it's been dirty ever since." Again the jury could not determine whether the plot to take a bribe had started with Merrill or Corbin, so they acquitted the sheriff. After shaking hands with the jurors, Merrill said, "I was a big saphead, but I've really had a lesson and I feel like a free man again." Subsequent trials of the other defendants produced only two convictions.

At the next election, both Sheriff Merrill and County Attorney Corbin lost their bids for office in the primaries. Merrill moved to Mohave County, where he operated a cocktail lounge in Bullhead City and the Gateway Bar in Kingman until his death in 1953.

The Two Faces of Jerry Martin

Pima County Sheriff Jerome "Jerry" Patrick Martin became the only Arizona sheriff to date to serve time in Florence State Prison. Martin had resigned from the Southern Pacific Railroad to join the U.S. Navy during World War I. After his discharge, Martin worked for the railroad until World War II, when he saw service with the Seabees in the Pacific. Martin received many decorations for his service in both world wars.

Martin served as a deputy sheriff under Pima County Sheriffs Walter Bailey, John Belton, and Ed Echols before accepting an appointment as the first town marshal of

Pima County Sheriff Jerome "Jerry" Martin.

the newly incorporated city of South Tucson in 1936 (he was also working for the railroad during this time). He continued to serve as a Pima County deputy sheriff. Martin, who spoke fluent Spanish, received $200 per month in total for the marshal and sheriff jobs.

South Tucson had just adopted its first traffic ordinance. Speeders were warned, if they persisted in "making knots" on South Sixth Avenue, they were likely to encounter Martin's "Five Dollar Smile." Martin, with a big smile, would haul the speeder off to Mayor Frank Norton's lumberyard office, where the culprit would pay $5. Furthermore, the ordinance proclaimed the speed limit to be twenty-five miles per hour. Cars were not to turn in mid-block or make sudden loops from the center traffic lane, back to curbside beer parlors they had just driven past. No longer were drivers even to think about parking on a sidewalk, and the law intended to prolong the life of pedestrians by taking a definite attitude toward their immunity while walking in a pedestrian lane.

Martin won a seat in the sixteenth Arizona state legislature, where as a representative in 1943–1944, he served on the child welfare, accounting and business methods, appropriations, and labor committees. In 1946, after five consecutive terms, Sheriff Ed Echols lost the Pima County shrievalty to Jerry Martin. Martin accomplished much during his administration as sheriff, including acquiring five new Dodge patrol cars and reorganizing the sheriff's department into jail, criminal, and civil functions. He purchased ten electric flares to serve as road markers at accident scenes and named Frank C. Johnson as the first black deputy sheriff.

Martin also instituted the Knothole Gang, for kids from ages nine to sixteen, and made arrangements for all of its members to be admitted to city league baseball games and Tucson High School and University of Arizona football games at 10 cents per head. He also persuaded the Tucson Rapid Transit Company to furnish them with free transportation.

Martin started the first volunteer Pima County Rescue Patrol, after Guy D. Rockefeller Jr., a young boy, became trapped on a ledge under a projection in Sabino Canyon on August 9, 1948. Deputy Sheriff John D. Anderson, who had previously lost a leg during a motorcycle accident, descended twenty-five feet by rope and brought the boy up to where deputies could pull the boy to safety. Unfortunately, when Anderson started to climb back up, the rope caught in a narrow crevice and jerked out of his hands, and he plummeted five hundred feet to his own death.

Martin organized the Pima County sheriff's mounted posse, which made its first appearance in Tucson's 1949 La Fiesta de los Vaqueros parade. All of the posse riders wore distinctive red-and-gold uniforms and rode palominos. Martin got the idea of a mounted posse when friends presented him with Honey-Boy, a beautiful palomino horse, plus a glittering silver-and-black saddle, at a surprise Christmas banquet in 1948.

Budget problems plagued Martin's office during the end of his first term. At one point he threatened to lay off all but seven of his staff because of a $44,500 shortage. During his second term, Martin's patrol car, driven by his underage son, hit and killed twelve-year-old Theresa Mendibles. Judge Mercer J. Johnson dismissed a $50,000 lawsuit against the sheriff, and a coroner's jury cleared Martin's son.

In November, Martin defied a court order that specified that twenty-one slot machines belonging to civic organizations should be returned to their owners, because the sheriff had not obtained search warrants. Judge C. W. Gardner lashed out at Martin, demanding to know why certain clubs were raided while others went unmolested. The judge called upon the Democratic Party to rid Pima County of Martin. What the Democratic Party did not do, the county's Republican voters did. Martin lost the next election to Frank Eyman, and in the same election County Attorney Bryce Wilson lost to Robert Morrison.

Both men went out of office and into serious trouble. During thirteen sessions, a grand jury heard testimony from forty-nine witnesses in its investigation of vice, graft, gambling, and the general breakdown in Pima County law enforcement. Indictments were brought against former Pima County Attorney Bryce Wilson, former Pima County Sheriff Jerry Martin, and former Undersheriff Maurice Guiney.

Wilson testified that he had received money from a prostitute, Dolores Raines, as payment for legal services. At this time, county attorneys were still allowed to pursue private practices. However, the court ruled that the evidence as a whole indicated that Raines, who ran a "disorderly house," had paid Wilson for protection from prosecution. The Arizona Supreme Court heard tapes of conversations between Wilson and Raines, and saw compromising photographs and payment receipts from Raines. The court ordered that Bryce Wilson be disbarred from further practice of law in the state of Arizona.

The state examiner, who had been called in to audit the office, found the sheriff's records to be in a deplorable condition. In April 1951, a grand jury indicted Martin on three felony counts: receiving a bribe, receiving the earnings of a prostitute, and conspiracy to obstruct justice. Two Tucson madams, Alice Miller and Dolores Raines, were arrested and held in the Pima County Jail as material witnesses. On March 21, 1951, Martin appeared in court. The charge stipulated that Martin had asked for and received bribes from Raines and Miller. In return, Martin agreed to refrain from arresting Raines and Miller for running houses of prostitution.

Raines admitted that she paid money to both Wilson and Martin and testified to running a house of prostitution on Ina Road, known as the Tamarack Ranch. A pimp testified that he heard Raines complain to Wilson that Miller was running her out of business and that Miller's girls near Davis-Monthan Air Force Base were giving venereal diseases to the soldiers. Wilson responded that he could not do anything about the sheriff's office.

Wilson even went so far as to accuse the prosecutor, Pima County Attorney Robert Morrison, of paying for an abortion for Raines at St. Mary's Hospital. When asked if this was true, Raines replied, "I guess so. I didn't pay anything. I was broke." During Martin's trial, Raines, in return for testifying against the former sheriff, received absolute immunity from prosecution, but she had to waive her right to object to testifying on the grounds of self-incrimination.

Deputy Sheriff Leslie O. Moore testified that when he investigated a complaint against Raines, he told her that she would have to close up. She offered to pay $100 a week for protection. Moore testified that when he told the sheriff about her offer, Martin sent him back to Raines to collect the money. Moore put the money in an envelope and gave it to Undersheriff John Phebus, stating, "Here is a present for the boss."

Martin allowed Raines and Miller to operate their houses of prostitution, under the guise of massage parlors, without fear of arrest, but the women had to share their profits with the sheriff. Martin appealed his guilty verdict to the Arizona Supreme Court, claiming numerous errors regarding the admission of evidence and uncorroborated testimony. The court rejected his appeal. On August 20, 1952, Judge Porter Murry sentenced Martin to a term of not less than two years and not more than five years at the state prison in Florence.

Upon the urging of friends and family, Martin was paroled on November 10, 1953. For a little over two years, Martin worked his cotton farm, but his health deteriorated. He tried to rehire with the railroad, but Southern Pacific refused to reinstate him on the basis of "dishonesty." On June 21, 1956, former Pima County Sheriff Jerome Martin died at a local hospital.

A gathering of peace officers; Waldon Burr (Pima County sheriff 1958–1971) is seated second from left.

Flashy Sheriff Waldon Burr

Sheriff Frank Eyman put the Pima County Sheriff's Office back on stable ground. When Eyman left the sheriff's office to accept a position as warden of the state prison at Florence, the supervisors named former U.S. Marshal Benjamin J. McKinney as Pima County sheriff. James Clark beat out McKinney in the next election, but lost the subsequent election to Waldon Burr in 1958.

Pima County Sheriff Waldon Vivian Burr was a big man who wore cowboy boots, a white Stetson hat, and a prominent, flashing diamond-studded badge. His campaign motto stated, "It takes a big man to cover a big county." Burr did much good for Pima County—catching and incarcerating numerous criminals, pushing for highway safety measures (including flashing lights at railroad crossings), and staying within his budget—but he would resign in disgrace on September 24, 1971.

Born in El Paso, Texas, on August 25, 1907, Burr arrived in Arizona in 1918, and he worked on his father's Tucson ranch. Burr's formal education included Brophy College Preparatory, a Phoenix-area Jesuit school founded in 1928, and the University of Arizona in Tucson, where he majored in poultry husbandry but never graduated.

In 1937, Burr joined the Arizona Highway Patrol, and he served as director of its Southern District in Tucson in 1940. During World War II, Burr headed the Highway Patrol's training program in southern Arizona and escorted General George C. Patton, whose troops had been training in the Yuma desert, and his regiment across the state. His Arizona Highway Patrol superintendent relieved Burr of his command after a political dispute on September 30, 1949, but he successfully appealed and was reinstated on April 4, 1950.

The flamboyant sheriff personally escorted prisoners to jail, making certain that the press recorded the event. Burr changed the uniform, added a shoulder patch with a Pima County outline, and replaced the five-pointed star badge with the six-pointed star. As a prerogative of the office, Burr had his badge embellished with diamonds. He got a new county jail and, to save money, he laid off 10 percent of the staff and gave the remainder a 10 percent cut in pay. In November 1966, he turned down an offer to become U.S. marshal for Arizona.

On April 1, 1969, Burr appointed Michael Barr as chief deputy to assist Undersheriff James Wyckoff. Wyckoff resigned six months later to recuperate from a gunshot wound that he received from his housekeeper, Catherine Lenahan, during a domestic disturbance at his home. Richard C. Williams replaced Wyckoff as undersheriff. Wyckoff's problems were but a prelude to greater disasters in the sheriff's office. During the 1960s an undercurrent of rumors continually alleged misconduct in the department. When the Pima County Board of Supervisors attempted to investigate the complaints, Burr hired attorney H. Earl "Bud" Rogge to represent him during the investigation.

When the supervisors asked Burr to testify under oath in 1966, Rogge successfully got an order restraining the three Republican members—Thomas Jay, Dennis Weaver, and Pete Rubi—from asking Burr about money missing from the Pima County Jail store, the Fraternal Order of Police funds, and the sheriff's welfare fund. In spite of his problems, Burr won reelection in 1968. A few days before the election, Deputy Sheriff Kirk P. Coshatt presented the Republican candidate, Rocky Andresano, with a notarized affidavit stating that he had paid Burr $600 for his job as deputy and that deputies paid for their promotions. Coshatt claimed that Burr received monies from the deputies' emergency fund and from the jail store, and that deputies who moonlighted were expected to give Burr 10 percent of their earnings, to be paid either through payroll deductions or in person to Sheriff Burr. If a deputy refused to make a payoff, he would not receive any more outside assignments. Coshatt also accused Burr of depleting the deputies' emergency fund.

In response to these accusations and at the request of Pima County Attorney William J. Schafer III, Judge Robert O. Roylston ordered that a twenty-one-member grand jury be empaneled to investigate Burr's misconduct. The grand jury accused Sheriff Burr, Captain Richard C. Williams, and Lieutenant Albert M. Felix of "willful or corrupt misconduct in office." Nine other deputies were alleged to have received their positions in exchange for "an emolument, gratuity or reward or promise thereof for doing an official act." However, on February 24, 1969, Judge Alice Truman dismissed the accusations on the basis that the statute of limitations had expired and that the misdeeds of a past office term could not be brought to bear once that term of office had ended.

At the same time, Deputy Sheriff Allen P. Defosse produced an affidavit in which he charged that he had paid Burr $900 for his job and his promotion to sergeant. Burr immediately fired Defosse on the grounds that the deputy had performed poorly on the written examination. Burr claimed that Defosse had not paid for his job, but had contributed to the sheriff's election campaign. A new grand jury brought charges against the sheriff and several of his staff. On February 11, 1971, Pima County Sheriff Waldon Burr, Undersheriff Richard C. Williams, Captains Manuel Medeiros, James McDonald, and Albert M. Felix, and Deputies William Freed and Nickolas Manners were arrested by state agents. Burr, the last to be arrested, said the action was politically motivated by Republicans.

For reasons she never made public, Pima County Attorney Rose Silver offered Burr and his deputies a choice of resigning or staying on and taking the consequences. If they resigned she would drop the eighty-six felony charges. Burr and all of his deputies chose to submit their resignations. The resignations made the operation of the Pima County Sheriff's Department look like the unfolding of a cheap novel. Charges included conspiracy, taking bribes from prostitutes, selling appointments to positions in the sheriff's department, and encouraging others to commit perjury. Albert Felix, a former captain, said that every two years the deputies were threatened with the loss of their jobs unless they supported the sheriff for reelection.

Chief Deputy Michael S. Barr took over as acting Pima County sheriff and served until the Pima County Board of Supervisors appointed William Coy Cox. As for the charges, all County Attorney Rose Silver would ever say was that there was a "dangerous situation" in the sheriff's office. Both the Pima County Sheriff's Department and the County Attorney's Office may have had a vested interest in the records, since they were sealed and turned over to the Department of Public Safety. The once-gregarious, flamboyant sheriff became a total recluse. Waldon Vivian Burr died at age eighty-one on December 6, 1988.

Five years after he represented Burr during

Pima County Attorney Rose Silver.

the investigation by the Board of Supervisors, on

September 3, 1971, Burr's counsel H. Earl Rogge left home in his wife's car. Three days later, Rogge's body was found on a dirt road off the Old Spanish Trail east of Tucson. An autopsy concluded that he had committed suicide by shooting himself in the head, and rumors maintained that the suicide was related to the Burr investigation.

Voters have no way of knowing what character flaws will appear in their selected office holder. None of the sheriffs who wore tarnished badges were entirely bad. And, in fact, many of them did much that was good. Apparently they simply felt that it was not wrong to take payoffs or look the other way when it came to publicly tolerated vices. These attitudes had arisen decades earlier during the failed experiment of Prohibition.

That point having been made, a closer look at political trends in the last few decades would indicate that a more conscientious Arizona citizenry is running "background checks" on candidates for sheriff. Because the people are making more and more demands on their public servants, they want to determine if the hopefuls boast the necessary credentials—in education, community involvement, and law enforcement. Positive results have been noteworthy, with a number of recent and current sheriffs being reelected for multiple four-year terms and several outstanding sheriffs serving for twenty to thirty years. At the same time, serious scandals and dismissals have declined markedly—a good sign of integrity in our sheriff's offices. Isn't it ironic? We always expect our law enforcement personnel to be a cut above the society that produced them.

CHAPTER 9.
Freedom of Religion

Short Creek raid, July 1953, the Richard Jessop family.

On the morning of July 26, 1953, Arizona Governor Howard Pyle came on the radio with an announcement: "Before dawn today," he said, "the State of Arizona began and now has substantially concluded a momentous police action against insurrection within its own borders."

Arizona officials, including the governor, the attorney general, and the Mohave County sheriff, chose July 26, a Utah state holiday known as Mormon Pioneer Day, for the raid on the Mormons of Short Creek in Mohave County, who practiced plural marriages as a part of their religious convictions. The officials knew that most of the people would be in town on that day.

During the Short Creek polygamist raid, Mohave County Sheriff Frank Porter had to deal with the unique dilemma of protecting the freedom-of-religion rights of a group of fundamentalist Mormons, while at the same time enforcing the laws of the state of Arizona. Churches must conform to building codes, fire regulations, and sanitation laws, but under the United States Constitution's First Amendment, freedom of religion is protected, and the government may not place religious constraints on people's freedom to act upon their beliefs. However, in the 1878 case *Reynolds vs. the United States,* the United States Supreme Court ruled that laws against polygamy are constitutional. Porter, who worked his way up through the ranks, brought impressive credentials to the sheriff's office. He had graduated from the University of Missouri and the FBI's National Academy.

Polygamists of Northern Arizona

Because of its Mormon heritage, the Colorado Strip area of northern Arizona actually has more in common, culturally, with Utah than with Arizona. Short Creek, now renamed Colorado City, is tucked away in a remote corner of Mohave County near the Utah-Arizona Border. The "twin cities" of Colorado City, Arizona, and Hildale, Utah, hug the state border. The fringes of these rural communities, with their large and somewhat run-down-looking houses, stand in stark contrast to the magnificent backdrop of the Vermillion Cliffs.

Today, the large dormitory-like houses are concealed behind trees. One road leads into Colorado City from Fredonia, Arizona, and another road enters the town from Utah. Small sawmills, cattle raising, and farming provide the principal sources of income. The few visitors will not see shorts, halter tops, or women in pants. Weary, work-worn women wear mid-calf dresses, stockings, and aprons. All females, including little girls, wear their long hair in braids.

The Short Creek fundamentalists claim to be the true Mormon followers of Joseph Smith. They settled in this isolated area specifically so they could practice plural marriages. A man's first marriage may be a legal ceremony conforming to state laws, but subsequent marriages are "celestial" marriages, with the rituals performed by the community elders. In 1831, Joseph Smith claimed to have received a vision from God encouraging plural marriages in order to better emulate Old Testament directives to multiply and replenish the earth. Members of the Church of Jesus Christ of Latter-day Saints (the Mormons) openly practiced polygamy in the United States between 1852 and 1890, but the church renounced polygamy when it saw that the practice kept Utah from attaining statehood. However, some Mormons, including ancestors of the Short Creek group, refused to give up the practice of polygamy.

Around the start of the twentieth century, Jacob M. Lauritzen and his family moved from St. George, Utah, to Short Creek. Lauritzen was soon joined by Lorin Covington, O. Colvin, and Frank Johnson. Mohave County supervisors gave

Lauritzen $50 to start a school and appointed him as justice of the peace, and the U.S. government established a post office there. In 1935, several families moved to Short Creek from northern Utah. Each man had two or three wives and several children. The parents taught their children that Short Creek was the "Land of the Bountiful," as described in the *Book of Mormon*, and the spot where Jesus Christ blessed the little children when he visited North America.

When Mohave County Attorney Elmo Bollinger received reports of polygamy around 1935, he charged several polygamists with open and notorious cohabitation. Three men and a woman—John Y. Barlow, L. C. Spencer, Price Johnson, and Silvia Allred—fled to a mountain cave, where they lived on dried corn until they were arrested. Allred was not prosecuted, but the men were tried and sentenced to prison terms.

In 1935, Mormon Church members from Hurricane, Utah, called the people of Short Creek, Arizona, and Hildale, Utah, to a meeting, and asked the men to sign a statement supporting the official Mormon Church and disavowing polygamy. Twelve of the men refused to sign, and they and their families were excommunicated. Five years later, these twelve polygamists incorporated under the United Effort Plan, whereby no individual could own any real or personal property in Short Creek. Officers of the plan included John Y. Barlow, J. Marion Hammon, Leroy S. Johnson, Joseph W. Musser, and Rulon Jeffs. Like the original Mormons, the Short Creek fundamentalists sought to establish a trust that dictated the holding of real property, any wages earned by members, the duties of the officers, and the members' rights. Even today the fundamentalists are governed by the United Effort Plan. Under this edict, the child and the mother give unquestioning obedience to the father. If the child is a girl, she must obey men simply because the community considers men as superior human beings.

In 1944, the FBI arrested and charged thirty Short Creek men with violating the Mann Act, which forbids transporting women across state lines for immoral purposes. The accused were tried and found guilty. Several convicts served time in the Utah State Prison, while others were incarcerated in a Tucson-area federal prison camp. They returned home as heroes with several new recruits, whom they had converted while in prison.

Young girls, by the age of ten, may hear talk of their being pledged to a particular man. In 1945, a man in his sixties married the twelve-year-old daughter of a younger man. The younger man accepted the older man's fifteen-year-old daughter in return. Girls are generally given to men over the age of thirty, and young men were evidently often harassed to leave the community to find wives on the outside. At the Short Creek council meetings, an elder would announce that a fourteen-year-old girl was ready [for a husband] and that one of the older men desired her. The girl would then be pledged to the man in a celestial marriage. Judge Norman Tullar, who had replaced Faulkner, commented, "It was if they all sat back and watched their stock grow."

POLYGAMY FORBIDDEN BUT NOT PENALIZED

Although the Arizona Constitution forbids polygamy, it provides no legal penalty for the practice. Defrauding the welfare system is a crime, however, and several Short Creek mothers, many under sixteen years old, gave the name of the same husband while requesting financial assistance for their children. They contributed their welfare checks to the United Effort Plan, and as a result adult men benefited from the money. The Short Creek community also demanded expanded school facilities from Mohave County, while at the same it claimed exemption from paying taxes (including school taxes) because its members belonged to a religious organization.

The Crackdown of 1953

At the insistence of Judge Jesse Faulkner, Arizona Attorney General Fred Wilson began an investigation in the 1950s. He planned a raid but aborted it when a wire service leaked the news. Faulkner tried again under Attorney General Ross F. Jones. By 1953, about 385 people lived in the Short Creek-Hildale area on both sides of the Arizona–Utah border.

In response to Arizona Governor Pyle's request for help, Utah Governor J. Bracken Lee said, "You do whatever you have to do but we are not going to become involved." Lee did, however, agree to help with Arizona's extradition proceedings if the polygamists fled across the border. At all times, Pyle kept the Mormon Council of Twelve and Utah state officials apprised of the proceedings.

A prosecutor from the Attorney General's Office, Paul LaPrade, bluntly stated that as a result of the plural marriages, all of the children were inbred. Some men had two generations of related women—mothers and their daughters—as wives. Attorney General Jones concluded that every member of the Short Creek's United Effort Plan had participated in a conspiracy against the State. Five non-Mormons living in Short Creek who did not practice polygamy, including Mohave County Deputy Sheriff Alfonso Nyborg, were excluded from the raid.

After completion of the investigation, Governor Pyle, Attorney General Jones, and Sheriff Porter met to plan the raid. They discussed the protection of human rights and freedom of religion as well as the possibility of violence. Pyle accepted personal responsibility for any problems related to the raid. He informed the official Mormon Church of his investigation, and the Mormon bishops and Relief Society began looking for volunteers to house the Short Creek children after their parents were arrested.

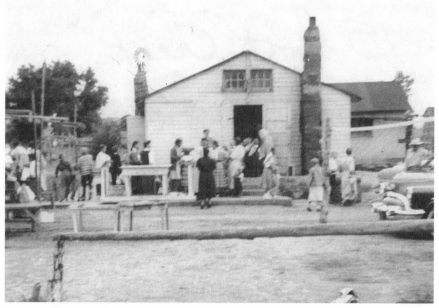

Short Creek building appropriated by law enforcement to use as a juvenile court.

The posse, led by Attorney General Jones and Sheriff Porter, consisted of all of the Mohave County Sheriff's Department, sixty state highway patrolmen, a dozen liquor agents, five matrons to care for the women and children, six welfare workers, three judges, the Arizona attorney general with three of his deputies, and the National Guard, which would set up food stations.

Arizona Highway Patrol Superintendent Greg Hathaway announced that a traffic school would be held at Williams, Arizona, on July 25, 1953. Only upon arriving in Williams did law-enforcement personnel learn that they would participate in a raid on the Short Creek polygamists. The Attorney General's Office deliberately leaked news of the raid to the press, so a horde of reporters and photographers also converged on Williams, and the posse convoy moved out with all "the ponderous secrecy of an elephant on a skating rink" (according to an article in *Time* magazine).

Half of the posse approached Short Creek by way of Hurricane, Utah, and the other half entered via Fredonia, Arizona. The caravans traveled in total darkness and timed their entry to coincide with the total eclipse of the moon. In the predawn hours, as the officers approached Short Creek, sentries David Broadbent and two brothers, Joseph and Dan Barlow, set off three blasts of dynamite to warn the residents of the impending raid. (At age twenty-one, Dan Barlow already had three wives and several children.)

The polygamists insisted that the dynamite explosion was only a warning, but it may have been a threat. One dynamite stick exploded only ten feet from a patrol car.

Fearing an attack, the officers turned on their flashing red lights and sirens just before entering Short Creek. Because Sheriff Porter was concerned over the possibility of bloodshed, he ordered that the press remain outside of Short Creek until he had rounded up all of the residents.

The officers found most of the Short Creek population had gathered in the dark school yard after hearing the dynamite go off; they were singing "Come, Come, Ye Saints" and "The Star-Spangled Banner" while awaiting their fate. Leroy Johnson, who had five wives, stepped forward to greet Sheriff Porter as he emerged from the lead posse car. Johnson told the sheriff that the polygamists were not going to run anymore and that they stood ready to shed their blood if necessary. So that everyone could hear, Porter responded in a clear voice that he did not want any violence but that he was there to do a job. Sheriff's deputies fanned out and slowly served warrants for each adult member of the Short Creek community. The cases of the fifteen wives under age eighteen would be heard by Judge Lorna Lockwood from Tucson. Eleven juvenile boys (who also had plural wives) would be treated as adults. Charges included rape, statutory rape, adultery, bigamy, open and notorious cohabitation, polygamy, contributing to the delinquency of a minor, income tax evasion, failure to comply with Arizona corporation laws, misappropriation of school funds, improper use of public facilities, and falsification of public records. Two of the accused men had six wives, the others each had from two to five wives. Four of the child brides were under thirteen, two were fourteen, and two were fifteen years old.

The Mormon Church, which originally had given verbal consent to the raid, now sympathized with the polygamists. President David O. McKay announced that the official Mormon Church had no part whatever in the planning or carrying out of the Arizona operation, and did not know about it until a few days before the occurrence. (In 1991, an anonymous source informed this author that "Governor Pyle made a mistake when he did not get written approval from President McKay."

PHOENIX PRESS PUMMELS PYLE

Phoenix newspapers came down hard on Pyle, calling the raid "a humiliation to the citizens of this state" and an "insurrection with diapers and volley-balls." However, the more sympathetic *Arizona Daily Star*, in Tucson, reported that the Short Creek polygamists lived in "poverty that forces them to feed their large broods on homemade wheat bread and potatoes for many months a year ..."

On July 28 and 29, court photographers and a Mohave County deputy sheriff photographed all of the Short Creek polygamist wives with their children in front of their houses. The adult men and eight older childless women were bused to Kingman, where the men were incarcerated in the Mohave County Jail and the women were housed in a Kingman dormitory barracks. Women with small children remained with their charges at Short Creek under the matrons' supervision.

The sheriff's department bugged the jail cells of male polygamists, and Sheriff Porter learned from tapes that the men were planning to escape and to kidnap their families and move to either Utah or Mexico, where there were substantial polygamist colonies. After learning of this, officials decided they would transport the women and their children from Short Creek to Phoenix the next day. However, that night about fifty Short Creek women and children, led by three teenage boys, slipped past guards and across the border into the mountains of southern Utah. Utah's Washington County Sheriff Antone Prince arrested five of the fleeing Short Creek women, but released them the next day so they could care for their children. Prince and Deputy Sheriff Israel Wade searched the cliffs, and a few days later Utah officers apprehended a truckload of the escaping women and children.

Once the accused were incarcerated, Sheriff Porter's job was done. Now the case rested in the hands of the courts. In November, twenty-five male polygamists pleaded

July 1953 raid on Short Creek. The white-bearded man is patriarch Joseph Smith Jessop.

guilty to one count of open and notorious cohabitation in return for dismissal of all other charges. Judge Tullar sentenced each of the men to a one-year suspended jail sentence. He was afraid that if he gave them harsher sentences, they would become martyrs in their community. Tullar ordered them to report monthly to their probation officer, and to swear that they had not participated in polygamy. On March 3, 1955, the court ordered seventeen children returned to their parents, and two weeks later the remaining 147 children were returned to their parents as well.

Until 1953, students from Hildale had attended the Short Creek school, and the Washington County (Utah) school district reimbursed the Mohave County school district for their education. Upon demands by local ranchers, who had strenuously objected to the polygamy practices, Mohave County authorities closed the Short Creek school in 1953. A new school opened on the Utah side of the border, with three Short Creek polygamists as teachers: Clyde Mackert and Louis Barlow (who both had plural wives), and Jerold Williams (who believed in polygamy, although he had only one wife at the time).

On April 5, 1954, the Arizona State Board of Education gave the teachers until July 31 to sign an oath stating that they would not practice polygamy from that day forward, or else their certificates would be revoked (which would also make them invalid in Hildale). The teachers petitioned for a review under the guarantee of freedom of religion. Maricopa County Superior Court Judge Robert E. Young ruled that the teachers could retain their certificates, and that the school board had exceeded its powers when it sought to compel them to sign the oath renouncing polygamy. The Short Creek school was subsequently allowed to reopen.

In 1954, Mohave County provided money to operate a high school but no funds to build it, so the Short Creek polygamists built it themselves. Students made adobe bricks for the school during their summer vacation, and the community's sawmill provided the lumber. Edson Jessop said, "We don't get support for our high school. By our own choice we run it and support it so that our children can have the kind of education we think they ought to have."

In May 1957, Mohave County Deputy Sheriff Al Nyborg confirmed claims made by a non-polygamist Short Creek teacher, R. E. Brown, that plural marriages still flourished. Attorney General Robert Morrison asked Sheriff Porter to investigate three teenage pregnancies in Short Creek, but no legal action was taken against the polygamists.

Colorado City

In 1985, the residents of this remote enclave successfully petitioned to be incorporated as Colorado City. They felt that the name Short Creek, a community that had never incorporated, had negative connotations because of the polygamy arrests. As a result of the incorporation, the Mohave County Sheriff's Office removed the one deputy residing in Colorado City. The town, with a population of about seventeen hundred people, most of whom espoused polygamy, would now have to take care of law enforcement with its own police.

They chose Sam Barlow to serve as town marshal. Barlow, who had begun his law-enforcement career in 1968 as a deputy in Arizona and later also worked in law enforcement in Utah, had three wives and thirty-six children. When the Arizona Law Enforcement Officers Advisory Council attempted to strip Barlow of his certification, his attorneys argued that prohibition of polygamy violated Barlow's right to freedom of religion. Utah had already denied a renewal of his certification. Other complaints against Barlow included allegations that he used his law-enforcement power to enforce the United Effort Plan. Despite the 1990 U.S. Court of Appeals ruling that neither the state nor the U.S. Constitution protected the practice of polygamy, in 1992 (after a five-year legal battle) charges for decertification of Barlow's law-enforcement accreditation were dismissed. Over the years Utah and Arizona both attempted to have Barlow decertified as a peace officer, and Barlow resigned as Colorado City town marshal in October 2005, after learning that once again authorities were attempting decertification.

The polygamists also faced threats from another group, which professed to be the "true" Mormon Church. Ervil LeBaron's Church of the Lamb expressed its beliefs through "violence with blood atonement." LeBaron had been convicted of the 1980 murder of Rulon C. Allred, a Salt Lake City polygamist who had relatives in Colorado City. LeBaron had even sent several of his followers to Allred's funeral to kill his own brother, Ross LeBaron.

In early 1986, although Ervil LeBaron had died in a Utah state prison in 1982, Colorado City Marshal Sam Barlow received a letter from the Church of the Lamb warning the followers of ninety-seven-year-old religious leader Leroy Johnson to forsake him by April 1 "or be destroyed by the sword of the Lord." The letter contended that Short Creek residents were guilty of sins that could only be forgiven through the ordinance of blood atonement. Mohave County Sheriff Joe Bonzelet turned the matter over to the FBI. He said, "I haven't got the money or the manpower for a holy war. I hope the FBI has something by April 1." Utah's Washington County Sheriff Ken Campbell took the threat seriously and sent fifteen deputies into the area. Jerry Miller, an agent of the Bureau of Alcohol, Tobacco, and Firearms office in Salt Lake City, confirmed that law-enforcement officials had learned that the Lamb of God Church in Mexico might bring machine guns into Colorado City. Luckily, April 1 came and went without any problems.

In 1987, Leroy Johnson died of natural causes, leaving at least fifteen widows and almost fifty children. Rulon T. Jeffs assumed leadership of the Colorado City polygamists. Three years later, Mohave County Supervisor Dale D'Alessandro claimed that the polygamists were still abusing the welfare program and that underage children were forced into polygamous marriages. Today the communities of Hildale and Colorado City (and their practice of polygamy) are flourishing. In May 2006, Hildale's religious leader, Warren Jeffs, was added to the FBI's Ten Most Wanted list (he was apprehended three months later in August); in early August of that same year, Ervil LeBaron's daughter Jacqueline Tarsa LeBaron was also placed on the Most Wanted list, in connection with four 1988 murders in Texas.

Miracle Valley Church Causes "Most Difficult Case"

In 1982, an apparent struggle for freedom of religion (with overtones of racial conflict) had tragic results in Miracle Valley in Cochise County. A shoot-out between Cochise County sheriff's officers and members of the all-black Christ Miracle Healing Center and Church ended with the death of two members of the church and nine injured deputies. There was no peace in the early 1980s in the Miracle Valley community, which straddles Arizona Highway 92, about five miles north of the U.S.–Mexico border, against a backdrop of the Huachuca Mountains in the beautiful San Pedro Valley. Miracle Valley came to represent an impasse of conflicting religious ideologies as well as racial prejudice on both sides. Sheriff Jimmy Judd had to protect the religious freedom of the church members, while still attending to the law-enforcement needs of the rest of Cochise County.

Miracle Valley has long attracted religious groups. In 1912, two brothers, Ben and Urbane Leiendecker, homesteaded 2,400 acres of land in Miracle Valley. In 1958, Urbane attended an evangelist meeting in Phoenix led by Reverend Asa A. Allen, after which Urbane claimed to have received a vision from God ordering him to help Allen. When Allen told the revivalists that he needed a site for his headquarters, Urbane offered him 1,200 acres of the Leiendecker holdings in Miracle Valley. Allen accepted the offer and built a church and a bible college on the land. During the 1950s and early 1960s, Allen's early-morning radio show provided great jazz gospel music. After Allen's death in 1970, most of the church members moved away.

Another person captivated by Allen's preaching was Frances Thomas, from Chicago. After hearing one of his sermons she felt the call and assembled a congregation in Chicago, known as the Christ Miracle Healing Center and Church. She would later claim that Allen had ordained her as a minister. In 1979, Reverend Thomas told her parishioners that they had to follow her to Arizona because Chicago would be destroyed like the Sodom and Gomorrah of biblical times.

Thomas and her three-hundred-member Christ Miracle Healing Center and Church moved in 1981 from Chicago into Miracle Valley, across the road from the old

Allen property. Members of the church were required to pay Thomas $100 a week. With these monies Thomas purchased one large home, a church building, a store building, and twenty-five vacant lots. Church members lived in trailers or in the buildings near the church.

Thomas permitted both local and national reporters to attend her Pentecostal three-hour services. The church celebrated with frenzied dancing, rapturous singing, and expounding the glorification of persecution. Many parishioners testified as to the positive results of Thomas's faith-healing rituals and professed to have found salvation as members of her church.

Sheriff of the Year

Miracle Valley came under the jurisdiction of Cochise County Sheriff Jimmy V. Judd, whose roots ran deep on both sides of the border. When Pancho Villa ordered Judd's father, a Chihuahuan rancher, out of Mexico (some time in the early 1900s), he allowed the Judd family to take only one wagon, one trunk, and a team of mules. The Judds moved to El Paso, Texas, and to Farmington, New Mexico, before finally settling in Arizona's San Pedro Valley.

Jimmy Judd grew up and attended schools in St. David, where he excelled as an all-state football and baseball player, and an honorable-mention basketball player. After high school graduation, he worked as a civilian at Fort Huachuca, served two years in the Navy, worked briefly as office manager for the Cochise County schools, and finally began his career in law enforcement as an insurance investigator. He went on to serve as Benson justice of the peace and, in 1973, as chief deputy sheriff under T. J. "Jim" Willson. In 1976, Cochise County voters elected Judd as sheriff and in 1981, the Arizona Sheriffs and County Attorneys Association named him Sheriff of the Year. Judd would later state, "My most difficult case involved the Miracle Valley religious cult."

During their early days in the community, church members committed a few misdemeanors that were overlooked or dealt with lightly by law enforcement. Area whites resented what they perceived as partiality, however, and resentment built up against the black church members. Church members set up security teams armed with handguns, rifles, and clubs, who patrolled Miracle Valley and stopped and interrogated people driving on public roads. Reverend Thomas said that her congregation patrolled the area because Judd did not provide sufficient protection against white vandals and burglars, and that firearms were simply a psychological deterrent.

Tensions between the Miracle Valley whites and the black members of the Christ Miracle Healing Center and Church sharply escalated in 1981. In July, 150 church members surrounded eight Cochise County sheriff deputies after the officers entered the area to investigate reports that the blacks stopped and verbally abused motorists on the highway. Several white families had moved elsewhere, while others kept their children out of the nearby Palominas Public School.

The U.S. Department of Justice and Governor Bruce Babbitt set up a panel that same summer to discuss the Miracle Valley problems and possible solutions to defuse the situation. The Phoenix Police Department lent Captain Harry Hurtt, a black officer who specialized in community relations, to the panel. Judd and Cochise County Attorney Beverly Jenney represented Cochise County, Robert Johnson represented the National Association for the Advancement of Colored People (NAACP), and Director Ralph Milstead represented the Department of Public Safety (DPS). Reverend Thomas represented her church.

The church and law-enforcement representatives signed a Memorandum of Understanding, which held out high hopes for peace. Judd proposed setting up a sheriff substation in Miracle Valley to deal with problems as they arose. He also agreed to hire more blacks. Not long after the Memorandum of Understanding was signed, black church members assaulted and threatened white residents with abusive language. Judd asked Governor Babbitt to bring in the National Guard, but the governor stated that while he was concerned about the events in Miracle Valley, he considered it a local matter to be resolved at a local level. Local man James Melton warned Babbitt that the Miracle Valley residents who were not church members had held a community meeting and were openly discussing forming an armed vigilante committee.

Judd moved a force of fifty officers into Miracle Valley to show that the sheriff's office was operating in full force. However, two sheriff deputies backed off from citing a church member for a traffic violation after they were surrounded by approximately two dozen hostile church members. The sheriff insisted on charging the driver, who turned out to be a "church security specialist." After considerable negotiations with Reverend Thomas, deputies served the summons on said driver, George L. Smith.

About the same time, the sheriff's office also served truancy papers on about ninety children whose parents had kept them out of school. Church members requested permission to set up their own parochial school, because their children failed at too high a rate at the public school and were subjected to racial prejudice, both in and out of school. The Cochise County School Board asked the church's attorney, Rubin Salter Jr., to provide documentation that the church could satisfy the Arizona statutory requirements for establishment of a school. Meanwhile, white parents requested that a twenty-four-hour guard be placed at the Palominas Public School and that patrol cars accompany the school buses.

Church members practiced faith healing and resisted all efforts by the Department of Economic Security to take over the medical care of their children. One six-year-old child died untreated, except by prayer, from a strangulated hernia. Cochise County health officials speculated that at least four other children who died during the year might have been saved if they had received proper medical attention.

Growing Violence

In early September, sheriff's deputies arrested a black church member for assaulting a white woman, who had driven into Miracle Valley to take children home after a day of fishing. He grabbed her arm and when he tried to hit her, a sheriff's deputy blocked the punch. Church members Sherman McCain and Dorothy Ann Collins were arrested and incarcerated in the Sierra Vista Jail. McCain was charged with obstructing government operations and carrying concealed weapons—an automatic gun and a knife. McCain also struck a deputy, who called for order when George Smith attempted to block Highway 92. Sheriff's deputies jailed Collins for carrying a concealed weapon—a pair of nunchakus (Oriental fighting sticks linked by a chain), which are illegal in Arizona. Officers spotted the weapons when she pounded them on the counter in the Miracle Valley substation and demanded the release of McCain.

On the evening of September 10, 1981, a van registered to Reverend Thomas and carrying four passengers exploded about two miles west of Miracle Valley on Highway 92, killing Steven Lindsey. Lindsey's body was badly disfigured, and the blast tore off his hands, severed his legs, blew out the windshield, and buckled the roof. Three injured church members, Julius Gillespie, Clinton Gillespie, and Frank Bernard, sustained minor injuries and were released from the Sierra Vista hospital after treatment.

The DPS found evidence of four homemade bombs in the exploded vehicle. All of the bombs contained sticks of dynamite, which had been wired with batteries and fuses, but only one bomb had exploded. Lindsey, who had no experience with explosives, may have neglected to insulate the bomb contacts and so inadvertently detonated the electric blasting caps. The investigation also revealed pieces of a clip and .30-caliber ammunition of the kind used in automatic and semiautomatic rifles, such as an M1, on Lindsey's body.

For several months the Bureau of Alcohol, Tobacco, and Firearms had known that the Christ Miracle Healing Center and Church had legally purchased a large quantity of dynamite, ostensibly for a church mining operation. Church member Amos Thompson bought the dynamite on August 12 from the Apache Powder Company in Benson. Thompson had also purchased, on a separate occasion, fifty pounds of Amogel No. 3 dynamite, the same type found in the exploded van. Records revealed that church members had purchased five M1 semiautomatic combat rifles, a dozen handguns, three hunting rifles, and three shotguns within the previous year. The minister's son, William Thomas Jr., had bought an M1 carbine with fifty rounds of ammunition.

An anonymous church member, who had become disgruntled with the church operations, told the sheriff's office that the vehicle was probably on its way to the Sierra Vista Jail, where the passengers would attempt to force the release of incarcerated church members McCain and Collins.

Reverend Thomas appeared to cooperate with law enforcement and told officers about the locations of more explosives, including a cache at the Palominas Public School. She insisted that the dynamite had been planted in the van by whites while its occupants were shopping. A few days after the explosion, Thomas traveled to Chicago to raise money. She was more than $11,000 in arrears on paying the mortgage on the church's Miracle Valley property. Although members were supposed to contribute $100 a week to the church, most of them were out of work and had seen their life savings disappear into the church coffers. Relatives in Chicago advised their Miracle Valley Church kin to pack their bags and come home.

After removing the dynamite, Sheriff Judd had the unenviable task of assuring parents that the Palominas Public School was secure. During a bitter diatribe at a parent–teacher meeting, parents cited cases when deputies had retreated from the attacking church members. Judd responded, "This is not get-your-sheriff night. I am here to tell you it is safe to send your children to school today." Nevertheless, most of the parents did not believe him. James Melton's group of non-church members formed the Citizens for Equal Justice. They demanded that law and order be restored to Miracle Valley and accused Judd of not moving "vigorously" against lawbreaking black church members. In June, Stanley Hill and G. Severe Cole, representing the church, filed a $75 million federal civil-rights case against eight Cochise County officials, including Sheriff Judd.

On October 23, 1982, violence erupted when two deputies, backed by thirty-five other law-enforcement officials, attempted to serve a summons on a church member for a traffic violation. When the deputies refused to leave, church members attacked them with rocks and boards. The deputies did not draw their weapons until William Thomas Jr. raised a rifle. Deputy Sheriff Ray Thatcher ordered him to put his weapon down. When he refused, Thatcher opened fire and killed Thomas. When Arguster Tate tried to pick up Thomas's rifle, Thatcher shot and killed him. Church members claimed that Tate and Thomas were shot in the back, although autopsy reports refuted this accusation. William Thomas Jr., the eldest son of the minister, was the father of five children, and Arguster Tate was his father-in-law. After the shootings, several church members joined the fracas and Reverend Thomas drove her car into the middle of the mob.

Finger-Pointing and Settlement

Thomas's daughter called the *Chicago Sun Times* and insisted that the deputies came in and shot people down like dogs. More than one hundred law-enforcement officers from various agencies converged on Cochise County to aid the sheriff—including the Pima County Sheriff's Office, the Department of Public Safety, and the U.S. Border Patrol and Customs Service. Governor Babbitt's spokesman said the governor had no plans to become involved.

On November 11, 1982, the charismatic Reverend Jesse Jackson, accompanied by two Chicago attorneys, arrived in Miracle Valley to conduct a fact-finding mission and to serve as a peacemaker. Jackson started a campaign to raise legal defense funds for the nine men and one woman of the "Miracle Valley 10," as they came to be known. The accused were each held on thirty-seven felony charges stemming from the October shoot-out with Cochise County sheriff's deputies.

Captain Harold Hurtt, the black officer from the Phoenix Police Department who had worked hard to establish harmony, harbored no illusions that further efforts at mediation would serve any useful purpose. White non-church members were advocating, "Move them out or kill them all." Jackson insisted that the $7,500 allowed by Cochise County to defend the accused was far too little. And he pointed out that as long as the ten defendants stayed in jail, they would drain the Cochise County coffers.

After the shooting, Thomas and most of her church members returned to Chicago for the funerals, but the Miracle Valley 10 remained in jail. Jackson also interviewed and listened to the Miracle Valley whites, who complained of the church's belligerence and armed patrols. He described the law-enforcement actions as overly aggressive and concluded that Sheriff Judd had not used proper methods for crowd dispersal.

In November 1982, Superior Court Judge Matthew W. Borowiec ordered a change of venue for the trial of the Miracle Valley 10. All of the defendants were removed from the Cochise County Jail in Bisbee to the Pima County Jail in Tucson. The judge refused to reinstate the Chicago attorneys, whom he had charged with a violation of ethics. He claimed that they made improper comments by referring to the deaths of the church members as assassinations. Borowiec also removed himself as judge, because he questioned his ability to sit as a fair and impartial jurist in the case.

As the court's investigation progressed, defense attorneys tried to show law-enforcement persecution of a black minority church, creating an atmosphere of fear and terror in Miracle Valley. The defense team also unsuccessfully attempted to prove that the members were victims of a police riot of such a magnitude as to constitute justification of all of their actions. In the end, however, the federal grand jury declined to indict either the Miracle Valley 10 or Sheriff Judd and his deputies.

In June 1985, Cochise County and church officials reached a $500,000 out-of-court settlement in the $75 million civil-rights suit. In 1987, twenty-six members of the Christ Miracle Healing Center and Church sued Reverend Frances Thomas for more than $2 million. The lawsuit, filed in Chicago, claimed that Thomas defrauded her parishioners by using their money to purchase the Miracle Valley property, which she put in her name only. Thomas countered that the plaintiffs had no right to the money because they had abandoned the church. The plaintiffs included the widows of the two slain church members (including Reverend Thomas's own daughter-in-law). A former church member, Julius Gillespie, maintained that Thomas had been responsible for many of the conflicts with the officers and white residents of Miracle Valley. This lawsuit was later dropped.

In retrospect, both Cochise County Sheriff Jimmy V. Judd and Mohave County Sheriff Frank Porter were confronted with religious organizations that felt that they were above the laws of the land. Even so, both sheriffs had to protect the constitutional rights of these groups. Unfortunately, in each of these celebrated cases, it would appear that group members broke Arizona state laws under what they considered their religious rights. At the same time, the two religious organizations gained a considerable amount of public sympathy by pointing to an "excessive" show of force on the part of sheriffs and other law-enforcement agencies. Then the county judges and state courts, somewhat curiously, were not too helpful to law enforcement in the attempted resolution of both cases, failing to penalize most of the lawbreakers by calling draws in deference to sympathetic public opinion. Finally, the mesmerizing quality of the messages offered by leaders of both churches swayed many minds for many years—until they ran afoul of their membership and the public through their own illegal actions.

Mohave County Sheriff Frank Porter.

CHAPTER 10.
Young Criminals Present New Challenge

Maricopa County Sheriff Thomas Agnos.

When Arizona's Maricopa County Sheriff's Office responded to a 911 call on that sweltering morning of August 10, 1991, they were unprepared for the gruesome sight inside the Wat Promkunaram Buddhist temple west of Phoenix. Nine people—including six monks, one acolyte, one temple helper, and a seventy-five-year-old nun, all clad in saffron robes—lay facedown, drenched in pools of blood. After the murderers sprayed the Buddhists with shotgun pellets, they had systematically shot each victim through the head with a rifle. Some bodies formed a rough semicircle, with their heads pointed toward the center and their hands clasped over their heads in an attitude of prayer. The word "bloods" had been carved into a hallway wall.

Earlier that morning two Thai women, Chawee Borders and Primshat Hash, had gone to the temple to bring flowers for the Buddha and meals for the monks. When

Borders discovered the victims' bodies, she picked up the telephone to call for help. When they discovered that the telephone line had been cut, the women fled to a nearby home, where they called 911.

Maricopa County Sheriff Thomas Agnos, recently recovered from open-heart surgery, was already putting in long hours on the job. He had taken over an office that had been criticized as incompetent, amid allegations that former sheriff Richard Godbehere had staged drug busts. Agnos had run for sheriff because he wanted to give the sheriff's office "a sense of unity and direction."

A Divisive Investigation

By virtue of the position, the county attorney serves as legal advisor to the sheriff. Most of the time, Arizona county attorneys and Arizona county sheriffs cooperate with each other in a joint effort to produce satisfactory investigation and prosecution of criminal cases. The botched investigation of what became known as the "Buddhist temple murders," however, would pit Maricopa County Attorney Rick Romley against Maricopa County Sheriff Agnos. Although both men worked hard to maintain a professional demeanor during the debacle, the public could not help but see that they were often in disagreement over the investigation of the murders. With time, the divisiveness became even more apparent.

The case, which included false arrests and accusations of coerced confessions, ultimately contributed to Agnos's election loss in 1992. By the time he left office, Agnos and the Maricopa County Sheriff's Office would face a barrage of lawsuits totaling millions of dollars. Moreover, later investigations would show that if the Maricopa County Sheriff's Office had conducted a more careful investigation, it might also have prevented the unrelated murder of Alice Cameron.

The Buddhist temple murders would also focus national attention on the frightening growth of violent juvenile crimes. The largest mass murder in Arizona's history had been committed by teenagers, with the cold premeditation of hardened adult criminals

The Maricopa County Sheriff's Office, the second-largest law enforcement agency in Arizona (after the Arizona Department of Public Safety), has a special division that deals with juvenile crimes. In 1990, the sheriff's office employed over 1,700 people and operated with an annual budget of approximately $86 million. Criminal cases occupied about 70 percent of the sheriff's office workload, and the rest of the time was spent on civil cases.

Agnos, a twenty-six-year veteran Phoenix police officer, had worked his way up from patrol officer to assistant chief of the Criminal Investigation Division in the police department. At the same time, he attended Arizona State University at night,

JUVENILES BECOME ADULTS IN MURDER CASES

By definition a juvenile is a person under eighteen years of age. Technically, a juvenile suspected of a crime is "detained," but not arrested. Whereas adults are charged with crimes, officers file police reports and prosecutors file complaints alleging delinquent conduct against juveniles. A juvenile accused of a crime has the same rights as an adult, except the right to bail and a jury trial. In Arizona, the county attorney must prosecute the juvenile as an adult if the juvenile is fifteen, sixteen, or seventeen years of age and is accused of first-degree or second-degree murder.

and at the age of forty-one, received a bachelor of science degree in political science. When the temple murders made national and international headlines, Agnos came under national and international political pressure to solve the case.

Media reporters and government officials from London and Bangkok bombarded the sheriff's office with telephone inquiries; before long, many of these same officials arrived in Arizona. President George H. W. Bush sent condolences to the people of Thailand. The Thai people started a campaign to raise $44,000 to send the bodies of the victims back to Thailand for proper Buddhist cremation. Thailand's royal ambassador to the United States, Birabhongse Kasemsri, visited Phoenix twice to press for a speedy investigation.

The Wat Promkunaram temple had been started by Thai, Laotian, Cambodian, and American Buddhists in 1983, at first meeting in a temporary temple. Two years later the temple board of directors bought a piece of land near Waddell, Arizona, where the permanent temple was constructed. Immediately after the temple murders, the Council of Thai Bhikkus in the United States appointed monks to take over the administration of Wat Promkunaram temple.

Rumors ran rampant as to the motive for the crime. Many people were bewildered at what might have precipitated this slaughter of a religious group, whose teachers taught that through Buddhism one found inner peace by meditating. Some people speculated that the temple might have been a distribution center for heroin. Others thought that robbers might have sought the gold purported to be concealed in the temple. People in Thailand, who believed the murders were a consequence of racial or hate crimes, demonstrated in front of the U.S. embassy in Bangkok. Arizona already had a black mark for poor racial relations for its long refusal to recognize a Martin Luther King holiday (although Congress enacted the holiday in 1983, it was not approved in Arizona until 1992).

The Investigative Team

Agnos put a large portion of his staff, known as the Maricopa County Major Crimes Task Force, on this one case. Captain Jerry White served as task-force commander, while Sergeant Russ Kimball coordinated various aspects of the investigation. Patrol officers were taken off the street to answer the ever-ringing telephones. Duane Brady, public-information officer, set up a reward fund and fielded hundreds of inquiries. Surplus funds in the Maricopa County Sheriff's Office were diverted to this task force, for the purchase of computers, copiers, and office furniture.

At the end of the first week, Sheriff Agnos expressed disappointment that the task force had not yet solved the temple murders. Outside forces pressured him to release the temple so that its carpet could be cleaned and the Buddhists could observe proper religious ceremonies. By the end of August the task force was no closer to solving the case, despite the large assignment of manpower. At this point, many investigators believed the crime to be drug-related. In March, two men had been arrested in Hong Kong for allegedly attempting to smuggle heroin into the United States in Buddha statues. According to the Drug Enforcement Agency (DEA), monks traveling to certain temples would carry heroin into the United States—but investigators could find no evidence of drugs anywhere in the Phoenix temple.

An international liaison team opened up communications to Thailand in an effort to contact relatives. The sheriff's task force often worked as long as twenty hours, slept for two hours, and then went back to work again. Tempers exploded, and the super effort produced more chaos than resolution.

Before long, the task force involved ten agencies. The FBI and DEA (Drug Enforcement Administration) each loaned two agents to the task force. The Immigration and Naturalization Service in Los Angeles sent a Thai interpreter. The U.S. State Department sent three officers. The Phoenix Police Department loaned three officers, including an Asian gangs specialist. The Arizona Department of Public Safety, the Air Force Office of Special Investigations (OSI), the Scottsdale Police Department, the Tucson Police Department, and the Pima County Sheriff's Department also all participated at some point in the investigation.

The Air Force OSI formed its own task force and began checking out Thai families on Luke Air Force Base. On August 19, Air Force police stopped a car on base carrying Jonathan Doody and Rolando David Caratachea (both age seventeen) for suspicious behavior. The officers noted a partially concealed .22-caliber rifle in the back seat and reported this information to task force detective Richard Sinsabaugh. Because the rifle was not fully concealed, which would have been against the law, the youths were released.

The next day the Air Force police stopped the same car and saw the rifle again. They gave this information to the Maricopa County Sheriff's Office on September 10, but several more days passed before sheriff's deputies confiscated the rifle. Caratachea's .22-Marlin rifle—which did indeed turn out to be the final murder weapon—then languished for six weeks in the testing process. Meanwhile detectives focused on a hot tip that had just come in from Tucson.

The Tucson Tangent

On September 10, Tucson police informed the Maricopa County Sheriff's Office that they had received a tip from a patient in the Tucson Psychiatric Institute. This man, who had identified himself only as "John," told the officers that he felt guilty and suicidal about having participated in the temple murders. "John" offered to snitch on another accomplice, Kelsey Lawrence. "John" was Michael Lawrence McGraw (age twenty-four), who had a long history of psychiatric disorders and had previously led the Tucson police on a wild-goose chase involving drug activity.

The Tucson police questioned McGraw in the Tucson Psychiatric Institute. McGraw allegedly mentioned the word "bloods" on the wall. Supposedly this information had not leaked out, and thus McGraw seemed to have uncommon knowledge of the crime. McGraw told the police that he waited outside in the getaway car, while several others from Tucson and Phoenix went inside and robbed the temple.

Department of Public Safety officer Larry Troutt and Maricopa County Sheriff's Deputy Don Griffiths drove to Tucson to pick up McGraw. The hospital director warned the officers about McGraw's suicidal tendencies before giving them permission to remove him from the institution. En route to Phoenix, the officers read McGraw his Miranda rights and arrested him.

McGraw told his story again to sheriff's deputies. He claimed that he had gone to Phoenix to serve as a lookout while Victor Zarate (age twenty-eight), Mark Nuñez (nineteen), Dante Parker (twenty), and Leo Valdez Bruce (twenty-eight) killed the nine Buddhists and robbed the temple. McGraw explained that he had admitted himself to the mental institution because of his guilt over the slayings.

Baffled Tucson police officers could not find Kelsey Lawrence. When confronted with this complication, McGraw finally admitted that he was both "John" and Kelsey Lawrence. He continued to insist that he had participated in the temple murders. On September 11, Agnos's task force arrested Bruce, Zarate, Parker, and Nuñez, who became known as the Tucson Four, for probable cause. On September 17, Victor Zarate was released after videotapes showed that he had been in Tucson on August 9 during the time of the murders, but the others were detained.

The Phoenix task force wanted a "soft raid," wherein officers would knock on doors, present their warrants, tell the residents that they were going to search the house, and then politely request that the suspect come to headquarters for questioning. However, this area came under the jurisdiction of the Tucson Police Department, and they decided to raid the southside homes SWAT-style, by kicking in doors, hand-cuffing the suspects, and then spiriting them away to Phoenix.

Two days later at a press conference, Sheriff Agnos, in the presence of the Thai ambassador, Birabhongse Kasemsri, proudly announced the arrests of Michael McGraw, Mark Nuñez, Dante Parker, and Leo Bruce. Referring to a weapon confiscated from Bruce's home, the sheriff asserted that the temple murder weapon had been recovered, although ballistics subsequently proved that it was not the rifle used in the temple slayings.

Upon their arrests, all of the suspects were read their rights. Under the Miranda ruling, any law-enforcement officer making an arrest must warn suspects that they have the right to counsel, they have the right to remain silent, and that anything they say can and will be used against them. However, suspects are often questioned extensively before they are charged with a crime. Technically they are "free" during this time. Detectives, working in shifts, subjected each of the Tucson suspects to intensive grilling over long periods of time. None of the suspects had counsel during these interrogations. Finally, exhausted and frightened, Nuñez, Bruce, and Parker confessed to the murders. Parker went so far as to admit that the monks had resisted the invasion. Zarate always maintained his innocence.

Before long, detectives noticed that something was very much amiss with the Tucson Four confessions. The suspects confessed to using the wrong weapons and the wrong vehicles. Often, they merely parroted details of the murder that they had been fed by the detectives. After twenty-one hours of questioning, Bruce, who did not have a criminal record, confessed to killing all nine persons. The next day he retracted his confession.

Three secret grand juries felt that they had heard enough evidence to indict Bruce, Nuñez, and McGraw. Parker's grand jury hearing was held in open court so that the public could determine the strength of the case against the Tucson Four, and ultimately Parker was also ordered to stand trial. The day after the Tucson Four were booked into jail, McGraw admitted to reporters that he had falsely accused the others and that they were all innocent.

Romelia Duarte, Mark Nuñez's mother, picketed the Tucson courthouse and demanded that Sheriff Agnos release her son. Families and friends of the Tucson Four staged rallies protesting their innocence and accusing the Maricopa County Sheriff's Department of obtaining the confessions by threats. Confessions induced through fear of personal injury or an expectation of personal benefit are not admissible as court evidence. Sheriff Agnos admitted that the Tucson Four suspects had been threatened with the gas chamber if they did not help with the investigation, but he said it was just to show them what might happen if they did not cooperate. The sheriff regretted that a deputy had told one suspect that he would not look good in a lake with an anchor tied around his neck. When Maricopa County Attorney Rick Romley insisted on transcripts of the interrogations, he discovered that the tapes were of poor quality and unintelligible. Romley and his staff met with Agnos, and the angry county attorney protested that his office had not been involved from the beginning.

Romley, an Arizona native son, had graduated from Arizona State University law school and served with the U.S. Marine Corps in Vietnam. He had just finished handling the AZSCAM scandal—in which seven state lawmakers were indicted on corruption charges—which had catapulted Arizona into unfavorable national headlines. In the 1990s, the Maricopa County Attorney's Office operated on a $40 million-per-annum budget, with a staff of six hundred, including three hundred deputy county attorneys. Romley's diversion program for first-time drug offenders—Do Drugs, Do Time—was selected as a national model in the president's War on Drugs. Now he had to deal with a botched murder investigation, wherein wrongful arrests might make it more difficult to prosecute the real murderers. On September 30, McGraw, Bruce, and Nuñez pleaded "not guilty" to all charges. On October 3, Dante Parker pleaded "not guilty" after a judge ruled that probable cause existed to try him for robbery and murder.

Dissension within the Maricopa County Sheriff's Office emerged between the two camps of those who believed in the Tucson link and those who did not. Several investigators resented the high-handed manner of Chief Deputy George Leese, whom Agnos had brought in over more experienced sheriff's deputies. Early in the investigation, Romley worried about Leese's methods and accused him of bungling the case.

With the unfavorable press and accusations of forced confessions by the Tucson Four, Sheriff Agnos appointed Deputy John Coppock to replace George Leese. Agnos hoped that Coppock would be able to lead the task force and salvage the investigation. When Sergeant Mark Mullavey expressed an opinion to Coppock that the Tucson Four might not be involved with the case, he was escorted off the case because his belief in the innocence of the Tucson men could poison the investigation.

Anyone who disagreed with Agnos's premise of a Tucson link felt threatened with removal from the case. Paranoia swept through the Maricopa County Sheriff's Office. When investigators expressed fear that their reports might be altered, Sergeant Kimball told them to keep their own set of reports.

Results from Ballistics

On October 24, while testing firearms, officers of the Arizona Department of Public Safety matched the Marlin .22-caliber semiautomatic rifle, which had been seized from Doody and Caratachea, to shell casings found at the temple. That same day, deputies traveled to Colorado and interrogated Jonathan Doody's stepfather, Brian, and his younger brother, David, a former temple acolyte. Investigators thought David, who had lived in the temple for several weeks, might have uncommon knowledge of temple items and the temple arrangement. He might also know if any temple items were missing. According to David, the monks had a safe that held about $2,000. He also asserted that each monk carried rolls of money, and that he had held what he believed to be a solid gold Buddha statue belonging to the head monk.

Jonathan, born in Thailand, had been adopted by his American stepfather, who had married Jonathan's Thai mother. The younger David moved to Colorado when their father was transferred from Luke Air Force Base, but seventeen-year-old Jonathan stayed with Alessandro Garcia's family in Arizona. Both youths attended Agua Fria High School, where Jonathan's favorite class was Junior ROTC. Jonathan, who spoke English with an accent, did fairly well in high school. Military arms and uniforms fascinated him.

With the ballistics information on Caratachea's rifle, investigation efforts concentrated on the new suspects, Rolando Caratachea, Jonathan Doody, and their friend Alessandro "Alex" Garcia, all members of a gang known as the AM Posse. The name came from their penchant for wreaking mayhem during the early-morning hours. Caratachea, the leader, called himself Shakespeare. Yet Agnos remained adamant that efforts concentrate on finding a link with the Tucson Four, who were still in the Maricopa County Jail.

On October 25, Rolando Caratachea was arrested without incident for other unrelated offenses, including burglary and theft. After several hours of intense grilling, with his mother present, he screamed that he was innocent of the murders. He insisted that he had just loaned the rifle to Doody and Garcia.

Deputies picked up Doody at the high school and brought him to headquarters in his ROTC uniform. Doody nervously twisted his beret, while officers read his Miranda rights. He agreed to talk without a lawyer or his parents present. Doody denied the temple murders and claimed that he and Garcia had simply borrowed the rifle to test their home-made silencers.

In the early hours of October 26, officers picked up Alex Garcia at his home. Garcia's father agreed to let them take his son to headquarters for questioning. After reading him his Miranda rights, investigators grilled him. Garcia arrogantly denied the murders, but he corroborated Doody's statement that they had borrowed the rifle to test silencers made out of potatoes and pop bottles.

About 3:30 a.m. this same morning, Doody broke down and confessed that he, Garcia, Caratachea, and five or six other Phoenix youths had assembled at the Agua Fria River on August 9 to carry out the temple robbery. He snitched on Garcia and Caratachea, but said he did not know how many others were in the temple or who had pulled the trigger. Doody said that it was a robbery gone wrong and that they just wanted to see if they could beat the temple's alarm system.

Through thin walls, Garcia heard Doody confess to the murders, and he decided that he would not take all the blame. Garcia said that Doody fired the rifle, and Garcia fired the shotgun. When a monk recognized one of them, Doody stood on the sofa and systematically fired his rifle into the victims' heads. (They had already been sprayed with shotgun pellets by Garcia.) Garcia also provided uncommon knowledge, such as where the nun's dentures were located. Garcia said Doody had started planning the robbery several months earlier when he and his Buddhist mother visited his brother, David, in the temple.

Garcia exonerated the Tucson Four and admitted that just he and Jonathan Doody had been at the temple on the night of the murder. County Attorney Romley, who was listening from another room, knew then that they had the wrong suspects in jail. The Maricopa County sheriff's commanders ordered the interrogators to get tough with Garcia in an effort to make him confess to a link with the Tucson Four. They did, but he denied the link.

Doody implicated another acquaintance, George Gonzalez, and Rolando Caratachea as accomplices. Gonzalez went free for lack of evidence, but officers detained Caratachea on unrelated theft charges. Eventually he was cleared of any participation in the murders. Investigators swooped down on the Garcia house, where they found a Stevens shotgun and several items including cameras and stereos belonging to the temple. Ballistics connected the shotgun with casings and pellets found in the temple. Detectives also matched Garcia's military boots with a shoe print from the crime scene.

Romley gave Agnos a two-week deadline to provide evidence to charge the Tucson Four. Captain Jerry White reportedly urged Garcia's father to make his son confess to the Tucson Four's involvement, implying that otherwise Alex would go to the gas chamber. One indication that Sheriff Agnos's case was unraveling appeared when the sheriff met with Thai community members. Local media were barred from the meeting, but a Los Angeles Thai newspaper reporter surreptitiously made an audio tape, in which Agnos said, "There are some bits and pieces that indicated that these guys probably were connected, but didn't know one another, but it is not evidence we can take into court."

Despite Agnos's insistence, many investigators realized that the Tucson men were not involved. On November 22, 1991, Romley, over Agnos's opposition, dropped all charges against Dante Parker, Leo Valdez Bruce, Michael Lawrence McGraw, and Mark Felix Nuñez. He dismissed the charges without prejudice, meaning that the men could be arrested later if new evidence turned up. Romley contended that the moral issue was that people cannot be held in jail while authorities operate in hopes of gathering evidence.

Maricopa County Attorney Richard Romley.

At this point, several investigators publicly voiced their anger with Romley. DPS detective Ritchie Martinez said that the investigation lost momentum because the rug had been pulled from under it. Russ Kimball accused Romley of lying when the county attorney said that he had read the transcripts of the Tucson Four interrogations. The detectives claimed that Romley ignored investigative leads and followed a politically safe course because of the public outcry. Romley also met strong pressure from two of his top prosecutors, K. C. Skull and Myrna Parker, who did not want the Tucson Four released.

Nuñez and Bruce were greeted with hugs and cheers from families and friends as they left the Maricopa County Jail. McGraw avoided the crowds and left through another exit. The sheriff's office detained Parker for extradition to California, for parole violation.

Agnos, who refused to give up on the Tucson Four link, faced reelection in 1992. He formed an advisory panel to intercede on his behalf with Governor Fife Symington. Former U.S. Attorney Melvin McDonald chaired the panel, which included criminal attorney Jeremy Toles, former Phoenix Police Chief Ruben Ortega, former FBI agent Bud Gaskill, and Bernard Garmire, former police chief from Tucson, Arizona, and Miami, Florida.

The panel asked Symington to remove Romley from the case. They proposed that the governor give Agnos a sixty-day extension to find a Tucson Four link. They also asked him to assign a special prosecutor, or turn the case over to Attorney General Grant Woods. Symington agreed to study the proposals, but ultimately both Symington and Woods declined to get involved.

In July 1992, Agnos met with McGraw in Colorado, and again McGraw incriminated himself and the Tucson Four in the temple murders. Upon his return to Phoenix, the sheriff sent investigators on a wild-goose chase to a rest area on Interstate 10 and to Tucson's "A" Mountain area to search for shell casings that McGraw said had been buried in these locations.

On August 4, attorneys for Bruce, Zarate, and Nuñez filed suit in Pima County Superior Court, claiming that their civil rights had been violated. (Meanwhile, Doody's attorney, Peter Balkin, asked the judge to appoint a mental-health expert to review the tapes of Doody's confession. Balkin wanted to determine if Doody had the "ability to give truthful and rational answers to questions" after a "brutal" and "gruesome" fourteen-hour interrogation by sheriff's deputies.)

On the first anniversary of the temple murders (August 10, 1992), Agnos still wanted to file charges against Dante Parker. Agnos claimed that Parker had an earring that matched the description of one worn by the slain nun and that Parker implicated himself by describing a spiral-designed ring worn by the nun. Romley, however, said that Parker's description of the ring was not similar to the nun's ring. Also, deputies had seized a Buddha-like figurine from Zarate's home, and according to Agnos, a woman had recognized the Buddha as belonging to one of the dead monks. But according to the county attorney, Thai community members had said that the sheriff's deputies misinterpreted the woman's statements, and that she had not recognized the Buddha figurine.

Publicly, Agnos insisted, "We have solved the case. It's just a matter of rounding up all the players." In November, Agnos lost his reelection bid, but Romley won a second term. The new Maricopa County Sheriff, Joseph Arpaio, who took office January 1, 1993, promised to restore the office's tarnished image with an internal investigation into interrogation techniques.

Bargains and Confessions

On February 6, 1992, a Maricopa County Juvenile Court judge ruled that Jonathan Doody, age seventeen at the time of the murders, should be tried as an adult. On March 14, a judge ruled that Alex Garcia, age sixteen at the time of the murders, would also stand trial as an adult.

Garcia pleaded guilty to the temple murders and plea-bargained to save his life by agreeing to testify against Doody. A clause stipulated that Garcia's plea bargain could be rescinded if authorities found that he was guilty of crimes that he had not admitted. In January 1993, while his attorneys were trying to get a plea bargain by having him testify against Doody, Garcia admitted to yet another murder. Garcia confessed that he and his girlfriend, Michelle Hoover (age fourteen), had murdered Alice Marie Cameron at a Verde River-area campground on October 18, 1991.

Upon being picked up for questioning, Hoover said she committed murder when Garcia asked her to prove her love for him by killing Cameron. After Hoover shot Cameron in the back, Garcia and Hoover muffled the dying woman's cries for help for almost an hour. Then they robbed her of her billfold. Hoover pleaded guilty to second-degree murder and was sentenced to fifteen years in prison.

Had Garcia been arrested right after the temple murders on evidence of ballistics tests on Caratachea's rifle, Alice Cameron might still be alive. The Cameron case had also not been handled all that well: Had investigators checked at Cameron's bank, they would have found photographs of Garcia and Hoover attempting to use Cameron's credit card for cash at an automated teller machine. Once again the Maricopa County Sheriff's Office had earlier arrested and incarcerated the wrong man, George Peterson Jr., a transient diagnosed with dysthymic disorder, who suffered bouts of extreme depression and anxiety. A judge ruled that this innocent Vietnam veteran, who had by now spent sixteen months in jail, was competent to stand trial for the murder of Alice Cameron.

After he confessed to the Cameron murder, investigators got Garcia to describe the temple murders. Garcia said they drove to the temple in Doody's 1983 Ford Mustang about 10:00 p.m. Both he and Doody wore military camouflage pants and shirts, hoods, brown gloves, military boots, knives, and scarves over their faces. Doody and Garcia waited outside and talked about the robbery for about fifteen minutes. Garcia told the detectives that Doody had insisted, "We can't have no witnesses—just go and shoot everybody."

Then they burst into the temple and for about an hour Garcia and Doody took turns holding the Buddhists hostage at gunpoint, while plundering the temple of about $2,650 in currency, $140 in coins, and electronic equipment that they placed in two military bags. When they could not open the safe, they vented their frustration by shooting the Buddhists. Garcia confessed that he carved the word "bloods" on a wall. Garcia said, "He [Doody] went around and shot everybody in the back of the head to make sure they were dead."

In a maximum term possible under the plea bargain, Alessandro Garcia was sentenced to 271 years in prison for his part in the temple murders and the unrelated murder of Alice Cameron. His defense attorney, Luis Calvo, argued for leniency because Garcia's testimony had freed the Tucson Four and would help convict Doody. At the sentencing, Maricopa County Superior Court Judge Gregory Martin said, "It is the court's intent that he [Garcia] not be released from prison ever." Ironically, Garcia's sentence was only ten years less than that of Jonathan Doody.

As the star witness at Doody's trial, Garcia provided the most damaging testimony. In July 1993, a jury convicted Jonathan Doody of nine counts of first-degree murder, nine counts of armed robbery, one count of burglary, and one count of conspiracy to commit armed robbery. The Maricopa County Attorney's Office argued for the death penalty, but the judge reasoned that he could not order Doody's execution because he could not conclude beyond a reasonable doubt as to whether Doody or Garcia had pulled the trigger in the executions.

In a letter to the court, Thailand's royal ambassador to the United States, M. L. Birabhongse Kasemsri, said that there had been waves of emotional reaction to the massacre but that in Thailand revenge was not being sought. Buddhists in Thailand even sent emissaries to Phoenix to plead for Doody's life.

On September 7, 1996, the three-judge Arizona Court of Appeals, in a unanimous ruling, upheld Doody's conviction and his 281-year prison sentence for the Buddhist temple murders. Doody's lawyers, which included famous appeals attorneys Alan Dershowitz and his brother Nathan, argued that the jury should have suppressed Doody's confession, because the officers had coerced him to confess. The appellate court ruled that Doody had confessed voluntarily.

The Maricopa County Board of Supervisors approved a $2.8-million out-of-court settlement to resolve the lawsuits of the Tucson Four and a $1.1-million lawsuit on behalf of George Peterson Jr., who had been falsely charged in the murder of Alice Cameron. Nuñez and Bruce were paid $1.1 million each. Parker and Zarate each got $240,000. Romelia Duarte, the mother of Nuñez, got $120,000.

Many people wrung their hands over the youth of the perpetrators. However, sociologists have long known that most violent crimes have always been committed by males between the ages of sixteen and twenty-five. The propensity for violent crimes falls off exponentially after age twenty-five. Garcia's mother sadly approached the judge for leniency for her son. She said that he had been a shy, quiet child, and she could not understand why he had gone on this rampage. Like many parents, she had not learned to recognize criminal behavior in her own son. She could not accept the fact that her child was capable of committing multiple heinous murders.

Temple life at Wat Promkunaram goes on. The temple has increased security, with fenced grounds and an alarm system triggered by infrared motion sensors. The temple, once open to anyone twenty-four hours a day, is now closed at night. Photographs of the nine victims—Foi Sripanprasert, Phra Somsack Sopha, Phramaha Siang Gingaeo, Surichi Anuttaro, Chirasek Chirapong, Phra Pairuch Kan Thong, Matthew Miller, Phramaha Chalerm Chantapim, and Booncheay Chaiarach—along with the urns containing their ashes, are enshrined in front of the temple. After the murders, Phra Wichiendhammakunathan, who had served as head monk in the Los Angeles temple, arrived to take responsibility for Wat Promkunaram during its troubled times. Today the three-hundred-member congregation, consisting of Thais, Laotians, Cambodians, Vietnamese, and American Buddhists, continues to go about its work of teaching people to live in peace and harmony with the world, in a place once marred with brutality.

As a reflection on the near-incomprehensible changes encountered by Arizona sheriffs since they first rode the range in the 1860s, the Buddhist temple case clearly provides a powerful mirror. It shows that basic expectations remain the same, whereas the challenges of today's fast-paced society are almost entirely different.

Our sheriffs in the early decades might spend weeks on end away from their offices, leading posses in pursuit of notorious outlaws—usually veteran gunslingers who had earned their reputations over many years. In sharp contrast, our 2006-vintage sheriffs oversee innovative crime-prevention programs, administer personnel decisions, and make use of personal computers as well as technological breakthroughs such as state-of-the-art communications networks and automated fingerprint-matching machines. Meanwhile, the well-trained sheriff's deputies—detectives and patrol officers in late-model autos—pursue the most-wanted criminal suspects, more often than not little-known, psychotic teenagers whose sudden craving for wanton violence and notoriety results in dark headlines.

The tragic temple murders symbolized the reasons behind our latter-day sheriffs' big push for more parental involvement in the lives of children and more effective anti-drug efforts in our schools and communities. In the old days, far fewer residents voiced far fewer demands; sheriffs could pretty much maintain the peace simply by keeping robbers out of homes and gunmen off the streets.

Despite tremendous societal changes, some bedrock human values, good and bad, have stuck with Arizona's sheriffs. For example, the desire for justice always has motivated our lawmen in response to the public's outcry. On the other hand, that laudable desire occasionally has been sidetracked by sheriffs in an ill-fated "rush to judgment." Posses in bygone days, overeager to "get their man," once in a while wound up hanging the wrong suspect from the nearest tree, necessitating the sheriff's ouster when justice eventually prevailed. In the recent temple case, a Maricopa County sheriff's "rush" to implicate the "Tucson Four" from Pima County not only deterred justice but also resulted in costly lawsuit penalties, a divisive morale breach in the sheriff's department, and his failure to win reelection.

Happily, as the pages of *Arizona Sheriffs* have documented, the vast majority of these top lawmen, while perhaps not flawless, has consisted of good men and true (plus three women of like stature). Their personalities have covered a broad spectrum and their lengths of service have varied, yet their records of accomplishment have revealed an innate ability to adapt to changing laws (as well as times) and to produce commendable performances. And even the few tarnished badges, to their credit, have managed good deeds before the bad.

The trail has been long and winding, and our sheriffs have followed it well. The people of Arizona should be forever grateful.

The Last Full Measure—Killed
in the Line of Duty

1865—May 3. Yuma County Sheriff Cornelius Sage and two friends ambushed and killed by Yavapai Indians.

1871—September 20. Yuma County Sheriff James T. Dana killed by a Yuma Mojave Indian, Que-Cha-Co, while attempting to make an arrest.

1877—October 21. Yavapai County Deputy Sheriff George Spencer killed in an ambush between St. Johns and Springerville.

1880—Pima County Deputy Sheriff Milton McDowell shot at Charleston; died several years later as a direct result of these wounds.

1880—April. Apache County Deputy Sheriffs David Creaghe and James Richmond killed by Indians.

1881—October 17. Yavapai County Deputy Sheriff J. A. Bryant shot and killed by a man named Miller at Flagstaff while he attempted to make an arrest.

1882—May 26. Coconino County Deputy Sheriff John Snodgrass shot and fatally wounded by a bartender by the name of Hazel.

1882—July 5. Cochise County Deputy Sheriff "Kip" Phillips killed while attempting to arrest Filomino Orante for causing a disturbance in a Tombstone bar.

1883—December 8. Cochise County Deputy Sheriff D. J. Smith shot and killed during a holdup of the Goldwater-Castañeda store in Bisbee.

1885—June 10. Cochise County Deputy Sheriff William A. Daniels, who also served as a U.S. Customs Inspector, killed by Apaches.

1885—November 26. Cochise County Deputy Sheriff Casper Albert killed by Apaches at Galeyville.

1885—December 20. Yavapai County Deputy Sheriff John M. Murphy shot and killed by Dennis Dilda.

1887—February 6. Apache County Deputy Sheriff George Lockhart and two members of his posse killed by Navajos when the posse attempted to arrest them on charges of horse stealing.

1888—August 12. Cochise County Deputy Sheriff Cesario Lucero shot by members of Geronimo Baltierez's gang of train robbers and murderers.

1888—December 3. Graham County Sheriff Benjamin Crawford and two other men killed by Apaches near Solomonville.

1889—November 2. Gila County Sheriff Glenn Reynolds and Deputy William "Hunky-dory" Holmes killed by Apache prisoners while transporting them to Yuma Territorial Prison.

1890—June 1. Gila County Sheriff Jerry Ryan drowned while trying to rescue a young woman who had fallen into Pasco Pond near Wheatfields.

1893—December 21. Apache County Deputy Sheriff Ed Wright shot by Juan Garcia while he attempted to arrest Garcia.

1896—August 12. Cochise County Deputy Sheriff Frank P. Robson shot while serving as a member of a posse in pursuit of the Black Jack Ketchum gang.

1899—Cochise County Deputy Sheriff and Pearce Constable Chauncy "Chet" F. Ainsworth shot and killed while attempting to arrest the Haldiman brothers, Tom and Bill, for cattle rustling.

1899—Coconino County Deputy Sheriff William Montgomery shot by Navajos while serving on a posse and attempting to arrest the Navajos for poaching deer.

1900—March 27. Apache County Sheriff's Deputies Frank LeSueur and Gus Gibbons murdered by unnamed desperados while serving on a posse.

1901—January 8. Yuma County Undersheriff Matthew E. DeVane shot and killed while attempting to arrest Thomas Hart for the theft of a case of whiskey from a Yuma saloon.

1901—October. Arizona Ranger Carlos Tafolla and Apache County Deputy Sheriff William Maxwell shot and killed during a fight with the Bill Smith gang on Reservation Creek in northern Graham County.

1902—Yavapai County Deputy Sheriff Joe Hawkins killed at Jerome by two local toughs named Crocker and Chew.

1903—May 16. Cochise County Deputy Sheriff Tom Vaughn killed in a gunfight at Douglas.

1904—February 9. Cochise County Deputy Sheriff (who was also former Graham County Sheriff) Arthur Wight shot and killed while trying to prevent a mob from freeing a prisoner at the Black Diamond Mine in the Dragoon Mountains.

1908—January 10. Gila County Deputy Sheriff Charles Edwards shot and killed by John Cline about twelve miles north of Roosevelt.

1908—July 17. Coconino County Deputy Sheriff Escapula Dominguez shot and killed by bartender James Duncan at the Fred Harvey House in Williams.

1908—December 15. Pima County Deputy Sheriff Riley Bennett stabbed and shot by Ramon Mendoza and Mendoza's son when he attempted to mediate in a wage dispute at the Berkelow Ranch near Redington.

1911—May. Pinal County Deputy Sheriff E. L. Drew shot and killed in a saloon near Ray, Arizona.

1912—September 23. Greenlee County Deputy Sheriffs Alberto Mungia and Jack Campbell shot and killed in ambush by Eusebio Arviso along Eagle Creek, about twelve miles from Morenci.

1913—January 20. Pima County Deputy Sheriff Joe Meek shot and killed by Calistro Villareal, after the deputy tried to quell a disturbance in an Ajo saloon.

1913—August 12. Cochise County Deputy Ed Miller shot and killed by U. D. Richart in a dispute over the location of a telephone pole.

1914—August 20. Pinal County Deputy Sheriff Phineas Brown murdered by horse thieves near Ray, Arizona.

1914—November 5. Pinal County Deputy Sheriff and Railroad Special Agent John C. Power shot and killed by a roustabout from a circus train.

1917—July 12. Cochise County Special Deputy Sheriff Orson P. McRae killed during the infamous Bisbee Deportation.

1918—February 10. Graham County Sheriff Robert Franklin McBride and his deputies Kane Wootan and Martin Kempton killed in the Power shoot-out.

1918—April 9. Gila County Deputy Sheriff John Franks shot and killed at Christmas, Arizona, while attempting to arrest Augustine Sanchez.

1918—May 13. Pinal County Deputy Sheriff Joe Donelson shot and killed by a Mexican arrested for bootlegging in Sonora, Arizona.

1918—July 16. Special agent and Yavapai County Deputy Sheriff James Lowry shot and killed by Porfirio Hernandez at the United Verde Mine in Jerome.

1921—July 8. Yavapai County Undersheriff Edward F. Bowers shot and killed by a drunk, Frank George.

1922—April 9. Maricopa County Deputy Sheriff Almon W. Dana killed in a collision with motorcycle officer Frank Bell while in pursuit of a speeder. Bell seriously injured.

1922—July 13. Santa Cruz County Sheriff George White killed in an automobile accident while transporting prisoners to the state prison at Florence. Deputy Leonard A. Smith died July 17 from his injuries.

1927—August 13. Pinal County Deputy Sheriff William Conoley shot and killed during a domestic-violence incident in Casa Grande.

1928—October 23. Pima County Deputy Sheriff Clifford Nelson killed in an airplane crash in the Santa Catalina Mountains while on a search-and-rescue mission.

1930—January 28. Maricopa County Deputy Sheriff Lee Wright killed by Pennsylvania fugitives in a gunfight near Chandler.

1932—June 16. Cochise County Sheriff Fred Kenney killed in an automobile crash near Las Cruces, New Mexico, while picking up prisoners from El Paso, Texas.

1937—July 21. Maricopa County Deputy Sheriff Edward J. Roberts killed by Jose Castellano, who was high on drugs and shooting randomly in a cotton camp west of Litchfield Park.

1938—June 8. Pinal County Deputy Sheriff Jack Hickox shot to death at Ray, Arizona, during a prison break.

1942—February 28. Apache County Sheriff John Nunn killed while attempting to hold back a crowd from a butane-tanker explosion in St. Johns. Nunn was struck by a piece of metal blown off the truck.

1946—September 13. Gila County Deputy Sheriff Mitchell Smith killed in a motorcycle crash.

1948. January 24. Yuma County Deputy Sheriff Sylvestre Villa shot while tracking a burglary suspect.

1948—February 3. Yuma County Deputy Sheriff Walter Akers shot by a drunk in Parker.

1948—August 3. Pinal County Deputy Sheriff Edward Smith killed in Eloy by Willis Bishop, who had escaped from the Pinal County Jail.

1948—August 9. Pima County Deputy Sheriff John D. Anderson killed in a fall while rescuing a stranded hiker in the Santa Catalina Mountains.

1951—January 8. Maricopa County Deputy Sheriff Burtice W. Wickstrum killed in a three-car collision.

1953—November 17. Pima County Deputy Sheriff Jack Russell Brierly killed in an automobile accident.

1955—May 14. Pinal County Deputy Sheriff Carlos Escamilla shot while trying to settle a bar fight.

1957—October 6. Maricopa County Deputy Sheriff Gerald Barnes killed in an airplane crash on a search mission. Two other deputies injured.

1963—October 21. Mohave County Sheriff Robert M. Tarr shot by fleeing car thieves near Coyote Holes on Route 93.

1965—August 31. Maricopa County Deputy Sheriff Robert Dorn shot by occupants of a vehicle he had stopped for a traffic violation.

1969—December 7. Cochise County Deputy Sheriff Leroy Brown shot and killed by Andreas Griego in a restaurant near Bowie. Brown had previously arrested Griego.

1969—December 30. Mohave County Deputy Sheriff Bobbie Ray Walker suffered a heart attack during a hand-to-hand fight with three teenagers suspected of DUI.

1971—January 18. Maricopa County Deputy Sheriffs Warren LaRue and Rex Stone shot while serving a writ of attachment on a trailer. Stone's son, Phoenix Police Officer Dale Stone, had been killed in an accident while on duty December 28, 1970.

1972—June 13. Maricopa County Deputy Sheriff Ralph Butler killed in a collision with a tractor-trailer rig while en route to an accident.

1973—February 25. Pinal County Deputy Sheriff James M. Morgan killed in an airplane crash in the Superstition Mountains while searching for a lost hiker.

1973—September 3. Apache County Deputy Chief Delbert L. Berry shot by a member of the American Indian Movement (AIM) at the Lupton Trading Post.

1973—November 8. Mohave County Sheriff Deputies Lloyd D. Heilman and Frank E. Howard killed in a plane crash in the Cerbat Mountains while on a search mission.

1974—July 22. Mohave County Deputy Sheriff James M. Lewis shot to death during a domestic disturbance.

1978—March 1. Maricopa County Reserve Deputy Sheriff James L. Epp drowned while attempting to rescue two men whose car had gotten stuck in a flooded wash.

1982—September 6. Coconino County Volunteer Deputy Sheriff Dr. John B. Jamison shot to death east of Flagstaff.

1983—May 26. Coconino County Deputy Sheriff Michael Young killed in a gunfight at Fredonia.

1983—July 21. Pima County Deputy Ernest Calvillo shot and killed by a would-be robber while guarding motion picture equipment outside an Avra Valley bar.

1983—September 27. Cochise County Deputy Sheriff Jeffrey Brown was beaten during a jail riot and died eleven months later as a result of those injuries.

1985—May 13. Maricopa County Deputy Sheriff Darrell B. McCloud killed in an automobile accident.

1986—January 23. Pima County Deputy Sheriff Randall Graves killed in an on-duty undercover motorcycle accident.

1987—February 10. Mohave County Deputy Sheriff Steve Gariboy killed in a head-on collision with a car driven by Bullhead City policeman David Lee; Lee seriously injured. Both officers were in pursuit of a fleeing suspect.

1988—June 30. Maricopa County Deputy Sheriff Vernon P. Marconnet shot and killed at the northwestern end of South Mountain Park.

1989—January 2. Navajo County Deputy Sheriff Robert Varner shot three times by fleeing suspects on I-40 near Winslow; died two days later.

1994—September 2. Santa Cruz Deputy Sheriff Patrick Thompson killed when his car was broadsided a mile south of Patagonia on Route 42. Thompson had earlier received life-threatening injuries from gunshot wounds inflicted by an insane man in 1990.

1995—August 28. Maricopa County Deputy Sheriff Eduardo Gonzales killed in an automobile accident.

1995—September 28. Maricopa County Deputy Sheriff Kenneth Blair shot and killed while investigating a domestic disturbance.

1996—September 2. Navajo County Sheriff's Captain Charles Welch Lane, age 75, succumbed to injuries sustained three days earlier during a fall while searching for a lost child.

2001—May 4. Pinal County Deputy Sheriff Jason Patrick Lopez shot and killed while attempting to serve a warrant near Casa Grande.

2001—August 13. Yuma County Senior Deputy Sheriff Michael Benjamin Meyer killed in a single-vehicle accident while on patrol.

2002—August 24. Pinal County Deputy Sheriff Donald Mauldin succumbed to gunshot wounds to the head, received nine years earlier.

2005—August 10. Pima County Deputy Sheriff Timothy Graham and two others (a fleeing suspect and a helpful passerby) struck and killed by an automobile after scuffling on the median, then falling off into oncoming traffic on Ajo Road in Tucson.

Arizona Sheriffs by County

Apache County Sheriffs
Alejandro Peralta, 1879
Luther Martin, 1879–1880
Ebenezer S. Stover, 1881–1882
Tomas Perez, 1883–1884
J. Lorenzo Hubbell, 1885–1886
Commodore Perry Owens, 1887–
1888 (also served in Navajo
County)
St. George Creaghe, 1889–1890
A. B. (or O. B.) Little, 1891–1892
William R. Campbell, 1893–1894
James Scott, 1895–1896
W. W. Berry, 1897–1898
Edward Beeler, 1899–1900
Leandro Ortega, 1901–1902
Sylvester Peralta, 1903–1904
Dionicio Duran, 1905–1906
Sylvester Peralta, 1907–1914
Jacob Hamblin Jr., 1915–1916
E. W. Grimes, 1917–1918
Jacob Hamblin Jr., 1919
J. A. Mineer, 1920
John E. Eagar, 1921–1922
Marion O. Haws, 1923–1924
H. L. Butler, 1925–1926
Andrew Maxwell, 1927–1928
M. L. Hall, 1929–1930
Marion O. Haws, 1931–1934
A. Hartley Greenwood, 1935–1936
John Nunn, 1937–1942 (killed in the
line of duty)
Alma C. Naegle, 1942–1948
Harris Miller, 1949–1950

John T. Crosby, 1951–1954
Grant Hamblin, 1955
Emilio Garcia, 1956–1960
Edgar B. Merrill, 1961–1972
C. Arthur Lee, 1973–1999 (retired)
Brian R. Hounshell, 1999– (appointed
and reelected)

Cochise County Sheriffs
John Behan, 1881–1882 (also served in
Yavapai County)
J. L. Ward, 1883–1884
Robert Hatch, 1885–1886
"Texas" John Slaughter, 1887–1890
C. B. Kelton, 1891–1892
Scott White, 1893–1894
Camillus S. Fly, 1895–1896
Scott White, 1897–1900
Adelbert Lewis, 1901–1904
Stewart R. Hunt, 1905–1906
Jack White, 1907–1912
Harry Wheeler, 1912–1918
Guy Welch, 1918
J. F. McDonald, 1919–1920
J. E. Hood, 1921–1922
James McDonald, 1923–1926
George Henshaw, 1927–1930
Fred A. Kenney, 1931–1932 (killed in
the line of duty)
I. V. Pruitt, 1932
Tom Voelker, 1933–1934
I. V. Pruitt, 1935–1952
Jack Howard, 1953–1958
C. A. Stewart, 1959–1960

Phil Olander, 1961–1964
T. James Willson, 1965–1976
Jim V. Judd, 1977–1992
John Pintek, 1993–1996
Larry Dever, 1997–

Coconino County Sheriffs
Ralph H. Cameron, 1891
John W. Francis May, 1891–1892
J. J. "Sandy" Donahue, 1893–1894
Ralph H. Cameron, 1895–1897
Fletcher Fairchild, 1898–May 1899
   (removed from office after being
   declared insane)
James A. Johnson, 1899–1903
   (appointed)
Harry Henderson, 1904–1905
John W. Francis, 1906–1912
Tom Pulliam, 1912–1914
W. G. Dickinson, 1915–1918
John O. Harrington, 1919–1920
Bill Campbell, 1921–1924
John O. Parsons, 1925–1928
Jack Kester, 1929–1930
Art Vandevier, 1931–1940
J. Perry Francis, 1941–1954
Cecil Richardson, 1955–1972
Joe Richards, 1973–2004
Bill Pribil, 2005–

Gila County Sheriffs
William Murphey, 1881
William Louther, 1881–1882
Ben Pascoe, 1883–1886
Ed Hodgson, 1887
George Shute, 1888
Glenn Reynolds, 1889 (killed in the
   line of duty)

Jerry Ryan, 1890 (killed in the line
   of duty)
J. H. Thompson, 1891–1896
Dan Williamson, 1897–1898
W. T. Armstrong, 1899–1900
J. H. Thompson, 1901–1902
Edward Shanley, 1905–1906
Will Shanley, 1906
J. H. Thompson, 1907–1912
Frank Haynes, 1913–1916
Thomas Armer, 1917–1918
Eugene Shute, 1919–1920
Tol Kinsey, 1921–1922
Alf Edwards, 1923–1930
Charles Byrne, 1931–1940
W. H. Richardson, 1941–1949
Jack Jones, 1950–1964
Elton Jones, 1965–1968
Ted Lewis, 1969–1972
Lyman Peace, 1973–1984
Joe M. Rodriguez, 1985–2004
Bill Pribil, 2005–

Graham County Sheriffs
C. B. Rose, 1881
George H. Stevens, 1882–1884
Benjamin Crawford, 1885 (killed by
   Apache Indians)
William Whelan, 1889–1890
George A. Olney, 1891–1894
Arthur A. Wight, 1895–1896
Benjamin R. Clark, 1897–1900
James V. Parks, 1901–1906
Alphie A. Anderson, 1907–1910
J. B. English, 1911–1912
Thomas Alger, 1913–1916
Franklin McBride, 1917–1918 (killed
   in the line of duty)
Brig Stewart, 1918

J. Skaggs, 1919–1922

Samuel V. Pollock, 1923–1924

Homer M. Tate, 1925–1928

Seth Dodge, 1929–1932

Hugh Talley, 1933–November 20, 1936

Belle Talley, November 21–December 31, 1936

Emert Kempton, 1937–1940

Victor Christensen, 1941–1944

Houston Bowman, 1945–1952

Ezekiel R. McBride, 1953–1956

Houston Bowman, 1957–1968

Harold D. Stevens, 1969–1980

Roy F. Curtis, 1981–1988

Richard I. Mack, 1989–1996

Frank D. Hughes, 1997–

Greenlee County Sheriffs

Irving B. English, 1911–1912

John D. Patty, 1913–1914

James G. Cash, 1915–1916

Arthur G. Slaughter, 1917–1920

John Bradbury, 1921–1922

W. T. Witt, 1923–1928

Harvey T. Grady, 1929–1941

Ben Phillips, 1942–1943

Joe Chaudoin, 1943–1946

Joe Tea, 1947–1953

Fred Carrell, 1953–1962

Forrest Wilkerson, 1963–1976

Robert Gomez, 1977–1992

Allen Williams, 1993–2004

Steve Tucker, 2005–

La Paz County Sheriffs

Rayburn Evans, 1983–1988

Marvin L. Hare, 1989–2001

Hal Collett, 2002–

Maricopa County Sheriffs

William A. Hancock, 1871 (appointed)

Thomas Barnum 1871 (elected, resigned)

Thomas C. Warden (sometimes spelled Worden), 1871 (appointed)

Thomas C. Hayes, 1872–1874

George E. Mowry, 1875–1878

Reuben S. Thomas, 1879–1880

Lindley H. Orme, 1881–1884

Noah M. Broadway, 1885–1886

Andrew Jackson Halbert, 1887–1888

William Thomas Gray, 1889–1890

John Britt Montgomery, 1891–1892

James K. Murphy, 1893–1894

Lindley H. Orme, 1895–1898

David L. Murray, 1899–1900

Samuel S. Stout, 1901–1902

William W. Cook, 1903–1904

John Elliott Walker, 1905–1906

William W. Cunningham, 1906 (appointed)

Carl Hayden, 1907–1912

Jefferson Davis Adams, 1912–1916

William Henry Wilky, 1917–1918

John G. Montgomery, 1919–1922

Jerry Sullivan, 1923–1924

A. J. "Johnnie" Moore, 1925–1926

Jerry Sullivan, 1927 (died in office)

Jefferson Davis Adams, 1927–1928 (appointed)

Charles H. Wright, 1929–1930

James R. McFadden, 1931–1936

Roy Merrill, 1937–1938

Joseph L. Jordan, 1939–1944

Jewel Jordan, 1944 (appointed)

Ernest W. Roach, 1945–1946

Luther C. "Cal" Boies, 1946–1968 (appointed, then reelected)

John Gerald Mummert, 1969–1972
Paul Blubaum, 1973–1976
Jerry I. Hill, 1977–1984
R. G. "Dick" Godbehere, 1985–1988
Thomas Agnos, 1989–1992
Joseph Arpaio, 1993–

Mohave County Sheriffs
W. G. "Milt" Moore, 1864–1865
Thomas J. Mathews, 1866–1867
E. H. Smith, 1868
A. P. Prather, 1869
Thomas Wicks, 1870
Paul Breon, 1871
Daniel H. Smith, 1871
L. C. Welbourn, 1872
E. H. Smith, 1873–1874
A. Comstock, 1875–1880
John C. Potts, 1881–1882
Robert Steen, 1883–1888
W. H. Lake, 1889–1892
James Rosborough, 1893–1896
John C. Potts, 1897–1898
Harvey Hubbs, 1899–1900
Henry Lovin, 1901–1904
Walter Brown, 1905–1912
Joseph P. Gideon, 1913–1914
J. C. Lane, 1915–1916
J. N. Cohenour, 1917–1918
William P. Mahoney, 1919–1926
Jasper Brewer, 1927–1928
Ernest I. Graham, 1929–1944
Frank L. Porter, 1945–1960 (died in
    office)
Frances Porter, March–December 1960
D. W. Harris, 1961–1962
Robert M. Tarr, 1963 (shot in the line
    of duty)
Floyd L. Cisney, 1964–1972

Walter "Phil" Jordan, 1973–1977
David Rathbone, 1978–1980
S. O. "Bill" Richardson, 1981–1984
Joseph Bonzelet, 1985–1989
Joseph Cook, 1990–1996 (died in
    office)
Thomas Sheahan, 1997–

Navajo County Sheriffs
Commodore Perry Owens, 1895–1896
    (also served in Apache County)
Frank J. Wattron, 1897–1900
F. P. Secrist, 1901–1902
Chester I. Houck, 1903–1906
Joseph F. Woods, 1907–1914
R. L. Newman, 1915–1918
Charles W. Harp, 1919–1920
R.L. Newman, 1921–1922
L. Daniel Divelbess, 1923–1932
O. C. Williams, 1933–1936
Lafe S. Hatch, 1937–1938
L. Daniel Divelbess, 1939–1940
Lafe S. Hatch, 1941–1944
Cecil McCormick, 1945–1948
L. Ben Pearson, 1949–1960
Glen Flake, 1961–1966
Lyle E. Jenkins, 1967–1974
Marlin F. Gillespie, 1975–1984
Glen Flake, 1985–1988
Gary H. Butler, 1989–

Pima County Sheriffs
Berry Hill DeArmitt, July 7,
    1864–October 17, 1865 (appointed)
Francis M. Hodges, October
    17–December 31, 1865
Granville Wheat, 1866
Peter Rainsford Brady, 1867–1869
Charles Hylor Ott, 1870–1872

William Sanders Oury, 1873–1876
Charles A. Shibell, 1877–1880
Robert H. Paul, 1881–1886
Eugene O. Shaw, 1887 (died in office)
Mathew F. Shaw Sr., 1887–1890
James K. Brown, 1891–1892
Joseph B. Scott, 1893–1894
Robert N. Leatherwood, 1895–1898
Lyman W. Wakefield, 1899–1900
Frank E. Murphy, 1901–1904
Nabor Pacheco, 1905–1908
John Nelson, 1909–1914
Albert W. Forbes, 1915–1916
J. T. "Rye" Miles, 1917–1920
Benjamin F. Franklin, 1921–1922
Walter W. Bailey, 1923–1926
James Wm. McDonald, 1927–1930
Walter W. Bailey, 1931–1932
John F. Belton, 1933–1936
Edward F. Echols, 1937–1946
Jerome P. Martin, 1947–1950
Frank A. Eyman, 1951–January 17,
    1955 (resigned)
Benjamin McKinney, January 23,
    1955–1956 (appointed)
James Clark, 1957–1958
Waldon V. Burr, 1959–September 24,
    1971 (resigned)
Michael S. Barr, September 24–
    November 20, 1971
William Coy Cox, 1971–1976
Richard Boykin, 1977–1980 (resigned)
Clarence Dupnik, 1981– (appointed,
    then reelected numerous times)

Pinal County Sheriffs
Michael Rogers, 1875
Peter R. Brady, 1876–1877
John Peter Gabriel, 1878–1882

Andrew James Doran, 1883–1884
John Peter Gabriel, 1885–1886
Jere Fryer, 1887–1891
L. K. Drais, 1892–1893
William C. Truman, 1894–1903
Thomas N. Wills, 1904–1907
James E. McGee, 1908–February 16,
    1912
F. J. McCarthy, February 16–November
    13, 1912 (Charles Foreman elected
    but died before taking office)
James E. McGee, November 13,
    1912–1913
Henry Hall, 1914–1920
Enis Thurman, 1921–1924
W. A. Benson, 1925
Walter E. Laveen, 1925–1938
James Herron Jr., 1939–1946
Lynn Earley, 1947–1952
Laurence White, 1953–1962
Coy DeArman, 1963–1974
W. B. "Tex" Whittington, 1975–1976
Frank R. Reyes, 1977–2000
Roger Vanderpool, 2001–2005 (left
    office to serve as director of Arizona
    Department of Public Safety)
Chris Vasquez, 2005–

Santa Cruz County Sheriffs
William H. Barnett, 1899 (appointed,
    resigned)
Thomas F. Brodrick, 1899–1900
Thomas H. Turner, 1901–1904
Charles Fowler, 1905–1906
Harry J. Saxon, 1907–1910
William S. McKnight, 1911–1916
Raymond R. Earhart, 1917–1920
George J. White, 1921–1922 (killed
    in the line of duty)

Harry Saxon, 1922
Harold J. Brown, 1923–1928
H. J. Patterson, 1929–1930
Victor J. Wager, 1931–1932
Harold J. Brown, 1933–1938
John J. Lowe, 1939–1958
Robert Connor, 1959–1962
Ezekiel Bejarano, 1963–1977
Jaime Teyechea, 1977–1984
Alfonso Bracamonte, 1985–1992
Tony Estrada, 1993–

Yavapai County Sheriffs

Van C. Smith, January 17–February 17, 1865
Jerome Calkins, February 18, 1865–January 24, 1866
John T. Bourke, January 24, 1866–July 1, 1867
Andrew J. Moore, July 1, 1867–April 21, 1869 (resigned)
John L. Taylor, April 21,1869–January 1, 1871 (appointed)
John H. Behan (also served in Cochise County), 1871–1872
James S. Thomas, 1872–January 17, 1874 (resigned)
Henry M. Herbert, January 17, 1874–January 1, 1875 (appointed)
Edward F. Bowers, 1875–1878
Joseph R. Walker, 1879–1882
Jacob Henkle, 1883–1884
William J. Mulvenon, 1885–1888
William "Buckey" O'Neill, 1889–1890
James R. Lowry, 1891–1894
George C. Ruffner, 1895–1898
John L. Munds, 1899–1902
Joseph I. Roberts, 1903–1904

James R. Lowry, 1905–1908
James W. Smith, 1909–1911
Charles C. Keeler, 1912–1914
Joseph Young, 1915–1918
Warren G. Davis, 1919–September 6, 1922 (died in office)
Joseph P. Dillon, September 6–December 31, 1922 (appointed)
George C. Ruffner, 1923–1924
Edward G. Weil, 1925–1926
George C. Ruffner, 1927–July 27, 1933 (died in office)
Robert M. Robbins, August 2, 1933–1940 (appointed)
M. Willis Butler, 1941–1946
Orville Bozarth, 1947–1954
James Cramer, 1955–1962
Al Ayars, 1963–1974
Robert Scott, 1975–1976
H. "Curly" Moore, 1977–1988
G. C. "Buck" Buchanan, 1989–2004
Steve Waugh, 2005–

Yuma County Sheriffs

Isaac A. Bradshaw, June 18–September 10, 1864
William Werringer, September 26–December 15, 1864
Cornelius Sage, December 15, 1864–May 3, 1965 (killed in the line of duty)
Alexander McKey, May 3, 1865–April 2, 1866
William T. Flower, April 2, 1866–June 1867
David King, June 5–late 1867
Col. Marcus D. Dobbins, late 1867–June 1868
James T. Dana, June 3, 1868–September

22, 1871 (killed in the line of duty)
George Tyng, November 6, 1871–?
Francis H. Goodwin, May 3–December
    31, 1873
William Werninger, 1874–1875
Charles D. Baker, 1876–1879
Francis M. Hodges, July 12, 1880–June
    7, 1881
Andy Tyner, 1881–1886
Mike Nugent, 1887–1892
Mel Greenleaf, 1893–1898
John Speese, 1899–1900
Gus Livingston, 1901–1912

Mel Greenleaf, 1913–1918
James Polhanus, 1919–1922
James Chappell, 1923–1928
James Polhanus, 1929 (died in office)
J. C. Hunter, 1930–1934
Thomas F. Newman, 1935–1944
Jack Beard, 1945–1950
James Washum, 1951–1954
Thomas H. Newman, 1955–1960
Lee Echols, 1961–1962
Travis Yancey, 1963–1980
John R. Phipps, 1981–1992
Ralph Ogden, 1993–

Sources

Books

Adams, Ramon F. *Six-guns and Saddle Leather: A Bibliography of Books and Pamphlets on Western Outlaws and Gunmen.* Norman, OK: University of Oklahoma Press, 1969.

Axford, Joseph. *Around Western Campfires,* Tucson, AZ: University of Arizona Press, 1969.

Bailey, L. R., ed. *The A. B. Gray Report and Including the Reminiscences of Peter R. Brad, Who Accompanied the Expedition.* Los Angeles, CA: Westernlore Press, 1963.

Ball, Larry B. *Desert Lawmen: The High Sheriffs of New Mexico and Arizona 1846–1912.* Albuquerque, NM: University of New Mexico Press, 1992.

Bancroft, Hubert Howe. *History of Arizona and New Mexico, 1530–1888.* San Francisco, CA: The History Company, 1899.

Bashford, Coles (compiler). *Compiled Laws of the Territory of Arizona, Including the Howell Code and the Session Laws, from 1864–1871.* Albany, NY: Weed, Parsons, 1871.

Behr, Edward. *Prohibition: Thirteen Years that Changed America.* New York City: Arcade Publishing, 1996.

Bond, Ervin. *Percy Bowden: Born to Be a Frontier Lawman.* Douglas, AZ: privately published, 1978.

Bradley, Martha Sonntag. *Kidnapped From That Land: The Government Raids on the Short Creek Polygamists.* Vol. 9. Publications in Mormon Studies. Salt Lake City, UT: University of Utah Press, 1993.

Browne, J. Ross. *Adventures in Apache Country: A Tour Through Arizona and Sonora, 1864.* Tucson, AZ: University of Arizona Press, 1974.

Burgess, Glenn. *Mt. Graham Profiles: Graham County, Arizona, 1870–1977.* Vol. 1. Safford, AZ: Graham County Historical Society, 1978.

Calhoun, Frederick S. *The Lawmen: United States Marshals and Their Deputies, 1789–1989.* Washington and London: Smithsonian Institution Press, 1989.

Carlock, Robert. *The Hashknife: The Early Days of the Aztec Land and Cattle Company, Limited.* Tucson, AZ: Westernlore Press, 1994.

Carmony, Neil B. *Gunfight in Apache County, 1887: The Shootout Between Sheriff C. P. Owens and the Blevins Brothers in Holbrook, Arizona,* as described by Will C. Barnes. Tucson, AZ: Trail to Yesterday Books, 1997.

———, ed. *Whiskey, Six-Guns & Red-light Ladies: George Hand's Saloon Diary, Tucson, 1875–1878.* Silver City, NM: High Lonesome Books, 1994.

Cline, Platt. *They Came to the Mountain.* Flagstaff, AZ: Northland Press, 1976.

Dedera, Don. *A Little War of Our Own.* Flagstaff, AZ: Northland Press, 1988.

Devens, Charles. *Official Opinions of the Attorneys General.* Washington, D.C.: GPO, 1878. (See 6:466–74 and 16:466 for Attorney General Charles Devens' opinion conforming to the Posse Comitatus Act.)

Drago, Harry Sinclair. *The Great Range Wars: Violence on the Grasslands.* New York: Dodd, Mead & Company, 1970.

Dreyfuss, John J., ed. 1972. *A History of Arizona's Counties and Courthouses.* Tucson, AZ: Arizona Historical Society, 1970.

Duncombe, Herbert S. *Modern County Government,* Washington D.C.: Washington National Association of Counties, 1977.

Edwards, Harold. *The Killing of Jim McKinney.* Porterville, CA: Edwards Book Publishing, 1988.

Elliott, Wallace W. & Company, eds. *History of the Arizona Territory.* Flagstaff, AZ: reprinted by Northland Press, 1964.

Ellison, Glenn. *Cowboys Under the Mogollon Rim.* Tucson, AZ: University of Arizona Press, 1968.

Engelmann, Larry. *Intemperance: The Lost War Against Liquor.* New York: The Free Press, 1979.

Eppinga, Jane. *Henry Ossian Flipper: West Point's First Black Graduate.* Plano, TX: Republic of Texas Press, 1996.

Erwin, Allen A. *The Southwest of John H. Slaughter, 1841–1922: Pioneer Cattleman and Trail Driver of Texas, the Pecos, and Arizona and Sheriff of Tombstone.* Glendale, CA: Arthur H. Clark, 1965.

Farish, Thomas E. *History of Arizona.* San Francisco, CA: Filmer Brothers, 1918.

Fireman, Bert M. *Arizona: Historic Land.* New York: Alfred A. Knopf, 1982.

Forrest, Earle R. *Arizona's Dark and Bloody Ground.* Tucson, AZ: reprinted by the University of Arizona Press, 1984.

Gillette, Frank. *Pleasant Valley.* Privately printed, 1984.

Goff, John S. *Arizona Territorial Officials: Members of the Legislature.* Vol. VI. A–L, Cave Creek, Arizona: Black Mountain Press, 1996.

———. *Arizona Territorial Officials: The Secretaries, United States Attorneys, Marshals, Surveyors General and Superintendents of Indian Affairs 1863–1912.* Vol. IV, Cave Creek, Arizona: Black Mountain Press, 1988.

Grey, Zane. *To the Last Man.* New York: Harper & Row, 1922.

Haley, J. Evetts. *Jeff Milton: A Good Man With a Gun.* Norman, OK: University of Oklahoma Press, 1948.

Hayes, Jess G. *Apache Vengeance.* Albuquerque, NM: University of New Mexico Press, 1954.

———. *Sheriff Thompson's Day.* Tucson, AZ: University of Arizona Press, 1968.

Hirschi, Travis. *Causes of Delinquency.* Berkeley, CA: University of California Press, 1969.

Horton, L. J. *The Pleasant Valley War.* Typescript. Prescott, AZ: Sharlot Hall Museum, 1925.

Hughes, Stella. *Hashknife Cowboy.* Tucson, AZ: University of Arizona Press, 1985.

Hunt, Frazier. *Cap Mossman: Last of the Great Cowmen.* New York: Hastings House, 1951.

———. *The Long Trail from Texas.* New York: Doubleday, Doran & Company, 1940.

Kant, Candace. *Zane Grey's Arizona.* Flagstaff, AZ: Northland Press, 1984.

Keleher, William A. *The Fabulous Frontier.* Albuquerque, NM: University of New Mexico Press, 1962.

King, Jean Beach. *Arizona Charlie.* Phoenix, AZ: Heritage Publishers, 1989.

Kuykendall, Ivan Lee. *Ghost Riders of the Mogollon.* San Antonio, TX: The Naylor Company, 1954.

Lawton, Paul J. *The Last Full Measure: Law Enforcement Deaths in Arizona.* Tucson, AZ: Arizona State Lodge Fraternal Order of Police, 1987.

McBride, Darvil B. *The Evaders or Wilderness Shoot-Out.* Pasadena, CA: Pacific Book & Printing, 1984.

McCarty, Kieran. *Desert Documentary: The Spanish Years, 1767–1821.* Historical Monograph No. 4. Tucson, AZ: Arizona Historical Society, 1976.

Miller, Joseph C., ed. *Arizona: The Last Frontier,* New York: Hastings House, 1856.

Moore, Daniel G. *Enter Without Knocking.* Tucson, AZ: University of Arizona Press, 1969.

Morgan, Learah C., ed. *Echoes of the Past: Tales of Old Yavapai in Arizona.* Prescott, AZ: Yavapai Cow Belles, 1955.

Morris, Norval and David J. Rothman, eds. *The Oxford History of the Prison: The Practice of Punishment in Western Society.* New York: Oxford University Press, 1995.

Murphy, James M. *Laws, Courts, and Lawyers Through the Years in Arizona.* Tucson, AZ: University of Arizona Press, 1970.

Northern Gila County Historical Society. *Rim Country History.* Payson, AZ: Rim Country Printery, 1984.

O'Neal, Bill. *The Arizona Rangers.* Austin, TX: Eakin Press, 1987.

Peplow, Edward H. Jr. *History of Arizona.* New York: Lewis Historical Publishing Company, 1958.

Power, Tom with John Whitlatch. *Shoot Out at Dawn: An Arizona Tragedy.* Phoenix, AZ: Phoenix Books, 1981.

Russell, Don. *The Lives and Legends of Buffalo Bill.* Norman, OK: University of Oklahoma Press, 1988.

Sexton, Major Grover F. *The Arizona Sheriff.* South Bend, IN: Studebaker Corporation of America, 1925.

Sheridan, Thomas E. *Los Tucsonenses: The Mexican Community in Tucson 1854–1941.* Tucson, AZ: University of Arizona Press, 1986.

Sloan, Richard E. *Memories of an Arizona Judge.* Stanford, CA: Stanford University Press, 1932.

Smith, Cornelius C. Jr. *William Sanders Oury: History-Maker of the Southwest.* Tucson, AZ: University of Arizona Press, 1967.

Sonnichsen, C. L. *Billy King's Tombstone: The Private Life of an Arizona Boom Town.* Tucson, AZ: University of Arizona Press, 1980.

Stevens, Robert C., ed. *Echoes of the Past: Tales of Old Yavapai.* Vol. 2. Prescott, AZ: Yavapai Cow Belles, 1964.

Studebaker Corporation. *The Dash of the Sheriff.* South Bend, IN: Studebaker Corporation, 1926.

Thrapp, Dan L. *Al Sieber: Chief of Scouts.* Norman, OK: University of Oklahoma Press, 1995.

———. *Encyclopedia of Frontier Biography.* Glendale, CA: A. H. Clark Co., 1988.

Tinsley, Jim Bob. *The Hash Knife Brand.* Jacksonville, FL: University of Florida, 1993.

Wagoner, Jay J. *Arizona Territory 1863–1912: A Political History.* Tucson, AZ: University of Arizona Press, 1980.

Walker, Dale L. *Buckey O'Neill: The Story of a Rough Rider.* Tucson, AZ: University of Arizona Press, 1983.

Way, Thomas E. *The Parker Story.* Prescott, AZ: Prescott Graphics, 1981.

Weiner, Melissa Ruffner. *Prescott Yesteryears: Life in Arizona's First Territorial Capital.* Prescott, AZ: Primrose Press, 1978.

Wilhelm, C. LeRoy and Mabel R. *A History of the St. Johns Stake.* Orem, UT: Historical Publications, 1982.

Wilson, James Q. *Crime and Public Policy.* San Francisco, CA: ICS Press, 1983.

Wood, Elizabeth Lambert. *The Tragedy of the Powers [sic] Mine.* Portland, OR: Binfords & Mort, 1957.

Zachariae, Barbara. *Pleasant Valley Days: Young Arizona,* Young, AZ: privately printed, 1991.

Zarbin, Earl. *All the Time a Newspaper.* Phoenix, AZ: The Arizona Republic, 1990.

Newspapers

Research included numerous articles from back issues of the following: *Apache Critic, Arizona Cattlelog, Arizona Champion, Arizona Daily Star* (Tucson; also *Arizona Tri-Weekly Star, The Weekly Star*), *Arizona Miner, Arizona Record, Arizona Republic* (Phoenix), *Arizona Republican, Arizona Silver Belt, Arizona Weekly Enterprise, Clifton Copper Era, Courtland Arizonian, Daily Californian, Daily Tulare Register, Holbrook Times, Hoofs and Horns, Merced County Sun, Mohave County Miner* (also called *Kingman Daily Miner*), *The Morning Echo, New York Times, Nogales International, Phoenix Daily Herald, Phoenix Gazette* (also *Arizona Gazette*), *Prescott Courier, Prescott Journal Miner, Salt River Herald, Tombstone Epitaph, Tombstone Prospector, Tombstone Weekly Nugget, Tucson Daily Citizen* (also *Tucson Weekly Citizen, Tucson Citizen*), *Tulare County Times, Weekly Arizona Miner, Weekly Arizonian, The Weekly Delta* (Visalia, California)*, Wickenburg Sun News, Yavapai County Reporter.*

Arizona Historical Society, Tucson

Biographical files
William Sanders Oury, Robert H. Paul, Peter Brady, Thomas Jefferson Power and John Grant Power, Thomas Sisson,

Pete Gabriel, Joseph Goldwater, Robert Leatherwood, John Heith, Frank E. Murphy, Charles Bly (aka Frank Sherlock), Henry Lovin, Matthew Shaw.

Taped and written interviews
Joe Frank Wootan and Thomas Kane Wootan by E. F. Schaaf, April 27, 1976 (AV-0118); Robert William Wootan by E. F. Schaaf (AV-0119); James Frank Wootan by E. F. Schaaf (AV-0376); Thomas Jefferson Power by Kaye Zimmerman and Hugh O'Riordan, March 1969; Robert Voris by Clara Woody and Dale Stuart King, May 20 and July 29, 1957 (Woody Collection).

Unpublished manuscripts
Allison, Robert. *The Blevins Family: An Episode in the Pleasant Valley War*, 1908.
Barney, James M. *Arizona Sheriffs* (several articles, n.d.).
Davisson, Lori. *Arizona Executions* (n.d.).
Edmondson, Colin. *The Escape of Apache Kid: New Light on the Riverside Murders*, 1987.
Hankin, Harriet W. "The Bisbee Holdup and Its Aftermath" (n.d.).
Hazelton, Drusilla. *The Tonto Basin's Early Settlers*, 1977.
Henning, Lloyd. "Sheriff, Scholar and a Gentleman: Frank J. Wattron," 1941.
Malach, Roman. *Short Creek: Colorado City on the Arizona Strip*, 1982.
Palmquist, Robert F. *Election Fraud 1880: The Case of Paul vs. Shibell*, 1986.
Woody, Clara T. "Outlaw Valley," Woody Collection (n.d.).

Other materials
Transcript of the Reporter's Record of Evidence in deaths of Robert F. McBride, Martin R. Kempton, Thomas K. Wootan Deceased. Safford, Graham County Arizona W. C. D. Cochran, Reporter. February 12, 1918.
Wolfley, Lewis. Letter to the Senate Judiciary Committee re Robert Paul's appointment as U.S. Marshal. January 15, 1890.

Arizona Historical Society, Yuma

Rube, B. Johnny. *Yuma County Sheriff's Department* (unpublished manuscript, n.d.).

University of Arizona Library, Tucson

Hayden, Carl T. 1931 speech at the laying of the cornerstone of the county building in Phoenix (Arizona Collection).
Hollister, Charles A. 1946. *The Organization and Administration of the Sheriff's Office in Arizona* (master's thesis).
Papers of Joseph Thomas McKinney (Special Collections).
Pima County Court Records, Vol. 1-39 (Special Collections).
Wayte, Harold C. Jr. 1962. *A History of Holbrook and the Little Colorado Country* (master's thesis).
Weed, William. Court reporter's transcript, preliminary hearing, August 29-September 8, 1892. Territory of Arizona vs. Edwin Tewksbury, two volumes (Special Collections).

Sharlot Hall Museum, Prescott

Biographical file on William J. Mulvenon.

Arizona Department of Library, Archives, and Public Records, Phoenix

Dolores Moore papers.

Fish, Joseph. *History of Arizona* (unpublished manuscript), ca. 1896.

Flake, Osmer D. *Some Reminiscences of the Pleasant Valley War and Causes That Led Up to It* (unpublished manuscript, n.d.).

Legal Documents

State of Arizona vs. Jerome Martin. Case 4018.

State vs. Martin No. 1024 Supreme Court of Arizona, June 16, 1952.

State vs. Jonathan Andrew Doody CR 92-01232 Filed September 5, 1996 Division 1, Court of Appeals, State of Arizona.

Acts, Resolutions, and Memorials, First Legislative Assembly, 1864. Prescott.

Laws of the Territory of Arizona. First through Twenty-Fifth Sessions, 1864–1909.

Arizona Revised Statutes (various).

United States Marshal's Records, 1892–1927.

Coroner's inquest into the death of Ola May Power, December 8, 1917. Safford, Graham County, Arizona.

Personal Interviews

Michael A. Arra (Public Affairs Administrator, Arizona Department of Corrections), Maricopa County Sheriff Joseph Arpaio, Maricopa County Sheriff Thomas J. Agnos, Deputy County Attorney Paul Ahlers, Maricopa County Attorney Rick Romley, Larry Rogge, Judge Norman Tullar, Cochise County Sheriff Jimmy V. Judd, Pinal County Sheriff Frank Reyes, Russell Murdock.

Additional Sources

James H. McClintock Collection, Phoenix Public Library.

Judge, Barbara. *The History of the Maricopa County Sheriff's Department* (unpublished manuscript).

Provence, Jean. *Bloody Pleasant Valley* (unpublished manuscript), Phoenix Public Library.

Taylor, Ralph D. 1975. *History of the Pima County Sheriff's Department: 1864-1972.* Courtesy of the Pima County Sheriff's Department, Tucson.

Wheeler, Harry C., enlistment papers, National Personnel Records Center, St. Louis, Missouri.

Acknowledgments

Many fine institutions have helped with the research required on this book, including Special Collections in the University of Arizona Library in Tucson, the Charles Trumbull Hayden Library at Arizona State University in Tempe, the Arizona Historical Society in Tucson, the Sharlot Hall Museum in Prescott, the Arizona State Archives in Phoenix, and all of the Arizona sheriff and county attorney offices.

In the course of this research, I have formed wonderful friendships with people whose expertise and help went far above the call of the job. My long-time friend— Arizona Historical Society historian and member of the Peace Officers Died in Line of Duty Board, Lori Davisson—amassed an invaluable collection of law-enforcement history at the Arizona Historical Society. Russell Murdock, member of the Arizona Historical Society Board of Directors, had personal memories and stories of his uncle's part in the Power shoot-out.

Susan Abbey and Michael Wurtz of the Sharlot Hall Museum in Prescott were always punctual in finding obscure but pertinent bits of information on Yavapai County law-enforcement history. Loren Wilson, from the Mohave County Historical Society in Kingman, helped with Mohave County law-enforcement history. Pat Etter of the Charles Trumbull Hayden Library at Arizona State University in Tempe, and the late Barbara Judge, a historian with the Maricopa County Sheriff's Department, provided sources and primary documents pertaining to the Maricopa County Sheriff's Department. Maricopa County Attorney Rick Romley and the chief prosecuting deputy, Paul W. Ahler, from the Maricopa County Attorney Office in Phoenix, provided invaluable assistance and primary documentation on the 1991 temple murders.

Garnette Franklin of the Holbrook Historical Society contributed information on the house of the Blevins shoot-out during the Pleasant Valley War. Navajo County Sheriff Gary Butler provided original documentation in the form of the Criminal Complaint against George Smiley. Deloris Reynolds, a volunteer with the Bisbee Mining and Historical Museum in Bisbee, helped research sheriffs in Cochise County. Art Solano, formerly a guard at the Pima County Courthouse, allowed me to copy his excellent photographs of the Pima County Sheriffs.

Harold L. Edwards provided photographs of the California sheriffs involved in the shooting of James McKinney. Over the five years that I wrote for *The Arizona Sheriff* magazine, Carol Downey of the Arizona State Records and Archives was always prompt with material on Arizona law enforcement. The late Della Meadows, who retired as secretary at the Arizona State Prison, was a walking encyclopedia of Pinal County History. Michael Arras, Arizona Department of Corrections, helped with information on the procedures for executions in Arizona.

Special thanks to Emojean Girard, childhood friend and retired Pima County justice of peace, for guiding me through the legal terminology of my research. Thanks also to my good friend Bob Pugh, owner of Trail to Yesterday Books, who always points me in the right direction when it comes to Arizona history books. Thanks to Asa Bushnell, for excellent suggestions and for his wonderful foreword to this book. Finally, thanks to the Rio Nuevo Publishers staff, including Lisa Cooper, Carrie Stusse, Tracy Vega, and Susan and Ross Humphreys.

Index